COUNSELING AND COMMUNITY

**CONTEMPORARY CHRISTIAN
COUNSELING**

COUNSELING AND COMMUNITY

ROD WILSON, PH.D.

CONTEMPORARY CHRISTIAN COUNSELING

General Editor
GARY R. COLLINS, PH.D.

Library of Congress Cataloging-in-Publication Data:

Wilson, Rod.
    Counseling and community / Rod Wilson.
       p. cm. — (Contemporary Christian counseling; 12)
    Includes bibliographical references and index.
    ISBN 0-8499-1051-X
    1. Pastoral counseling. 2. Evangelicalism. I. Title. II. Series.
    BV4012.2.W485   1995
    253.5—dc20

               95-18888
               CIP

5 6 7 8 9 1 2 3 4 LBM 9 8 7 6 5 4 3 2 1

Printed in the United States of America

To my father,
Cecil John Kenneth Wilson,
(1924–1995)
who taught me the importance
of having high ideals for the church

and

to the community of faith
at Ontario Bible College
and Ontario Theological Seminary

Contents

Acknowledgments

To write a book on community and not acknowledge certain communities would be a contradiction in terms. I am particularly grateful to my colleagues at Ontario Bible College and Ontario Theological Seminary. They have provided a rich environment for the development of ideas and the stimulation of the spirit. I also am indebted to the students I have taught over the past seventeen years. Their questions and challenges have sharpened my perspective and made me realize that real learning takes place in community.

The faculty and student body of Conrad Grebel College provided a needed oasis during a sabbatical year. I will always be appreciative of the opportunity to be in a context where aspirations toward community go beyond rhetoric.

Numerous camps, parachurch organizations, and churches have given me the privilege of being involved with them as they seek to practice what it means to be a true community. Apart from any benefit that may have come through my influence, I have received much in return.

Our family's last two church homes have had a major impact on our lives. My thanks to the leadership of Hilltop Chapel and Forest Brook Bible Chapel who were willing to take some risks and provide me with opportunities for ministry and service that have deepened my understanding of God and his work in the church.

I am grateful to the staff at Word Inc., particularly Terri Gibbs, Editor of Academic and Reference Works, Lois Stück, copy editor, and Gary Collins, the general editor of this series, for their patience and contribution to the completion of this project as well as their commitment to communicating the message about community.

I have had the privilege of being involved in the lives of many people. As is true for most counselors, this opportunity to look behind the scenes has produced a high respect for the courage and perseverance that these individuals have demonstrated. Their integrity has pushed me on to understand the true meaning of community.

A number of individuals made unique contributions at various points in the project: Brian Cunnington, Bill and Julie Disesa, Bob Duez, John Franklin, Paul Friesen, Paul Johansen, Roy Matheson, John Miller, Jim Reimer, Lynn Smith, Peter Roebellen, Tim and Marilyn Sinclair, Mary Taylor, and Doug Webster. I want to particularly thank Glenn Taylor, for launching me on the community journey over sixteen years ago; Ian Rennie, for teaching me what it means to be the people of God; Rod Sawatsky, for introducing me to new ways of thinking about community; and Elizabeth Davey, for providing untiring editorial expertise.

Finally to my daughter, Jessica, and my wife, Bev, I will always be grateful for your patience, understanding, and love in the completion of this book.

Preface

On a number of occasions I have sat in an audience and heard a speaker ask, "Who has had the greatest influence in your life?" At times I find that hard to answer, and I cannot come up with one person or even a couple of people. Obviously, there are myriad people who have affected me in various ways, for good and for ill. By the time I come up with my one person, the speaker has moved on to his or her next point.

However, I would find it much easier to answer if that question were rephrased: "Which Christian community has had the greatest influence in your life?" This question makes me think of Christian communities that have invited me to live and experience the abundance that comes through faith in Christ. It also reminds me of Christian communities that have invited me to die in their negation of real life.

In thinking about this I decided to write down all the Christian communities where I have had any major involvement. I listed churches, theological institutions, camps, missions, and parachurch organizations. They totaled forty. This number did not include the infrequent contacts that I have experienced with many others. When I look at the list, I am conscious of the shaping and molding that took place through these communities. This is not to deny the influence of family, friends, or personal devotion, but it is to state a reality:

Communities are central in God's economy.

The thesis of this book is tied to this assumption: We need a counseling approach that is community-oriented rather than exclusively focused on the individual. When this is the case, we will be able to appreciate the biblical emphasis on the people of God. While he prizes a relationship with individuals, God's heart is with a body, a fellowship, a community. Fundamentally, Christian community is the visible manifestation of the work of God, through Jesus Christ, in the church.

There is a vast amount of literature, both Christian and secular, that has commented on community-individual tensions. We need to tie this literature to the field of counseling. Both pastors[1] and private counselors need to reaffirm the priority of community and its power in the healing process.

However, there is some confusion and separation between the world of private counseling and the church community. This distance can easily lead to suspicion so that communication between these two worlds is strained. A renewed understanding of the power of community will help to bridge this gap.

My model for this undertaking is the introductory textbook in a first-year course. A good one will give a cross section of the field, list some of the questions, and provide some of the answers. However, its most enduring contribution will be its ability to stimulate further study and reflection. It is my hope that this book will serve to motivate others to begin talking about the "second course" and maybe even begin writing the textbook. The absence of exhaustiveness in this undertaking should be a stimulus for others in the Christian community to grapple with the issues.

With this aim in mind, the book is divided into two parts. Part 1 looks at the evangelical struggle with community. At least three factors have contributed to our confusion with the term *community* and its implications for the counseling enterprise. First, our Western notions of help and healing have emphasized the solitary expert who tends to deal with the autonomous person's inner struggles and intrapsychic needs. Second, the therapeutic movement has picked up on the Western sensibility with the result that private counseling has developed into a form of sanctioned retreat. Third, many of us read the Bible out of an individualistic mind-set and have difficulty understanding the communal framework of Scripture.

In part 2 practical implications are provided for both pastors and private counselors. The communal framework is applied to the counselor, the counseling context, and the counselee. The underlying assumption in part 2 is that a commitment to a communal understanding will have an influence on all aspects of the counseling enterprise. Readers are encouraged to work through this material in the context of a small group since many of the suggestions lend themselves to communal interaction (see appendix A).

It is important to note that in all case illustrations used in this book, names and identifying information have been changed. Most of the examples are composites of several similar cases.

Finally, a word to the pessimistic reader who may construe an emphasis on community as naive and/or irritating. How could anyone in this culture advocate that the Christian community has the power to heal? Don't Christian communities tend to do exactly the opposite? Is it not true, in the words of Henri Nouwen, that "our Christian communities are little more than sodalities of well-intentioned people supporting each other in their individual interests?"[2] Maybe the *community* is the answer, but surely not the *Christian* community? Has it not done an incredible amount of damage over the years? Maybe Alan Bloom is right when he argues that "universities, rightly understood, are where community and friendship can exist in our times."[3] Does the modern Christian community fulfill its responsibility in these areas? Maybe Scott Peck is right when he suggests that "the church is not only not the Body of Christ, it is not even a body, a community. It must become a community before it can serve as the body of Christ."[4]

While I recognize that many of my readers will have experienced significant pain and trauma in the context of Christian communities, it is my hope that this book will make a contribution to our understanding of the power of Christian communities to bring healing. The reason? It is a topic that is close to the heart of God.

NOTES

1. The term *pastor* is used throughout the book as a title for those who are involved in leadership roles within a church or parachurch context. It is not limited to a particular position in the church.

2. Henri J. M. Nouwen, *Clowning in Rome: Reflections on Solitude, Celibacy, Prayer, and Contemplation* (Garden City, N.Y.: Image, 1979), 9.

3. Allan Bloom, *The Closing of the American Mind* (New York: Simon and Schuster, 1987), 382.

4. M. Scott Peck, *The Different Drum: Community-Making and Peace* (New York: Touchstone, 1988), 300.

PART I

Evangelicals and the Struggle with Community

Chapter One

What Does
Community Mean?

The most painful negative feature . . . is the underlying theological indifference toward the biblical teaching about the church. We simply have a poorly defined ecclesiology. Evangelicals tend to believe that a personal relationship with Jesus is the one thing that counts.
—Andrew Kuyvenhoven

W<small>HAT DO WE MEAN WHEN WE USE</small> the term *community*? Frequently we are referring to the area where people reside with some associations of social interaction and common ties. But while people may live in so-called communities, they often do not experience much connection. Brief interactions while cutting the grass or shoveling snow is the most many can hope for in their neighborhoods. Ironically, many people may have purchased a home in that particular area in response to an advertisement praising this new "lifestyle community." As Bernard says, the only thing that is communal may be the sewage system.[1]

If you live in a suburb near a major urban center, you will be familiar with the term *bedroom community*. The term implies a number of things. It probably means that because of economic factors you have bought a home quite a distance from the city. You leave the house around 6:00 A.M., to return sometime between 7:00 and 8:00 P.M. The positioning of *bedroom* and *community* in the same phrase makes little sense, but it does describe the locale where you live—or more accurately, where you sleep.

On the weekend you exercise with other individuals at the community center. However, although they live in the same community and are involved in the same activity, your knowledge of each other is negligible. Your common geographical connection means nothing in terms of common ties and social interaction. *Community* seems like an inaccurate use of the word.

At work you are encouraged to be more involved in the professional community, to strengthen that community's profile and strategy. All of this requires time, energy, and lifestyle decisions that compete with other responsibilities.

You are taking one course at the university every quarter, and the school paper talks about your commitment to the academic community. There are special lectures, fund-raising drives, athletic events, all put in the context of supporting the community.

Then there is your church. It is a community church attempting to connect with those who live in the neighborhood. However, many drive quite a distance to get there, and you wonder if the term *local church* has any relevance.

THE GOOD OLD DAYS

Because *community* does not seem to describe a sense of connection and relationship, we retreat into our own private world and dream fondly of the days when there was real community. I have found myself, for example, commenting about the absence of road hockey in my current neighborhood: "It seems that young people stay inside more than they did in my day." From there I wax eloquent on the good old days of community road hockey.

I remember it clearly. We would come home from school as quickly as possible, change into appropriate clothes, and be on the street by 3:40. They were great games. I still remember Darion's slap shot. He had one of those new plastic blades. He would heat it up over a burner and put a big bend in it. If you were in goal and Darion was breaking in, you could be sure that he would try to pick the top corner. You would crouch down low and hope that your glove hand would come up with the outstanding save. Or better yet, a car would come and somebody would yell, "Time."

Those games were significant for many reasons, but one was that in the mid-sixties they allowed young adolescent boys to connect, to relate, to be part of each other's lives. The road in front of Jim's house was the meeting place. It was much more important than home, school, or church. It was where you expressed friendship and camaraderie. It was the community center, in the literal sense of the word. Everyone seemed close.

In current culture this desire for community is seen in what seems to be an ever increasing desire to move from the city into the country. While urban life suggests individuality and isolation, rural life becomes associated with a simple community existence. By a shift in geographical location, we attempt to return to our roots and live communally.

People do the same sort of historical analysis with church. In response to the so-called lack of commitment on the part of the young, they go back to the days when people were not as busy, the building was filled, services were well attended, and people thought church was important.

In each of these situations *community* becomes a criterion for assessment. It is cherished as an integral part of the past. Its absence in the present is lamented. But what is really going on? A nostalgic view of the "good old days" takes over with all its fantasy and unreality. We forget that the "old days" were actually both good and bad. Was the community orientation that strong and vibrant?

There was more to those early teenage years than connection with friends playing road hockey. What about the identity questions? What about trying to understand sexuality? What about peer pressure? What about the loneliness? What about the social anxiety in school? Our struggle with community is not just a contemporary problem.

And what of the country? Is the idealized communal sense of rural life more a reflection of the urban sensibility? I like Christopher Lasch's comment on this issue:

Nostalgia finds its purest literary expression in the convention of the pastoral, with its praise of simple country pleasures. The charm of pastoralism lies, of course, not in the accurate observation of country life but in the dream of childlike simplicity and security. Pastoral evokes a world without work, marriage, or political intrigue—the carefree world of childhood, in effect. Since it makes no claim to depict rural life as it is, it can hardly be faulted for its lack of realism.[2]

What about church in the past? Did people really connect in a communal sense? Was there a sharing of joys and sorrows, a sense of connectedness when feelings ran deep? Did people come to church because of a desire to celebrate with the people of God? Clearly the presence of sin affected the church in the past as it does in the present. So a nostalgic pining for the good old days will not help us find community. Nostalgia is really an abdication of memory. Lasch goes on to point out:

Nostalgia appeals to the feeling that the past offered delights no longer obtainable. Nostalgic representations of the past evoke a time irretrievably lost and for that reason timeless and unchanging. Strictly speaking, nostalgia does not entail the exercise of memory at all, since the past it idealizes stands outside time, frozen in unchanging perfection.[3]

DEFINITION

We need to take the word *community* seriously so that it does not become, as Rosenthal puts it, "a warmly persuasive word describing no particular set of relationships at all."[4] Unfortunately, this is not easy in current Christian culture. Along with the term *family*, *community* often becomes a descriptor of what we wish were the case. How many Christians have stood in church singing about being glad to be part of the family of God while inside they felt alienated from everyone around them? And what of the missionary on the field? She is tired of being told she is part of the mission community when she has no experience of community from one year to the next. The simple use of the term is no guarantee that it is occurring. In fact, one might argue that excessive use of the term in a Christian context may not reflect reality. Ignatieff observes that "words like fraternity, belonging and community are so soaked with nostalgia and utopianism that they are nearly useless as guides to the real possibilities of solidarity in modern society."[5]

After extensive involvement in facilitating community building, Scott Peck describes a community as a "group of individuals who have learned how to communicate honestly with each other, whose relationships go deeper than their masks of composure, and who have developed some significant commitment to 'rejoice together, mourn together,' and to 'delight in each other, make others' conditions our own.'"[6]

Peck notes that these communities are characterized by three fundamental qualities: inclusivity, commitment, and consensus. Because the "great enemy of community is exclusivity," he writes, there must be a high commitment to inclusivity. Communities, in contrast to cliques, do not exclude members. Because there will always be differences within the group, there is also a premium placed on commitment. In fact, Peck suggests, a propensity to "individualism must be counterbalanced by commitment." Finally, decision making does not come through votes but through a consensus, a process that has "something inherently almost mystical, magical about it."[7]

As to the role of religion in the process of community building, he makes it clear that "any group of people (no matter what their religious persuasion or whether the word 'Jesus' is ever spoken) who are willing to practice the love, discipline, and sacrifice that are required for the spirit of community, that Jesus extolled and exemplified, will be gathered together in his name and he will be there."[8]

While Peck quotes Matthew 18:20 accurately—"For where two or three come together in my name, there am I with them"—he makes assumptions about the nature of the individuals who are gathered together. In the scriptural passage, the individuals under consideration are linked in the context of a Christian community. Peck believes true community can occur among "Christians and Jews, Christians and atheists, Jews and Muslims, Muslims and Hindus. People of any religious persuasion or none whatever can develop community." While he is right in disputing the contention that "a belief in Christianity is a guarantee of community,"[9] it is theologically questionable to posit that a Christian can have true community in the context of atheists and other religious groups who are in fundamental disagreement with the Christian faith. As Dietrich Bonhoeffer argues simply, yet powerfully, "Christianity means community through Jesus Christ and in Jesus Christ. No Christian community is more or less than this."[10]

Jean Vanier has captured this element of Christian community when he writes that communities are "groupings of people who have left their own milieu to live with others under the same roof, and work from a new vision of human beings and their relationship with each other and with God." Vanier's position is that communities do exist outside Christianity; however, "the message of Jesus invites his disciples to love one another and to live community in a special way." [11]

Christian community is the visible expression of the work of God, through Jesus Christ, in the church. The message that Christ has come is authenticated by the love Christians have for one another (see John 13:34–35; 17:21). We need to see the church as

- a place where the community is an expression of Christ's love,

- a place where the preaching and the administration of communion are affirmed in concert with the shepherding and care of others,

- a place where truth is expressed not just in doctrinal affirmation but in the relationships within the community.

If this is the case, then, as Snyder argues, the church is living as the people of God. It is modeling the example of Christ with his disciples, following the Christians of the early church, and adhering to the explicit teachings of Scripture.[12] The church, then, is not simply an institution but a mystical communion. As Avery Dulles asserts:

> People find the meaning of their lives not in terms of such institutions but in terms of the informal, the personal, the communal. They long for a community which, in spite of all the conflicts built into modern society, can open up loving communication. The Church, if it can perform this function, will be enthusiastically welcomed.[13]

In following the great commandments (Mark 12:30–31), the new commandment (John 13:34), and the Great Commission (Matt. 28:18–20), the community will be strong and the verbal message will be authenticated through a care for others.[14]

This means that local church leaders need to see the church as more than just a collection of individuals. It requires mission executives to consider the overall mission community when making decisions. It demands that Christian camps look at the moral and ethical framework their community represents.

This is also the understanding that needs to characterize the private Christian counseling movement. Individuals, couples, and families need to be anchored in their Christian community. Furthermore, the counselors also need to understand the communal responsibility and accountability that needs to characterize every individual Christian.

EVANGELICALISM AND PRIVATIZATION

Because of the presence of pluralism and relativism in our culture, it becomes more and more difficult to bring religious consensus to any issue. With so many belief systems, the Judeo-Christian claim on truth is now being seriously challenged. In this social context, at least two alternatives are possible. On the one hand, religion can become more organized and establishment centered; or on the other, it can tailor itself to the individual. This latter alternative has become the major choice in Western culture where people tend not to be connected with communities. Robert Bellah writes:

> But I believe the more dangerous threat today
> comes from the second alternative—the complete
> privatization of religion, so that religion becomes
> entirely personal with no collective expression at
> all. Indeed, in a significant sector of our population
> (which is not necessarily "secularized") that has
> already happened.[15]

Tension results, though, since religious people connect with communities. They attend church, are involved in various parachurch activities, and meet together under the umbrella of religion. Yet what is the nature of the community if a group of autonomous individuals come together? Do they lose their commitment to privatization and suddenly become community-centered? Bellah suggests that, "These individualist ideas turn the religious community into simply a club for the like-minded. In our society it is difficult even to understand the idea of the religious community as the people of God or the Body of Christ."[16]

One critic has suggested that of the four major movements in contemporary American evangelicalism at least three of them are characterized by this tendency.[17]

1. Baptist traditions have an individualized view of salvation with a stress on personal volition.

2. Holiness-Pentecostal traditions stress personal pietism and the work of the Holy Spirit in individual sanctification.

3. Reformational-Confessional traditions see salvation and faith in personal and rational terms.

Only the Anabaptists, with their elevation of the church community over the individual believer, are exempt from a leaning toward privatization.

Evangelicals have tended to make a separation between the spiritual and the social as well as between soteriology (that which relates to salvation) and ecclesiology (that which relates to the church). Some of this emphasis can be traced to a concern with propositional truth. This truth is contained in the pages of Scripture, which are the sole authority for faith and practice: the virgin birth of Christ, the perfection of his pilgrimage, his substitutionary death, the validation of his resurrection, and his bodily return. Our personal convictions need to be centered on this truth for Christianity to have validity. The truth, then, is a personal possession that becomes a part of who I am.

Since true Christianity seems to be personally oriented, the communal side of life is downplayed. Personal prayer becomes more spiritual than caring for others, and individual Bible study has a greater priority than resolving conflict in the church—in spite of explicit biblical statements to the contrary (e.g., Matt. 5:23–24). Propositional truth takes on an abstract, nonrelational aura even though its real purpose is presumably life related. Our relationship with God takes on much more significance than our relationship with others. It is not surprising that the contemporary caricature of Bunyan's Pilgrim is an attractive image because of its apparent emphasis on the solitary walk.

> Throughout the twentieth century, evangelical Christianity has been preoccupied with contending for propositional truth as revealed in Scripture. The price paid for militantly maintaining biblical truth has cost the church dearly in other areas, especially the interpersonal.[18]

Unfortunately, the separation of the spiritual and the social is a denial of who we are as individuals-in-community. Niebuhr writes that our "social nature makes this purely vertical relation impossible."[19] It also makes truth a body of knowledge that is more linked with personal conviction than vibrant lifestyle. Truth is not expressed in social relation but is resident in the self. The by-product of this for community is clear: The body of Christ does not authenticate the verbal message. John Driver exclaims:

> We are appalled by that unbiblical polarization between the "spiritual" and the "social" aspects of the

church's life and mission which has come to characterize much of modern Western Christian thought.
Is it not possible for the community which confesses
Jesus Christ as Lord to demonstrate with integrity
the wholeness of the gospel of peace which has come
through Jesus Christ?[20]

Such a dichotomy between the spiritual and the social may
find some of its roots in the emergence of science and secu-
larity in the seventeenth and eighteenth centuries. Science
became linked with public truth and facts, while religion was
relegated to private values. When the broader social implications of the Christian gospel were not as viable, the conversion of the individual soul became paramount. Personal
assurance of faith in Christ in this life, as well as the promise
of comfort in a future existence, were central. As a result,
there was a marked split between a fact-public orientation
and a value-private framework.[21]

While faith in Jesus Christ is not achieved by communal connections and responsibilities, faith in Jesus Christ needs to be
expressed by communal connections and responsibilities. To
develop a faith system that is not demonstrated in an earthly
relational framework is to offer a form of religion that is simply preparation for the future. The present becomes irrelevant,
and any sense of duty or obligation to others is unimportant.
All we have to do is get converted and move on to heaven.

This overly individualized approach to Christianity is not
the intent of the Christian gospel as it is presented in Scripture. Such a view can probably be traced to a combination of
the Western influence toward individualism as well as a narrow view of Scripture.[22] More than likely it reflects not just a
separation between the spiritual and the social but between
the church and salvation. Reflect on the following presentation of the gospel, one which could have taken place from the
pulpit in an evangelical church or on a local campus in a one-
on-one interaction:

*The Bible says that you have to deal with God as an
individual. Your family, friends, or colleagues at work are*

not the issue here. It is you and God. You have a need for God. Think of the pain you have in your life. Your anxiety and stress come from sin. If you will accept Jesus as your personal Savior, you will be saved. Your sins will be forgiven. You will experience peace within—a peace that will always be with you. When you have problems and difficulties, you will have someone to help you and support you. Not only that, but you will be prepared for heaven. Rather than spending eternity in hell, you will enjoy heaven forever. All you have to do is make a decision. Accept Jesus into your heart. He will meet your needs. I want you to pray this prayer after me. . . .

What does this approach to evangelism say about community? Notice, first of all, the emphasis on method. There is a rationalistic approach that does not seem to acknowledge a dynamic, spiritual process.[23] One simply has to make a decision. That decision is based on needs that God will meet.

The needs revolve around problems. While sin is linked with the problems, the message is clear. In coming to Christ problems will be dealt with. Needs will be met. Anxiety and tension plaguing this person will be relieved. Conversion will decrease, if not eliminate, struggles. More than that, there is the ongoing provision of someone to help when trouble occurs.

Clearly this is a good deal! I can bring all my concerns and needs to God, who will not only forgive everything I have done but will also meet all my needs. When I have problems he will be there, and I can expect to have inner peace for the rest of my life. All I have to do is make a decision.

In reading the four Gospels, one would be hard pressed to find a single evangelistic interaction that parallels this one. This fact is alarming since this packaged approach is typical in many evangelical circles today. Notable by its absence is any emphasis on the primacy of God in conversion. Conversion begins and ends with the created, not the Creator. Decision making has replaced discipleship as the major metaphor for conversion. You get the impression that getting into this is the most significant issue. What you do once you are in is given minimal acknowledgment.

It is possible that because of God's sovereignty conversion could occur through this method. But what do the new converts bring into Christianity? Why is it much easier to conceptualize God as serving us rather than the reverse? Should it surprise us that many Christians put the personal over the corporate? Why is church secondary to personal devotion? Why is there such a problem-centered orientation to Christianity? Why are there so many disappointed and disillusioned Christians? A privatized and individualized entry into the kingdom, with a focus on meeting needs,[24] will set the pattern for living the same way once you are in. Anderson observes:

> When conversion to Christ is understood first of all as a private and individual decision, incorporation into the community of Christ will become more of a religious or ethical duty. Now that you have been saved, the person is told, you ought to join a church, to become active in the body. It is not surprising that the liturgical events by which the community celebrates its own existence as the body of Christ are viewed rather diffidently by many people who come in by this route. However, for the person who has first of all experienced wholeness of person affirmed as a "gospel of belonging," enacted through rituals which reinforce this reality, growth in faith and knowledge will be supported and encouraged as a continuing event of this participation in community.[25]

An overly personal version of salvation will tend to create a noncommunal approach to Christianity. Hunter refers to this concern with emotional, psychological, and personal needs as "psychological Christocentrism."[26] A relationship with Christ is captured best by inner happiness and peace. Through an acceptance of the gospel you will gain a lot personally and have to give very little communally. As a result, links with a Christian community are not crucial. As long as there is an intrapsychic peace, the interpersonal becomes secondary.[27] You can determine and express your own beliefs autonomously.[28] "Jesus is mine" becomes a complete summary of the Christian faith!

CHRISTIAN COUNSELING AND PRIVATIZATION

In his outline of the history of pastoral care, Don Browning argues that prior to the modern period problems were put in a religious and spiritual framework. In essence, they were positioned in a communal context. It was the church community that took primary responsibility for the cure of souls. Eventually specific individuals began to take over this role. So in some cultures the witch doctor or the magician was invested with healing power. No longer would people rely on a corporate entity to bring healing but on the solitary healer.[29]

In the modern church period this is demonstrated in the increased number of private Christian counselors who work outside the church, individually or in agencies, and offer help to those within it. With the lack of a communal sensibility, problems are no longer conceptualized within the church framework. This position is often legitimized by claims that the clergy have neither the time nor the expertise to deal with the problems that people are experiencing. On top of that, there is a concern that problems may be denied or overly spiritualized when they are brought to the church. What is required, then, is a safe and confidential context where people can deal with their intrapsychic problems privately.

To focus on the individual, however, with a particular emphasis on the intrapsychic, is to provide an inaccurate anthropology. To become obsessed by personal needs, the alleviation of stress, or accurate cognitions is to miss the primacy of the communal. The evangelical counselor who does this is falling into the trap of the culture—a trap that makes the enterprise of counseling an individual rather than a sociocultural phenomenon. In fact, Dueck argues:

> We are not at all confident that the evangelical community possesses the cultural resources nor the ethical consent necessary for healing to occur in its midst. To the extent that evangelical psychologists

> uncritically accept these cultural assumptions, to that extent they may be unaware of the impact of specific social forces impinging on the healing process. We must ask to what extent we have accepted American culture as the benign context for healing.[30]

One of the reasons that Christian counselors do slip in this area is because of a narrow understanding of sin and spirituality. With the concerns of the individual in primary focus, it is easy to ignore the individual-in-community. *Sin* is seen as the opposite of personal piety or as something committed by an individual. It is much harder to conceptualize sin in terms of social structures, institutions, or ideologies, and, of course, most evangelical therapists have had little or no training in how to understand sin's expression in community contexts. There is a greater concern for individual, marriage, or family pathology than there is for social criticism, social ethics or institutional failures.[31] As a result of this, healing is separated from the community and becomes individualized.

It is important to note that community-oriented counseling is not tied to a particular counseling approach. We are not talking about whether one believes in cognitive-behavior modification or ego psychology. Nor are we pitting Larry Crabb against Jay Adams. Further, it is not enough to claim that as a certified marriage and family therapist you represent a theoretical system that is nonindividualistic. One can deal with marriages and families and still minimize the role and function of the Christian community. In fact, family systems may have moved away from the intrapsychic emphasis of much of the therapeutic enterprise, but the issue here is whether it has embraced the primacy of the communal framework.

Unfortunately, much of the Christian counseling movement is assessed by other variables. Critiques are based on anything from the presence of Scripture and prayer, to the degree to which it supports or does not support demonization, to the extent to which it integrates or does not integrate secular knowledge, to the support it has from research data. While these variables have their place, the community focus is noticeable by its absence. Somehow it does not seem to have been a key criterion in the assessment of the Christian counseling literature.

So What Is the Problem?

Community is a confusing topic, particularly in the evangelical world, which has tended toward privatization and produced an approach to Christian counseling that may be more individualistic than communal. But as Gerald Noyce explains:

> Religious faith in the Judeo-Christian tradition is a corporate and communal reality, binding people into mutual care. Representing that corporate nature of religious faith with integrity, as well as drawing on the communal resources of church and synagogue life, is incumbent upon the pastoral counselor with anything more than a shallow religious and theological understanding.[32]

Healing needs to be connected with a Christian community for it to be truly Christian. We cannot isolate the individual counselee and act as if he or she has no communal commitment, responsibility, or accountability. Nor can we let the community off the hook. In many so-called individual problems, the community from which they come plays a central role in the origin or maintenance of the difficulty. At the same time, the community may be part of the resolution of the problem. Often because of a lack of training and understanding the counselor may ignore the power of the community, but this does not eliminate its influence. Finally, the counselor cannot be disconnected from the Christian community. The mores, values, and ethics that come from this body must be embodied in the therapist so they are functioning in a way that is loyal to Christian principles. It is quite possible that the phrase "private Christian counselor" is a contradiction in terms.

Why do well-meaning evangelicals pay lip service to the corporate solidarity of the body of Christ? And why do

Christian counselors fall into the same trap? I suggest there
are three reasons:

1. *Culture*: Many of us have been trained in the context of
   Western individualism, so it is difficult to frame problems and their resolution in a communal paradigm. We
   are not only in the West, we are of it as well.

2. *Therapy*: The therapeutic enterprise, in its alignment with
   Western culture, has tended to emphasize the intrapsychic. Further, counseling has become a form of sanctioned retreat, where pain is privatized and removed
   from any community.

3. *Scriptures*: Many of us do not know how to read the
   Bible! We miss its communal framework and read it with
   our individualistic lenses so we can get something for
   ourselves personally.

SUMMARY

There is a danger in employing the word *community* because
it has lost much of its meaning. There is also a danger in utiliz-
ing the word without any explicit Christian sensibility. For the
purposes of this book, community that is Christian is the visible manifestation of the work of God, through Jesus Christ, in
the church.

Since privatization has not only gripped Western culture but
has also influenced evangelicalism, it is difficult for evangelical
Christians to fully understand the implications of community.
Many have come to faith in Christ with a methodology that has
downplayed the church and made conversion overly personal.
It is no surprise, then, that the Christian counseling movement
has had a strong commitment to privatization.

What are the contributing factors that have produced this
problem? We have been strongly influenced by Western culture,
with its emphasis on the individual, and this has in turn led to
approaches to therapy that focus on healing in the context of a
sanctioned retreat. As Christians this has been reinforced with
an overly personal reading of the Bible and an ignorance of its
communal emphasis.

NOTES

1. J. Bernard, *The Sociology of Community* (Glenview, Ill.: Scott, Foresman, 1973).

2. Christopher Lasch, *The True and Only Heaven: Progress and Its Critics* (New York: Norton, 1991), 83.

3. Ibid.

4. Peggy Rosenthal, *Words and Values: Some Leading Words and Where They Lead Us* (New York: Oxford, 1984), 220.

5. Michael Ignatieff, *The Needs of Strangers* (New York: Viking, Penguin, 1985), 138.

6. M. Scott Peck, *The Different Drum: Community-Making and Peace* (New York: Touchstone, 1987), 59.

7. Ibid., 61, 62, 64.

8. Ibid., 75.

9. Ibid.

10. Dietrich Bonhoeffer, *Life Together* (New York: Harper and Row, 1954), 21.

11. Jean Vanier, *Community and Growth* (London: Darton, Longman and Todd, 1989), 10–11.

12. H. A. Snyder, *The Community of the King* (Downers Grove, Ill.: Inter-Varsity, 1977).

13. Avery Dulles, *Models of the Church* (New York: Image, 1987), 59.

14. I am grateful to Bufford and Buckler for this linkage. Rodger K. Bufford and R. E. Buckler, "Counseling in the Church: A Proposed Strategy for Ministering to Mental Health Needs in the Church," *Journal of Psychology and Christianity* 6 (1987): 21–29.

15. Robert N. Bellah, "Conclusion: Competing Visions of the Role of Religion in American Society," in *Uncivil Religion: Interreligious Hostility in America*, ed. Robert N. Bellah and F. E. Greenspan (New York: Crossroad, 1987), 221.

16. Ibid., 229.

17. James D. Hunter, *American Evangelicalism: Conservative Religion and the Quandary of Modernity* (New Brunswick, N.J.: Rutgers University, 1983).

18. William T. Kirwan, *Biblical Concepts for Christian Counseling: A Case for Integrating Psychology and Theology* (Grand Rapids: Baker Book House, 1984), 130.

19. H. Richard Niebuhr, *Man's Nature and His Communities: Essays on the Dynamics and Enigmas of Man's Personal Existence* (London: Geoffrey Bles, 1965), 130.

20. John Driver, *Community and Commitment* (Kitchener, Ontario: Herald, 1976), 27.

21. For a detailed presentation of this argument, as well as its implications in a postmodern world, see Lesslie Newbigin, *The Gospel in a Pluralistic Society* (Grand Rapids: Eerdmans, 1989).

22. Julie A. Gorman, *Community That Is Christian: A Handbook for Small Groups* (Wheaton, Ill.: Victor Books, 1993), 65–70, has a short section on individualism's penetration of evangelicalism.

23. This link of method with rationality and modernity has been critiqued by Hunter, *American Evangelicalism.*

24. Crabb might be seen as doing this in his approach to the personal needs of security and significance: "A local church is not only uniquely designed to provide a vehicle for meeting significant needs, it is also a natural resource for developing Christian security." Lawrence J. Crabb, Jr., "Basic Biblical Counseling," in *Christian Counseling and Psychotherapy,* ed. David G. Benner (Grand Rapids: Baker Book House, 1987), 102.

25. Ray S. Anderson, *On Being Human: Essays in Theological Anthropology* (Grand Rapids: Eerdmans, 1982), 189.

26. Hunter, *American Evangelicalism,* 95.

27. This tendency has led Hesselgrave to conclude that "in individualistic-independency cultures . . . the decision to accept the heavenly Christ needs to be reinforced by practical and undelayed incorporation into his earthly family." David J. Hesselgrave, *Counseling Cross-Culturally: An Introduction to Theory and Practice for Christians* (Grand Rapids: Baker Book House, 1984), 370.

28. A 1978 Gallup poll found that 80 percent of Americans agreed that people should arrive at their own religious beliefs independent of church or synagogue. *The Unchurched American* (Princeton, N.J.: Princeton Religious Research Center, 1978).

29. For an excellent treatment of this particular issue see: Don S. Browning, *The Moral Context of Pastoral Care* (Philadelphia: Westminster Press, 1976).

30. Al Dueck, "Ethical Contexts of Healing: Peoplehood and Righteousness," *Pastoral Psychology* 35 (1987): 240.

31. For further arguments along these lines see: Timothy J. Johnson," Empowerment as a Christian Helping Strategy: Bridging the Chasm Between Client and Institutional Oppression," *Social Work and Christianity* 17 (1990): 66–78; Kenneth Leech, *Soul Friend: The Practice of Christian Spirituality* (New York: Harper and Row, 1977); Charles R. Ridley, "Cross-Cultural Counseling in Theological Context," *Journal of Psychology and Theology* 14 (1986): 288–97; and H. Steven Scudder, "Social Work and Pastoral Counseling Perspectives: An Exploratory Comparative Analysis," *Social Work and Christianity* 17 (1990): 37–51.

32. Gaylord Noyce, *Pastoral Ethics: Professional Responsibilities of the Clergy* (Nashville: Abingdon, 1988), 109.

Chapter Two

Western Individualism and Community

But we will remain isolated individuals, and the cooperating between us, though it may appear to satisfy our need of one another, will not really satisfy us. For what we really need is to care for one another, and we are only caring for ourselves.
—John MacMurray

I AM THE PRODUCT OF WESTERN CULTURE. If you have a problem with anything—whether it is physical, spiritual, or emotional—you go to a person who is competent enough to help you. From undergraduate psychology training through to a Ph.D. in clinical-counseling psychology, the message has been consistent. Help is offered by a sole expert. The community is rarely mentioned.

This process of socialization does not come from formalized, in-class teaching. It is part of the hidden structure of the culture. If you have a problem with your teeth, you go to a dentist. If you have a problem related to the law, you consult a lawyer. If you have a problem with your heart, you consult a physician. An increase in the seriousness of the problem requires greater expertise in the helper. Your dentist may refer you to an oral surgeon. Your physician may refer you to a cardiologist.

To most Western observers this approach seems right and proper. However, it assumes that expertise is found in individuals rather than in communities. The individual's family and friends play a minimal role in the healing process. Expertise rests with the experts, not with those in the person's communal network.

In our Western culture, the tension around this comes up in the debate over midwives. When women give birth do they require a trained and certified medical practitioner, or can this event be handled by the mother, her family, and a paraprofessional midwife? To involve a midwife is to question the strongly held assumption that the sole trained practitioner is the primary caregiver.

With this backdrop I went to Africa. I taught a counseling course to second-year students in an evangelical theological college. Most of them were preparing for pastoral ministry and were interested in what this Western counselor would have to offer. They expressed surprise at a number of things we did in North America. Why, for example, did we send people to trained counselors when they needed help? The Kenyans spoke of the importance of the family and the village and the need to receive the pooled wisdom resident in that group. Help, healing, and decision making were a mutual responsibility and often involved the individual, the family, and a broader social network. If the person were a Christian, the church had something to offer as well. There was no individual-community dichotomy.

I found this particularly striking when it came to decision making. Western notions of decision making usually involve the individual choosing a particular course. There may be some consultation with others, but excessive reliance on advice can be seen as dependent and reflective of an inability to decide. When a Christian overlay is added, it is often even more individualistic. God has told me what I am to do, so I am going to choose this course. It is his will, and I am going to walk down that road. It is still rugged individualism but dressed up in different clothes.

In that African classroom I heard of some tribal situations where an individual would be struggling with something. The elders of the church and/or village would be called together. The youngest of the group would speak first with the oldest giving the final word. Through this process the individual would receive help. It was not from an individual, and it was definitely not from a formally educated individual. To observe this prizing of the community and its ability to help was a shock to my Western way of thinking. I found out firsthand what Stephen Githumbi meant when he said that the "strongest element in the African church is its sense of community. It is in such community—lived out both within the church and before the world—that the African proverb is most realized, 'I am because you are; if you are not, I cannot be.'"[1]

Many non-Western cultures cherish the collective mode where maturity is not assessed by your distance from others but on your willingness to depend on the pooled wisdom of the group.[2] Being true to yourself is much less important than fidelity to the community. In contrast, our experience of Western culture has taught us to prize independence, self-reliance, and uniqueness so that freedom from others is paramount.

Frequently, cross-cultural comparisons uncover Western arrogance. Since we are the New World, the modern world, the developed and civilized world, the way we see it is the *right* way. Those poor people in other countries just do not understand. If they had broader exposure, they would know that our way is right and their way is wrong. Sadly, such arguments are used to analyze not only those who are at a distance geographically but also the neighbors next door. In Toronto, for example, I am amazed at the number of Anglo–North Americans who make scathing comments about Asian–North Americans who have two or three related families living in the same house. Since we have made separation from the extended family into a psychological virtue, we assume that such a stance is universal and should be adhered to by all.

Those of us who have had cross-cultural experience in countries where the community is valued more highly than the individual would differ with this perspective. We are tired of our Western obsession with privatization and have come to appreciate cultures where interdependence is not only prized but practiced. In fact, it is because of this awareness that returning missionaries often experience more tension coming home than they do returning to the field.

One caution needs to be noted, however. Many Western–non-Western comparisons in past days had an implicit urban-non-urban variable hidden in them. There were fewer people in cities in both Africa and South America in the 1930s compared to the 1990s.[3] If urbanization negates community and facilitates individuality, we may find that the world as a whole is moving more toward the latter than the former. It is possible that such cross-cultural distinctions may not even be viable in the next century.

WESTERN CULTURE

Our understanding of community is central to analyses of modern Western culture. In fact, many social critics will comment on the individual versus nonindividual paradigm, illustrating the centrality of this important concept: for most North Americans any desire they might have for community is in tension with the cultural climate of individualism.[4]

Individualism is the process of prizing the individual over the group. What matters to *me* is more important than what happens to *us*. My self concern has higher value than our common benefit. With the idea of self-reliance and independence fed to us in large doses, we have developed into people who seek our own good before that of another. And now that many Western cultures have a greater multicultural/ethnic/religious blend, pluralism and relativism have contributed significantly to increased autonomy.[5]

Pluralism describes a context where there are people of diverse backgrounds and persuasions. In order to exist within this kind of framework, tolerance and respect become central. Pluralism is a way of acknowledging diversity. It serves to protect individualism. I let you do your thing and you let me do mine. We can both carry on our lives privately without being concerned about our corporate identity. This gives us a loose framework for living in community. As long as we tolerate and respect our differences, we can live together.

However, problems do come. For example, how does a municipal government respond to an immigrant family that has four generations living in the same house when the law stipulates that only three generations may exist together? Or how does a school board respond when Moslem parents complain that their children are being exposed to teaching on the origins of Christmas? In both of these cases pluralism has an answer. We need to live together by respecting our differences.

Relativism plays a key role as well in its opposition to that which is absolute. So if we tried to make laws on what color shirts men had to wear on Mondays, there would be strong objections, for obvious reasons. To absolutize the color of shirts is to take responsibility away from individuals. In this culture, that would be inappropriate. So we allow individuals to choose the color of their shirt. We may not like what they choose. It may make us uncomfortable. We may not ever choose that color ourselves. However, in the spirit of relativism, we will allow others freedom to make their own decisions.

Clearly the color of your shirt is not important. However, combine pluralism and relativism with a more poignant topic, and the issues become more salient. When it comes to abortion, pornography, and homosexuality, the argument for individualism can easily be made with pluralism and relativism as the fundamental substantiation. Pluralism affirms our differences and the need to respect and tolerate these differences. It legitimizes differences between people. You have your viewpoint and I have mine. Both views are acceptable. Then relativism kicks in. Not only do you have your opinion and I have mine, but since truth is relative and not absolute, we do not need to judge each other. Your choice is valid and so is mine. What this creates, then, is a way to coexist individually. We allow each other to make choices (pluralism), and then we validate these choices (relativism). If you support abortion, pornography, and homosexuality and I do not, we can still coexist.

This development did not take place overnight. Prior to 1950, North American culture was much more community centered.[6] However, in the past forty years the individual has taken on greater power and authority, and the community has paid accordingly. Part of this is linked with the move of the workplace out of the home and off the farm. More people began to move to the city where the focus was more individualized and specialized. People were able to make choices and create their own economic, social, physical, and spiritual futures. The community did not dictate to them. They began to function independently, with positive results. There was a much higher standard of living with a greater sense of freedom and tolerance. However, like many social changes, the downside has begun to show itself. Fragmentation has developed, and while individual emancipation has been on the increase, social and community connections have been strained. People have begun to realize that meaning is not found solely in the pursuit of personal success and gratification.

This may describe where we are in Western culture today. Individualism, pluralism, and relativism are the backbone of our culture, but there is a gnawing sense that this is not going to work. Canada's current struggles over a national identity may be traced to this tension. Canadian sociologist Reginald Bibby's summary is an accurate one: "Individually, we have been emancipated; socially, we are in disarray."[7] We desperately want to let every individual and every province be their own master, but we also want to exist together. However, individualism does not provide an appropriate structure for community existence.[8] We have become "spiritual orphans"[9]— people who are abandoned, deprived, and alone, yet who desire to become attached and connected in relationship.

As a result, some have made a distinction between the home and society—a distinction that has historical roots. Because there is so much fragmentation in the latter, there is a need to strengthen the former. Needs for intimacy can be achieved in the family while the rest of the world is distant. The domestic sphere becomes a "haven in a heartless world,"[10] to use Christopher Lasch's phrase.

> Today the "experience" of community has to be found in the company of "family and friends," which satisfies the need for intimacy in a world governed by the impersonal dynamics of the market. . . . The "coexistence" thesis is not new; in one form or another, it has figured in discussions of community from the beginning. It was the hope of sealing off

private life as a protected sanctuary from the market
that led nineteenth-century moralists to sentimental-
ize the domestic circle.[11]

This approach, however, begs a number of questions:

Is removal from society at large and a retreat into marriage
and the family a genuine form of community?

Do problems with individualism disappear with an emphasis on the domestic sphere?

Where do we go when we experience difficulties in our
marriages?

> Men and women cannot solve their problems of
> power, responsibility, and relationship alone. We
> are, whether as individuals, couples or nuclear fami-
> lies, dwarfed by the task. We cannot evolve new
> roles and new familial arrangements without sup-
> port, without a caring and intervening community,
> and most certainly not without a social order and
> social policy that promotes these ends.[12]

Others cope with individualism by expanding their view
of community. In light of its disintegration and the separation we experience from each other, we need to have a
broader consciousness. Ironically, as our culture has become
more fragmented, we now use the word *world* as an adjective. So we have world-class cities, hotels, and ballparks;
world travel and communication; even world Christians. Tied
in with this global emphasis is our consciousness of broader
world issues: the earth, the environment, the ozone layer.
Even in our struggle with autonomy and disconnection from
others there is some sense in which we seem to be trying to
bond with anything and everything. Kolbenschlag observes:

> We are the children of the Enlightenment: our
> world is circumscribed by our notions of ego, per-
> sonal consciousness, and autonomy. The worldview

is now being radically altered. A perception of our radical inseparability and connectedness is emerging as the next threshold of social revolution. Indeed, the depth of our interdependence with the whole earth-cosmic system is now becoming a much more primary reality than our own autonomy or survival or salvation.[13]

One of the by-products of individualism is that we are a people who are into the moment. There is minimal appreciation for the past. A return to history goes no further than a nostalgic experience of fifties and sixties music. By the same token, economic, social, and political conditions make the future look bleak. No longer can college graduates be promised lucrative employment that will last forever. People in their forties are looking forward to being eased out of their jobs within ten years. They worry about pension plans that may be obsolete in thirty years.

What does all this produce? Historical discontinuity.[14] We become disconnected from the past and from the future. Our lives are informed not by what we have experienced or what we will experience but by what we are experiencing. In essence, life is that which is taking place now, at this moment. So we can live for today in the true sense of the word. And in living for today, the only major concern is myself.

Given the lack of impetus from the past and stimulation from the future, self-preoccupation is really a form of coping. When people have learned to retreat into themselves to cope with survival in the present, communal concerns are negated. Alan Bloom laments:

This indeterminate or open-ended future and the lack of a binding past mean that the souls of young people are in a condition like that of the first men in the state of nature—spiritually unclad, unconnected, isolated, with no inherited or unconditional connection with anything or anyone. They can be anything they want to be, but they have no particular reason to want to be anything in particular. . . . Why are we

> so surprised that such unfurnished persons should
> be preoccupied principally with themselves and
> with finding means to avoid permanent free fall?[15]

The self-preoccupation of Western culture is often con-
demned in ways that reflect a lack of understanding. It is not
that people are egotistical in the sense that they are obsessed
with how wonderful they are. Rather a retreat into self becomes
a form of narcissism—a way to cope given the perceived lack
of alternatives.

The distinction between egoism and narcissism is clarified
by the Greek myth of Narcissus, the young Thespian. One of
the prophets, Tiresias, predicted that he would live a long
time if he did not know himself. During the course of his life
a beautiful mountain nymph, Echo, loved him, but he rejected
her. She called on the gods to bring vengeance through un-
requited love. One day Narcissus was walking by a pool of
water and saw his reflection. He fell in love with it, became
enthralled and eventually died of anguish. What was the flaw
in the personality of Narcissus? In large measure it was his
inability to love others combined with a preoccupation with
his own image and importance. As a result, the term is often
used in clinical circles to describe people who appear invul-
nerable, devoid of feeling, and obsessed with their own
presentation and abilities. It is not self-preoccupation in the
sense of an egotistical self-absorption but rather an inability
to connect with others combined with a threatened sense of
self.[16] These are people who have self-dislike rather than
people who are in love with themselves.

The modern Westerner is seen, then, as someone who has become cut off from the past and the future. Self-preoccupation
becomes a survival mechanism since there is little else to absorb
the person's time and energy. Such narcissistic individualism
results in focus on self rather than others. In the process, the community becomes secondary to the needs of the individual.

This linking of individualism, narcissism, and needs is an
important one that is often ignored in this culture because personal needs have become instrumental to our understanding
of life. Marriage, for example, is often conceptualized in terms

of the meeting of needs. Job choices are made on the basis of individual needs, and leaving your job can easily be explained on the basis of needs not being met. In both cases of marriage and career there seems to be an inherent danger: a needs orientation may be a veiled form of individualism.

The link of individualism and needs is seen in the area of consumer purchases. Whereas advertising used to describe the strengths of a given product, now marketing strategies key in on a need for consumption. The upbeat lifestyle of sports heroes and entertainment figures linked with a given commodity make the product attractive. Since there is no past and no future, the consumer is living for today and for self. Somehow through the purchase of goods, a need for fulfillment, satisfaction, or pleasure will be met.

This consumer orientation has been facilitated, as Ivan Illich has observed, by the shift of *need* as verb to *need* as noun.[17] At one point need was a form of desiring or acting:

I need water.

I need money.

I need a car.

Need was connected with the acquisition of something. However, the term has taken on substance in and of itself:

I have a need for security.

I have a need for achievement.

I have a need for sex.

In these cases need has become an object in itself. Somewhere, lurking within, there is an entity that precipitates and motivates. It not only is described, as is illustrated by its use as a noun, but it also becomes a form of explanation: The reason I am working hard is because I have a need for achievement. What that entails, where it comes from, and its moral and ethical value are absent.[18] What is most important is that I, personally and individually, experience it. Need becomes a form of intrapsychic analysis.

The outcome for community is clear. If my needs and their fulfillment are central, then I have conceptualized life in terms that are self-oriented. My concern for the community, by definition, is limited.[19] However, if the culture were duty and responsibility oriented, needs would be conceptualized in different terms. Rather than working in the city to meet the needs of the poor and disadvantaged, the street worker would function out of a sense of preexisting love and acceptance. Personal and individual needs would be replaced by a sense of communal commitment and responsibility.

> Each time we experience ourselves as recipients of gift, then in that moment, however fleeting, we have ourselves seen the lie in all the chatter and babble about the purpose of life being no more than the challenge of meeting our own and others' needs. In that moment, which we usually call joy, we have seen beyond ourselves and our needs.[20]

One of the places this would be demonstrated is in parenting, where the meeting of children's needs has become sacrosanct. Rather than encouraging parents to meet the needs of their children, the emphasis would be on parental love and care. As Tony Walter points out:

> In a world where nothing seems certain, we latch onto one thing that does seem certain: that children have definite and identifiable needs. We can all agree that these needs must be met if they are to grow up into decent human beings, though as a society we haven't the faintest clue what a decent human being is. Nor have most parents. We don't know what these needs are needed for, but that they are needed has become unquestionable dogma.[21]

Western culture is need-centered, and in the process, another symptom of individualism is revealed. But what has contributed to this preoccupation? Why are we so oriented to needs both in ourselves and others? To some degree economic and social realities play a role, but there is no question that this has been facilitated by modern psychology. While we are interested in the universe, the earth, our country, and our neighborhood, our main interest is in our own psyches and their peculiar needs. As Ignatieff explains:

> The needs of our spirit have been re-born in the intensive search for the logic of our childhood, our dreams, our desires. We share with other tribes the idea that certain forms of knowledge are necessary to our health, but we are the only tribe which believes that such necessary knowledge can be private knowledge—the science of the individual. We have created a new need, the need to live an examined life.[22]

The most blatant example of this is the so-called hierarchy of needs.[23] Based on a progressive stage model, life is conceptualized around needs. At the foundation is a need for survival followed by needs for safety/security, belongingness/affection, respect/self-respect, and self-actualization. It is assumed that when the so-called lower needs are met, the rest can be fulfilled in turn. The explicit message is clear: Progress is achieved by the constant meeting of needs. There is also an implicit message: These needs are perceived to be givens. Natural and normal, they are part of everyone's existence. In the process we are drawn into a presupposition that is fundamental: Life is captured best by an intrapsychic emphasis with needs at the center.

SO WHAT IS THE PROBLEM?

Many of us are the product of Western culture. This has had a profound influence on the way we understand counseling. The fact that my East African experience was jolting is a testimony to the fact that my presuppositions regarding help and healing were well entrenched.

Why is it hard for us to understand the importance of the communal? When your culture enshrines individualism, pluralism, and relativism, you learn how to protect the individual.

When you are socialized to be self-preoccupied as a form of protection from a disconnected past and a bleak future, it is impossible to look for community links with others. When the meeting of needs becomes a primary focus, it is difficult to think outside of a narcissistic preoccupation.

In terms of help and healing, many of us—pastors and counselors alike—need to understand the importance of being in the West but not of it.

Summary

An overview of cultural issues will reveal that community is a key concern. However, there do appear to be differences in an understanding of community. While some non-Western cultures tend to place the person in their communal setting, the West seems to elevate the individual above the community.

Western culture, in its noncommunal orientation and historical discontinuity, is permeated by an obsession with the moment. A link between the past, present, and future is tenuous at best. What is happening now is most salient—particularly what is happening to me. We may be spiritual orphans unconnected with others, but we become true to ourselves by a focus on our own needs and a generalized intrapsychic preoccupation.

The Western context breeds a form of individualism that discourages communal understanding. The natural by-product is a focus on autonomous persons with their inner struggles and intrapsychic needs. Pastors and private counselors need to beware of this influence.

NOTES

1. Stephen Githumbi, "I Am Because You Are; If You Are Not, I Cannot Be!" *Theology, News and Notes* (1991): 7–8.

2. David J. Hesselgrave, *Counseling Cross-Culturally: An Introduction to Theory and Practice for Christians* (Grand Rapids: Baker Book House, 1984), distinguishes collectivistic-dependency cultures from individualistic-independency cultures.

3. For references that provide urban demographic trends as well as their implications for evangelism, see Ray Bakke, *The Urban Christian: Effective*

Ministry in Today's Urban World (Downers Grove, Ill.: InterVarsity, 1987); and D. Barrett, *World Class Cities and World Evangelization* (Birmingham, Ala.: New Hope, 1986).

4. This point is expressed well by M. M. Poloma, "Christian Covenant Communities: An Adaption of the Intentional Community for Urban Life," in *A Reader in Sociology: Christian Perspectives,* ed. C. P. De Santo, C. Redekop, and W. L. Smith Hinds (Kitchener, Ontario: Herald, 1980), 609–30.

5. This entire section, relating individualism to pluralism and relativism, is built on the work of Reginald W. Bibby, who critiques Canadian culture. Non-Canadian readers will find his concepts helpful even though his conclusions may not have the same application in other contexts. Reginald W. Bibby, *Mosaic Madness: The Poverty and Potential of Life in Canada* (Toronto, Ontario: Stoddart, 1990).

6. S. Lipsett, *Continental Divide: The Values and Institutions of the United States and Canada* (Toronto, Ontario: C. D. Howe Institute, 1989).

7. Bibby, *Mosaic Madness*, 15.

8. Bibby distinguishes between Canada and the U.S. on this point. In Canada the stress on pluralism serves to separate us but does nothing to bring us together. In contrast, the U.S. has an individualistic thrust in the context of a strong community commitment.

9. For this concept I am indebted to M. Kolbenschlag, *Lost in the Land of Oz: The Search for Identity and Community in American Life* (New York: Harper and Row, 1988).

10. Christopher Lasch, *Haven in a Heartless World: The Family Besieged* (New York: Basic Books, 1977), concludes that the outside world cannot be separated from the modern family. While he is critical of its influence, society's intrusion on the private sector cannot be denied. A different perspective is given by Philip Slater, *The Pursuit of Loneliness: American Culture at the Breaking Point* (Boston: Beacon Press, 1970), who suggests that privatization is expressed when there is a retreat to the domestic context.

11. Christopher Lasch, *The True and Only Heaven: Progress and Its Critics* (New York: Norton, 1991), 165.

12. Kolbenschlag, *Land of Oz*, 180.

13. Ibid.

14. See Christopher Lasch, *The Culture of Narcissism: American Life in an Age of Diminishing Expectations* (New York: Norton, 1978).

15. Allan Bloom, *The Closing of the American Mind* (New York: Simon and Schuster, 1987).

16. This discussion is brief; however, the reader may wish to pursue Christopher Lasch, *The Minimal Self: Psychic Survival in Troubled Times* (New York: Norton, 1984); A. Lowen, *Narcissism* (New York: Macmillan, 1983); and N. S. Xavier, *The Two Faces of Religion: A Psychiatrist's View* (Tuscaloosa, Ala.: Portals, 1987).

17. For further discussion on this issue, see Ivan D. Illich, *Toward a History of Needs* (New York: Pantheon, 1978).

18. For a short but penetrating book that is extremely helpful in this area, see Tony Walter, *Need: The New Religion* (Downer's Grove, Ill.: InterVarsity, 1985).

19. Michael Ignatieff, *The Needs of Strangers* (New York: Viking Penguin, 1985), gives a thorough presentation on the need orientation and the welfare state.

20. Walter, *Need*, 157.

21. Ibid., 73.

22. Ignatieff, *Needs of Strangers*, 78–79.

23. This notion is usually linked with Abraham Maslow, *Toward a Psychology of Being*, 2d ed. (New York: Van Nostrand, 1968), and Abraham Maslow, *Motivation and Personality*, 2d ed. (New York: Harper and Row, 1970).

Chapter Three

The Power of the Sanctioned Retreat

Whatever it means to be a Christian psychologist, it is surely not imposing a privatistic religious experience on a client for the sake of altering behavior.

—Ray Anderson

IN THE CHURCH WHERE I SPENT MY adolescent years, there were two individuals who had psychological problems. I did not know this at the time because the formal announcements about their situations were obscure and nonspecific. These two people were "having problems," "struggling," "away for a while," or "needing a rest." They would disappear for lengthy periods of time, and the conversation about this was at the level of a whisper. No one seemed to know what was going on, and those who did were unwilling or unable to talk about it. As a teenager this made a lasting impression. People with heart problems or strokes did not seem to create problems for the Christian community, but those with psychological problems did not fit. We had a language system to talk about birth, measles, and cancer, but concerns of the psyche were muted. It is possible that this may have been unique to that particular community of faith, but I suspect it is not atypical of much of evangelicalism.

Eventually, I found out that both of these individuals were struggling with clinical depression and that they were going for private counseling to non-Christians. As I got closer to both situations, I heard the quiet descriptions of what was happening and the speculation as to why. Some were concerned that these two people were not coming to church enough. When they returned, it was a sign that they were better. Others speculated on the degree to which this was attention-seeking behavior. A number made negative comments on the field of psychology and saw it as contributing to the difficulties rather than solving them. But all of this took place quietly, behind the scenes.

I found it ironic that many of the people in that church went to Christian mechanics, Christian real estate agents, Christian accountants, and Christian physicians, but many of them appeared to accept the involvement of private, non-Christian counselors. Further, no one that I heard talked about the potential role of that particular Christian community either in a possible contribution to the development of the problems or to their resolution. The healing was to take place in a private counseling context.

Interestingly, it was those two situations and the response of that particular community that stimulated my interest in the field of psychology, eventually leading to a Ph.D. in the field. I wanted to be part of the bridge between the church and the world of the private counselor.

THERAPY AS SOLUTION OR PROBLEM?

Modern social critics have concluded that the primary climate of Western culture has shifted from the religious to the therapeutic.[1] We frame life in terms that reflect a fundamental psychological awareness. That is not to say that everyone has had exposure to academic psychology. To operate with an orientation that is therapeutic is to be influenced by an ethos that goes beyond formal training, occurring at a subconscious level even within people who might choose otherwise if they were more aware of its influence. Christopher Lasch comments:

What matters is psychic self-improvement: getting
in touch with their feelings, eating health food, taking lessons in ballet or belly-dancing, immersing
themselves in the wisdom of the East, jogging,
learning how to "relate," overcoming the "fear of
pleasure." Harmless in themselves, these pursuits,
elevated to a program and wrapped in the rhetoric
of authenticity and awareness, signify a retreat from
politics and a repudiation of the recent past.[2]

What is the essence of the therapeutic climate? The development, maintenance, and well-being of the self. Groups, courses,
and books that hinge on this pursuit are endless. Lurking beneath them is a powerful assumption: Somehow by the mastery
of self one will find fulfillment and self-actualization. In fact, this
has become a prerequisite to proper relating. Unless the self is
in proper perspective, meaningful connections with others are
impossible. Bloom observes:

> For us the most revealing and delightful distinction—
> because it is so unconscious of its wickedness—is
> between inner-directed and other-directed, with the
> former taken to be unqualifiedly good. Of course, we
> are told, the healthy inner-directed person will really
> care for others. To which I can only respond: If you can
> believe that, you can believe anything.[3]

This is the built-in assumption of much of the therapeutic
enterprise. By focusing on the self, you will be able to care for
others. One becomes a foundation for the other. An interesting
corollary of this notion is captured in the title of a book—*A
Time for Caring: How to Enrich Your Life Through an Interest and
Pleasure in Others*.[4] Self-actualization is facilitated by involvement in community. Community, then, has become intertwined
with the pursuit of the self. But as Rosenthal has decried:

> It sounds as if we've gotten into community but are
> marching there to the same old beat of self-interest,
> moving just in a slightly larger circle encompassing

> others with a similar interest—as if, that is, in going
> from self-concern to community concern we haven't
> gone very far.[5]

What has happened is that the therapeutic sensibility has taken over from religion as a major form of salvation. So whether a person believes in sin or not, there is a general sense that people do experience conflict and problems. At times there is an existential tension that pervades life, and this drives us to some sort of answer. We look for a form of salvation. We want recovery. Help. Answers. Where do we go for these?

You only have to go back to my parents' generation to find religion providing many of the answers. For many people life was conceptualized in a theological framework that put God at the center. The driving concern was not the internal functioning of the human psyche but the dynamic relationship between the Creator and his community. When problems occurred they were placed in that framework—a framework that provided parameters for proper functioning. You did not look inside to find a cure. Your obligation was to God and his community, not yourself.

In modern culture, however, therapy provides the answers to many of life's questions. If therapy is a contributor to individualism, then, in the words of Paul Vitz, we may argue that "psychology has become more a sentiment than a science and is now part of the problem of modern life rather than part of its resolution."[6] Since therapy enhances individualism, our Western push toward autonomy is not going to be arrested. If anything, it may be facilitated and in the process, community will be negated.

Three sets of terms will help us understand the individual-community tension in more detail: Gesellschaft-Gemeinschaft, analytic-commitment, and autoplastic-alloplastic. We will examine each of these briefly.

GESELLSCHAFT-GEMEINSCHAFT

Toennies has distinguished between a form of social existence characterized by *Gesellschaft* (society) rather than *Gemeinschaft* (community).[7] The societal emphasis, or *Gesellschaft*, is more individualistic. People have varied interests, education, and occupations, and they reflect an urban mentality that is nurtured by technology, capitalism, pluralism, and a freedom from authority. In contrast, *Gemeinschaft* is communal in orientation and is characterized by a common belief system that is usually expressed in an agricultural context. Village life is central, and people exist by sharing resources rather than hoarding them. Faith and religion play an integral role in daily life.

Classic social theory captured *Gemeinschaft* well when it taught that the health and wholeness of the individual was tied directly to membership in a community. Philip Rieff points out that whether it was the Greek politician, the individual Hebrew, or the enlightened economic person of the eighteenth century, there was a link with the communal.[8] The good of the individual could not be separated from the good of the whole. By implication, therapy for the individual could not be conceptualized without the perspective of community. The only real cure that could occur was one that acknowledged the individual-in-community. Rieff goes on to say that "community cures through the achievement by the individual of his collective identity. To cure a man, one need only return him to his community or construct a new one."[9]

However, the social critics have made it clear that the religious bias is no longer the accepted way to understand people. A new grid is operative—one that reflects our current psychological mindedness. Simply stated, that grid is therapy. It is now the way to understand human functioning as it provides us with appropriate analyses of motivation and attitude. Ironically, it not only moves us from religion to psychotherapy, but it reflects a move from the community to the individual. In essence, Western psychology becomes one more form of individualism.[10]

ANALYTIC-COMMITMENT

It is in this broader context that we can distinguish between analytic therapies and commitment therapies.[11] Analytic orientations are based on the assumption that the well-being of the individual is linked with the ability to be just that—an individual. In fact, when people come for help they are seen as those who, given their lack of communal attachment, need to be helped toward self-management. The therapist functions in much the same way. He or she is not representative of any particular moral or ethical community. Therapy is constructed in such a way that the therapist's own character and lifestyle are incidental to the process. Competence and skill are central.

Let's illustrate the analytic therapy orientation from a Christian camping situation. One of the full-time staff finds another staff person doing drugs. Rather than dealing with the staff person in the context of the community, he or she is referred outside to a therapist who prizes individuality and autonomy. Instead of being a representative of the camp community, the therapist offers a morally neutral perspective that seeks to help the individual deal with the drug problem. The community sensibility and all that it represents becomes unimportant, and the therapist does not have to worry about being an exemplar figure. Success will be judged more in terms of therapeutic skill and the resultant change in individual behavior.

Commitment therapies are based on classic social theory or *Gemeinschaft*. Counseling occurs with a full recognition that an individual's well-being is dependent on his or her full involvement in the community. However, this does not just apply to the person desiring help but also to the helper. As a representative of a community, the therapist becomes the exemplar or sacral figure in that the ideals of the community are actualized. In this sense the community not only forms part of the counselee's support but is epitomized in the actions of the therapist.

> It is the function of the sacralist to help both an individual and an entire community carry out their pledges to some communal purpose. . . . He speaks for some corporate identity within which the individual can feel secure in his personal identity.[12]

Imagine if the camp had hired a full-time person who was given the responsibility of being the chaplain to the rest of the staff. Some of the chaplain's work might be informal and crisis-centered, but he or she would also set up formal meeting times if that were requested. The chaplain could begin meeting with the person regularly not only as a counselor but as a representative of that particular community. The counseling would be an implicit statement that both people work within that given community and that, while one has fallen short of the expected standards of behavior, the other is representative of the community mores.

AUTOPLASTIC-ALLOPLASTIC

The autoplastic-alloplastic distinction has been utilized in cross-cultural counseling situations.[13] To illustrate this, reflect on the missionary who struggles in her work because of a high need for privacy. She is in a context where this is not respected, and it has created a considerable amount of stress. She feels manipulated to share all her thoughts, feelings, and experiences with her fellow missionaries. The counselor who has an autoplastic orientation might interpret her struggle historically. Maybe she has a sense of insecurity and shame that expresses itself in a desire to stay more distant from others. The counselor focuses on this area with the ultimate view of helping her adjust to the setting she is in. Her problem, in essence, is intrapsychic, and change needs to occur internally.

Alloplastic counselors see the source of her dysfunction as inherent to the system in the mission organization. There is too much pressure to be vulnerable, and her resistance to doing so is a sign of strength, not weakness. Since the social structure is the source of the dysfunction, the counseling focuses on ways to initiate institutional change. The intrapsychic becomes secondary. What is important here is that the allocation of responsibility lies with the system, not the person. Furthermore, the system is not a cover for the blaming of another individual. It is the community that has an inherent dysfunction, not the psyche of the individuals within that community.

The community orientation is reflected in Gemeinschaft commitment therapies, and alloplastic approaches. Unfortunately, much of Western psychology is not resident in this milieu but reflects a view of therapy where individualism is enhanced by a noncommunal orientation.[14] The focus is on freeing the person from community restraints rather than advocating the individual-in-community paradigm. What becomes more important is the intrapsychic component.

INTRAPSYCHIC EMPHASIS

One place the intrapsychic emphasis manifests itself is in the deification of self and its capacity to make choices that will facilitate self-actualization. Our future fate is not in the hands of God. Nor is it resident in the community. Essentially it rests with us. We are in control of our own destinies. We can do what we want to do, be what we want to be. All of it is based on choice. This version of self-management is utilized in various forms of self-help groups as well as money-making schemes and dating services. Control is placed in the will, and all that is needed is the flexing of the volitional muscle. Subtly, the community is rendered nonexistent. All I need to function is myself.

The intrapsychic emphasis also shows itself in the deification of the emotive. What one feels takes precedence over what one believes. In fact, "I feel" has become synonymous with "I believe." So to say, "I don't feel comfortable with a lot of what the apostle Paul wrote," is to express a contemporary moral judgment. However, it lacks in substance and content and is not premised on any stated foundation. There is no historical connectedness with what the biblical community has done with Paul over the years. Nor is there any particular interest in how the faith community of the present deals with the apostle. The internal, intrapsychic orientation, with the domination of feeling, becomes the ethical and moral touchstone for biblical scholarship.

While this intrapsychic emphasis tends to minimize the communal, the modern therapeutic sensibility has built in a linkage between the two. Even though self-sufficiency, introspection, and individual freedom are paramount, they become the basis upon which the individual relates to the community. In other words, my own individuality becomes a prerequisite for connecting with others.[15] So it is not uncommon for secular books on counseling and relationships to push the development of self as a necessary and sufficient condition for relating to others. The following quotes capture this orientation vividly:

The self is the foundation of all relationships, so the goals of the first part of the book are self-discovery and self-satisfaction, with practical objectives of self-understanding and heightened self-esteem.[16]

Because the counselor's primary commitment is to individual growth and development rather than to the facilitation of group ends, the counselor is particularly concerned with those socialization processes that help the individual develop identity, self-awareness, values, and goals. . . . The counselor is not concerned with helping the individuals adjust to or resist those socialization forces, but rather with helping them learn to harness those forces in ways that will bring about maximum personal development in terms of a personal value system derived in a humanizing context of an open and pluralistic society. . . . The universe is mechanistically conceived and the human race is its master. . . . humans are essentially equal . . . humans are perfectible.[17]

Obviously, we need a degree of self-understanding and self-acceptance in order to relate to others. However, if the self becomes paramount and the primary basis upon which we relate to others, the community could simply become one more way in which self-development occurs. The theory would say that we relate better if we are intrapsychically sound, but the reality may be quite different. As Rieff has argued, "The modern individual can only use community as the necessary stage for his effort to enhance himself—if not always, or necessarily, to enrich himself."[18]

Lest the Christian reader think that such tendencies are only linked with the secular mind, reflect on a Christianized version of the same approach. You have probably heard the argument offered as follows: The Bible says you should love your neighbor as yourself. It also says that you should love God. In order to love God, you need to be able to love your neighbor. In order to love your neighbor, you need to love yourself. Those who do not love themselves cannot love their neighbor. Those who cannot love their neighbor cannot love God.

The argument is an appealing one and is part of the therapeutic sensibility in its emphasis on the intrapsychic. There are three relationships noted: you and God, you and others, and you and yourself. However, the initial project is your connection with yourself, and until that is in order the other two relationships will be hindered. So self-development becomes a prerequisite to community functioning. The appeal of this probably ties to its emphasis on the intrapsychic and to the fact that it appears to have biblical support (see Lev. 19:18; Matt. 19:19, 22:39; Mark 12:31–33; Rom. 13:9; Gal. 5:14; Eph. 5:28; James 2:8).

However, a number of questions need to be asked. Are there two commandments to love, or three? Is love of self assumed or commanded? Is the major project self-love or love of others and God? How do we understand love in this context? How does one cultivate self-love? What is the time frame if love of self is to precede love of others and love of God? If spending time and energy on self is a behavioral demonstration of love, then love of others and God can be predicated on such an assumption. We can be asked to spend time and energy on others and on God and in so doing reflect our love for them. On the other hand, if love is primarily an intrapsychic phenomenon that describes our feelings about ourselves, it may take some time before it is in proper condition to be channeled out to others.[19]

DIFFERENTIATION

Another conceptual issue that separates the intrapsychic from the communal is that of differentiation.[20] Since differentiation is an important concept in therapy, we need to reflect on its influence on our understanding of community. Based on the assumption that one needs to have a good sense of self before closeness with others can occur, differentiation conceptualizes life as a tension between independence and dependence. Since we begin our lives in complete dependence on our mother and other significant people, there is a constant struggle around who we are as individuals and who we are in relation to others. The so-called terrible twos are usually a time of conflict because the young child is going through a stage of self-assertion where dependence on parents is lessening. Some parent(s) will allow this assertion to occur and see it as part of the normal developmental process, while others will interpret it as bad behavior that needs to be eliminated. This often sets the tone for what will occur as the child gets older.

Children whose parents do not allow them to differentiate are told what to feel, when to feel it, and how to express it. Their behavior is monitored obsessively, and they learn that their own choices are not respected. This has a number of consequences. Because these children come to rely on their parent(s) in a dependent sense, a sense of insecurity may develop. After all, if someone else dictates how you should or should not respond, you soon learn that you cannot trust your own responses. In fact, this may provide a partial explanation as to why many children who come from "strong caring families" manifest insecurity. The care was sufficiently excessive that it taught them to doubt their own choices. If someone else is going to do everything for you, then you do not develop the skill to do it yourself.

For older children this dependence and insecurity can generalize to other social contacts. Feeling uncomfortable with their own values and ideas, there may be an excessive desire to be affirmed and loved. This may have an effect in marriage[21] or may even create a strain in their relationship with their parents.[22] It makes it hard for people to function because they are confused over what they believe and why. So much of life has been given to leaning on others that opportunities to stand on their own create fear and discomfort. Even when placed in a context where their opinion is considered valuable and is solicited, they will tend to defer to others, preferring the safer course of dependence. Unfortunately, these people often appear sensitive and caring, but in fact, they are simply covering up a confusion in personal identity.

While differentiation is a technical therapeutic concept, the process it describes is familiar to most in our culture. Whether we are parents or not, we all understand that growing up involves separation from our families of origin. To become an adult you need to move beyond your role as a child. Being an individual means standing on your own two feet, being able to make your own decisions in accord with your own value system. However, we need to step back from this and ask what this analysis communicates about the individual-community relationship. What does it say about the communal side of people?

Are we suggesting that being an individual is the ultimate in psychological health? What is the relationship between the self and the family?[23] Is the separation from the family community an appropriate definition of individuality? It is possible, for example, that an interdependent relationship with family is the ideal. This would not necessarily reflect passive dependence nor reactive independence but a healthy sense of self combined with a balanced view of family. While this sort of balance is not easily achieved, it may be more consistent with an anthropology that sees humanity-in-community. Unfortunately, therapeutic views of differentiation that separate the person from the family may be reflecting a Western preoccupation with individualism and the intrapsychic. In the process, the role of the community may be negated.

THERAPY AS SANCTIONED RETREAT

Anyone who has done counseling has been on the receiving end of this kind of feedback: "I really like coming here to see you. I find it safe. It is not like my church, family, marriage, or job. I feel like I can tell you anything and you will listen and understand. I do not feel accepted anywhere else." At first glance these sentiments can give a counselor a moral boost, a sense of well-being, a feeling that he or she is doing something right. They may also reflect the counselee's reality. It truly is a retreat from life—a home away from home.

These are profound comments about the nature of the therapeutic process. What are people saying when they describe the counseling hour as different from the rest of life? Are they suggesting it is not real or just that it is not like their reality? Can they expect a similar response from their community when they return to it, or is the therapeutic hour unique? Coming at it more pessimistically, is the therapist being genuine, or is he or she just playing a role in being so kind and understanding?

Our answers to these questions depend largely on whether we see therapy as a sanctioned retreat[24] or as a part of life. If the former, then we do not have to expect counseling to look like life. The fact that the counselor is caring, empathic, and understanding in providing a safe place is all that matters. The so-called moral neutrality of this environment is acceptable. Whether the rest of the world operates with similar principles is irrelevant. However, if counseling is conceptualized as part of life, then it needs to be looked at socially, politically, morally, and historically. It cannot be separated out from the rest of existence but must submit itself to the same analyses as the rest of the culture.

So one could well ask whether the counseling process reflects the individualism of the culture.

Does it tend to privatize pain and difficulty and localize it in the psyche rather than the community?

Is the moral and ethical context of the broader community important in counseling, or does the counseling context reflect the subjective morality of the therapist?

Which is given priority—the good of the broader culture or the good of the individual?[25]

To protect the therapeutic process from these questions is to compartmentalize, and therapy becomes immune to sociocultural analyses. Most important, it puts therapy into the realm of the individual rather than the communal. The broader concerns of the community, whether that community is religious or secular, are not taken into consideration. Therapy becomes a private affair, a sanctioned retreat, an enterprise that supplies its own mores and ethics. Note that in all of this what goes on in the counseling is not the major issue. We are not talking about what the counselor says or does not say, nor the particular behavior the client might engage in. The concern here is with the process and structure of therapy itself.

In some ways it may not be a surprise that modern therapy can be seen as a sanctioned retreat. If the field in general is individualized in its orientation and the intrapsychic is a major preoccupation, then one might expect that the process would be cut off from the community. It raises serious questions, however, about the degree to which therapy is simply a reflection of the culture where privatization is held in high esteem and communal connections are minimized. Again, therapy may have become part of our Western problem rather than part of its solution.

EXCEPTIONS

While we have argued that the therapeutic sensibility moves toward an individualistic orientation to help and away from a communal base, there are exceptions to this. One might argue that family systems therapy[26] fits this exception, but as has already been noted, such an approach does not necessarily emphasize the centrality of the Christian community. On the other hand, some writers have noted the importance of counseling in the context of the local church,[27] while others have discussed the role of that community in nurturing individuals who are hurting.[28] A recent article calls for the development of a specialty within psychology that will help congregations function effectively.[29] James Olthius has proposed a more relational therapeutic model that puts increased emphasis on relational issues and interconnectedness.[30]

However, while each of these approaches reflect a desire to move away from an emphasis on individualistic views of people, there are at least three therapeutic approaches that are built substantively on a communal orientation and have direct application to Christian communities: therapeutic community, live-in communities, and lay counseling. We will look at each of these briefly and note their sensitivity to community issues.

THERAPEUTIC COMMUNITY

The therapeutic community[31] literature advocates the cultivation of a social organization where the total system is emphasized rather than the deviant behavior of the individual. Every member is a full participant in the functioning of the community with a common interest in the healing of the whole person. Whereas typical healing communities like psychiatric wards or hospitals are based on roles and division of responsibility, this approach sees all the members as being responsible for healing. To advocate that the doctors are responsible for health while the support staff should confine themselves to cleaning and food preparation is to miss the point. Each individual has a unique role in the functioning of the social system.

This places the so-called deviant members in a different light. They are not perceived as the ones needing treatment as much as the ones who are part of the entire system. They are not dependent on others as much as they are part of an interdependent framework. This spreads the authority throughout the social organization so that no one person or group of individuals is charged with the responsibility of therapy. Care is a reciprocal process and not a patronizing gesture from someone who is higher on the status ladder.

In emphasizing the group above the individual, the emotional and physical climate becomes central to therapy. Healing is not resident in the expertise of a single therapist but is facilitated by the environment. The in-patients are not only treated when they go for a session with their counselors but when they interact in the lounge, eat in the cafeteria, or pay their bills at the accounting office. Each of these interactions can nurture the individual toward health or make this development more difficult. By the same token, the individual's behavior in these contexts will also have an effect on the general climate. It is not a linear cause-effect relationship, then, but one which is more circular. It is not simply a matter of who is helping me, or who am I helping, but what is the therapeutic climate in the entire group.

What is most significant about this approach to help is that it places premium value on the group. There is a sense of basic equality and relatedness between all members and a recognition that there is mutual responsibility. The traditional labels of *helper* and *helpee* do not apply in this social organization. Ideally all are helpers and all are being helped with the ultimate view of strengthening the entire group.

Because of this, therapeutic community has been applied in college settings[32] as well as local congregations.[33]

This is really what therapeutic community is all about. It is an attempt to break down the traditional hierarchical authority structures where only the privileged few are responsible for the care of many. Therapy is seen as the responsibility of the whole community. It is easy for a congregation, for example, to see the pastoral staff, elders, or deacons as responsible for all the care that occurs. If someone is not cared for, these groups often bear the brunt of the criticism. It is also often the case that one member, upon hearing a sordid tale from another member, will tell someone in authority in the hope that this individual will carry out his or her responsibility and do something about it. It is also the case, in some churches, that the strengthening of the community is seen as secondary. Again, a communal sensibility takes second place to other concerns.

While therapeutic community originated in the context of a psychiatric ward,[34] one might well argue that these principles work best in a religiously oriented group. As Almond points out:

> The greatest resource for bringing the healing group approach to a community is religious groups. . . . The central features of the healing community—shared beliefs; involvement with and caring about fellow-members; charisma; the sense of something out of the ordinary—all these describe the congregation well.[35]

LIVE-IN COMMUNITIES

Live-in communities provide a context where there is a mutual commitment to all members expressed by a willingness to live together.[36] The depth of relationships and extent of the mission are clearly enhanced by physical proximity. It is one thing to nurture a fellow pilgrim in a church context, but quite another to live with that person on a daily basis. Since both have left one sphere of living and come together to join a new body, there is the commencement of a new community that functions within different parameters. Typically, there is a dual commitment to reciprocal care of each other as well as a broader focus that puts the attention outside the community.

> Today there is a considerable desire for greater communality in living. But the reason most so-called communities usually cannot keep their members and exist on the fringes of society, often as its parasites, lies in a crucial misconception about communal life. Most of these communities are formed "to live the communal life," and therefore they concentrate on it. I am convinced communal life can flourish only if it exists for an aim outside itself. Community is viable if it is the outgrowth of a deep involvement in a purpose which is other than, or above, that of being a community.[37]

The Daybreak live-in community, just north of Toronto, is one of the L'Arche communities for developmentally disabled people established by Jean Vanier. Through the writing and speaking of Henri Nouwen, this group has become quite well-known. Of particular interest is Nouwen's own experience in moving into this community. As a professor at Harvard he experienced the push to be relevant and popular and found himself constantly leading others. When he moved into Daybreak he found that prayer had to replace relevance, ministry had to replace popularity, and being led had to replace leading. At the core of the change was a move away from a fundamental individualism that reflected the belief that "everyone has a right to live his private life privately." In the live-in community Nouwen found that

> this individualism was radically challenged. There I was one of many people who tried to live faithfully with handicapped people, and the fact that I was a priest was not a license to do things on my own.[38]

LAY COUNSELING

A third approach to therapy that purports to take the community into consideration is lay counseling.[39] In contrast to professionals, lay counselors do not have specialized training, education, or experience, but they are involved in helping others with personal problems. Usually the counseling is free and takes place in a relational context where there is less stigma, formality, and distance between the helper and the helpee[40] and where the context for help is a community where there are shared beliefs or commitments. Undergirding this enterprise is some research data suggesting that these counselors are as effective as those who have professional training.[41]

Because of the nature of the local church, this approach to counseling has been adopted as a viable people-helping method. Through a process of selection, training, and supervision, individuals are equipped to minister to those both within the church and outside of it. Questions as to its effectiveness, ethics, and relationship with professional counseling still linger,[42] but it remains as one of the communal models for therapy.

While therapeutic communities and live-in communities are rather obvious exceptions to the rule that Western therapeutic models are privatized, the lay counseling movement may be interpreted in different ways. The fact that it is set up in a communal setting, such as a school or church, does not guarantee a nonindividualistic approach. A lay counselor could meet privately in the office of the church and become absorbed with the intrapsychic component of the individual. We cannot assume that therapy is operating within a communal paradigm simply because the counseling happens to be located in the church building.

So What Is the Problem?

Originally I pursued the field of psychology to help within the context of a Christian community. Naively I had assumed that this training would help me bridge the gap between the ignorance of the church and the pain of individuals. However, I quickly learned that within a traditional therapeutic understanding there is minimal link with the community because of an emphasis on the individual and the intrapsychic. In fact, the treatment has become a form of sanctioned retreat with its accompanying negation of the communal.

There are three exceptions to this trend, but the predominant message in the therapeutic world is powerful. The
individual takes precedence over the community.

SUMMARY

In Western culture we have moved from a religious framework to one that is therapeutic. It is therapeutic in the sense
that the solutions for life and the framework in which they are
positioned are characterized primarily by self-management.
The cure to a person's difficulties is located within the self.

An emphasis on the intrapsychic is one of the major ways in
which this is facilitated. Whether it is a stress on the volitional
or the emotive, there is a desire to locate the issues of life within
people rather than in the community. This, then, becomes a
prerequisite for relating to others. My self has to be in proper
perspective or I cannot exist capably in community.

Given this tendency, it follows that therapy as a structural
social process is a private retreat that is sanctioned by modern
culture. With a privatistic thrust it helps individuals to examine what they are dealing with, while the community linkage
for both therapist and client may be missing.

That is not to say that all therapeutic approaches have this
leaning. Therapeutic communities, live-in communities, and
lay counseling all acknowledge the power and influence
of communal grids. However, the predominant model in
therapy is individualistic, with an emphasis on freeing individuals to be themselves rather than locating them back in
their communities.

NOTES

1. Robert Bellah et al., *Habits of the Heart: Individualism and Commitment in
American Life* (New York: Harper and Row, 1985); Reginald W. Bibby, *Mosaic
Madness: The Poverty and Potential of Life in Canada* (Toronto, Ontario: Stoddart,
1990); and Christopher Lasch, *The Culture of Narcissism: American Life in an Age
of Diminishing Expectations* (New York: Norton, 1978).

2. Lasch, *Culture of Narcissim*, 4–5.

3. Allan Bloom, *The Closing of the American Mind* (New York: Simon and
Schuster, 1987), 178.

4. G. Bach and L. Torbet, *A Time for Caring: How to Enrich Your Life Through an Interest and Pleasure in Others* (New York: Delacorte, 1982).

5. Peggy Rosenthal, *Words and Values: Some Leading Words and Where They Lead Us* (New York: Oxford, 1984), 231.

6. Paul C. Vitz, *Psychology as Religion: The Cult of Self-Worship* (Grand Rapids: Eerdmans, 1977), 9.

7. F. Toennies, *Community and Society* (New York: Harper and Row, 1957). I am indebted to Al Dueck for his reflections on Toennies' schema, "American Psychology in Cross-Cultural Context," *Journal of Psychology and Theology* 11 (1983): 172–80.

8. Philip Rieff, *The Triumph of the Therapeutic: Uses of Faith after Freud* (New York: Harper and Row, 1966).

9. Ibid., 70.

10. This point has been made by a number of people in the field: G. Albee, "The Protestant Ethic, Sex, and Psychotherapy," *American Psychologist* 32 (1977): 150–61; S. Sarason, *Psychology Misdirected* (New York: Free Press, 1981); and Dueck, "Cross-Cultural Context."

11. In this section I will be relying exclusively on Rieff, *Triumph of the Therapeutic*.

12. Ibid., 76–77.

13. Charles R. Ridley, "Cross-Cultural Counseling in Theological Context," *Journal of Psychology and Theology* 14 (1986): 288–97.

14. This point has been made by Rieff, *Triumph of the Therapeutic*, as well as Al Dueck, "Ethical Contexts of Healing: Character and Ritual," *Pastoral Psychology* 36 (1987): 69–83.

15. This has been critiqued by Bellah et al., *Habits of the Heart*.

16. Sharon L. Hanna, *Person to Person: Positive Relationships Don't Just Happen* (Englewood Cliffs, N.J.: Prentice-Hall, 1991), xi.

17. Rickey L. George and Therese S. Cristiani, *Counseling Theory and Practice*, 3d ed. (Englewood Cliffs, N.J.: Prentice-Hall, 1990), 28.

18. Rieff, *Triumph of the Therapeutic*, 52–53.

19. For an example of one approach reflecting Christian self-love, see Walter Trobish, *Love Yourself: Self-Acceptance and Depression* (Downers Grove, Ill.: InterVarsity, 1977). For a critique of this orientation, see Anthony Hoekema, *The Christian Looks at Himself* (Grand Rapids: Eerdmans, 1975).

20. This term is usually linked with the work of Murray Bowen, *Family Therapy in Clinical Practice* (New York: Jason Aronson, 1978).

21. David D. Waanders, "Ethical Reflections on the Differentiation of Self in Marriage," *The Journal of Pastoral Care* 41 (1987): 100–110.

22. Mary Vander Vennen, "The Encounter with the Family of Origin," in *Christian Counseling and Psychotherapy*, ed. David G. Benner (Grand Rapids: Baker Book House, 1987): 111–17.

23. With the great interest in marriage and family therapy one might conclude that this question is no longer important. However, for an interesting analysis of the relationship between the self and the family, see Michael P. Nichols, *The Self in the System: Expanding the Limits of Family Therapy* (New York:

Brunner/Mazel, 1987). He suggests that neither embeddedness in, nor separateness from, family can fully explain human behavior.

24. For this term I am indebted to Talcott Parsons, *Social Structure and Personality* (New York: Free Press, 1964).

25. Helpful in this area is Al Dueck, "Ethical Contexts of Healing: Peoplehood and Righteousness," *Pastoral Psychology* 35 (1987): 239–53.

26. Michael P. Nichols and Richard C. Schwartz, *Family Therapy: Concepts and Methods*, 2d ed. (Toronto, Ontario: Allyn and Bacon, 1991); R. Paul Stevens, "Analogy or Homology? An Investigation of the Congruency of Systems Theory and Biblical Theology in Pastoral Leadership," *Journal of Psychology and Theology* 22 (1994): 173–81.

27. William Backus, *Telling the Truth to Troubled People* (Minneapolis: Bethany House, 1985); Lawrence J. Crabb, Jr., and Dan B. Allender, *Encouragement: The Key to Caring* (Grand Rapids: Zondervan, 1984).

28. "People look to their faith communities to foster this sense of wholeness." William R. Miller and Kathleen A. Jackson, *Practical Psychology for Pastors* (Englewood Cliffs, N.J.: Prentice-Hall, 1985), 404. Frank B. Minirth, *Christian Psychiatry* (Old Tappan, N.J.: Revell, 1977), 30, sees the local church as providing "rehabilitative resources (fellowship and spiritual encouragement)."

29. A. A. Sappington, "Psychology for the Practice of the Presence of God: Puttting Psychology at the Service of the Church," *Journal of Psychology and Christianity* 13 (1994): 5–16.

30. James H. Olthius, "God-With-Us: Toward a Relational Psychotherapeutic Model," *Journal of Psychology and Christianity* 13 (1994): 37–49; "Being-With: Toward a Relational Psychotherapy," *Journal of Psychology and Christianity* 13 (1994): 217–31.

31. This term is frequently linked with the work of Maxwell Jones, *The Therapeutic Community* (New York: Basic Books, 1953); *Beyond the Therapeutic Community* (New Haven: Yale University Press, 1968). For an interesting history on this movement, see Michael Bloor, Neil McKeganey, and Dick Fonkert, *One Foot in Eden: A Sociological Study of the Range of Therapeutic Community Practice* (London: Routledge, 1988). For a good summary see R. Almond, *The Healing Community: Dynamics of the Therapeutic Milieu* (New York: Jason Aronson, 1974).

32. For further study in this particular area see Glenn C. Taylor, "The Christian Campus as a Therapeutic Community," *The Bulletin: Christian Association for Psychological Studies* 4 (1978): 17–23, and Glenn C. Taylor, "Therapeutic Community," in *Baker Encyclopedia of Psychology*, ed. David G. Benner (Grand Rapids: Baker Book House, 1985), 1149–54. Paul A. Grayson and Kate Cauley, eds., *College Psychotherapy* (New York: Guilford Press, 1989) discusses the uniqueness of the community setting on a college campus and some of the reasons why therapy needs to be approached differently.

33. For two examples of this see Leigh C. Bishop, "Healing in the Koinonia: Therapeutic Dynamics of Church Community," *Journal of Psychology and Theology* 13 (1985): 12–20, and Mary Pytches, *A Healing Fellowship: A Guide to Practical Counseling in the Local Church* (London: Hodder and Stoughton, 1988).

34. Particularly helpful here are Almond, *Healing Community*, and Jones, *Therapeutic Community* and *Beyond the Therapeutic Community*. It is also interesting to note the conclusions of M. Barry, *Bellevue is a State of Mind* (New York: Berkley, 1971), who found that when patients showed concern for each other they felt a sense of usefulness and increased self-esteem; and J. L. Crammer, "The Special Characteristics of Suicide in Hospital In-Patients," *British Journal of Psychiatry* 145 (1984): 460–76, who found that suicide among in-patients tended to increase when there was a significant lack of patient-patient connectedness.

35. Almond, *Healing Community*, 365.

36. For two examples of Catholic live-in communities, see M. M. Poloma, "Christian Covenant Communities: An Adaption of the Intentional Community for Urban Life," in *A Reader in Sociology: Christian Perspectives*, ed. C. P. De Santo, C. Redekop, and W. L. Smith-Hinds (Kitchener, Ontario: Herald, 1980), 609–30; and Jean Vanier, *Community and Growth* (London: Darton, Longman and Todd, 1989).

37. Bruno Bettelheim, *Home for the Heart* (London: Thames and Hudson, 1974), 307.

38. Nouwen's journey to Daybreak is described in Henri Nouwen, *In the Name of Jesus: Reflections on Christian Leadership* (New York: Crossroad, 1993) 36.

39. For the most thorough documentation of this approach, see Sian-Yang Tan, *Lay Counseling: Equipping Christians for a Helping Ministry* (Grand Rapids: Zondervan, 1991). *The Journal of Psychology and Christianity* devoted an entire issue to this topic in 1987 (vol. 6, no. 2).

40. This point is made by Everett L. Worthington, Jr., *When Someone Asks for Help: A Practical Guide to Counseling* (Downers Grove, Ill.: InterVarsity, 1983).

41. R. R. Carkhuff, "Differential Functioning of Lay and Professional Helpers," *Journal of Counseling Psychology* 15 (1968): 117–28; J. A. Durlak, "Comparative Effectiveness of Paraprofessional and Professional Helpers," *Psychological Bulletin* 86 (1979): 80–92; and J. S. Berman and N. C. Norton, "Does Professional Training Make a Therapist More Effective?" *Psychological Bulletin* 98 (1985): 401–7.

42. Gary R. Collins, "Lay Counseling: Some Lingering Questions for Professionals," *Journal of Psychology and Christianity* 6 (1987): 7–9; Siang-Yang Tan, "Lay Counseling: A Christian Approach," *Journal of Psychology and Christianity* 13 (1994): 264–69; and Y. M. Toh et al., "The Evaluation of a Church-Based Lay Counseling Program: Some Preliminary Data," *Journal of Psychology and Christianity* 13 (1994): 270–75.

Chapter Four

The Bible and Community

While today groups are often formed to enhance the individual, the biblical model reminds us that the individual enhances the group. Distinction comes from contributing to the advance of the group.

—Julie Gorman

RECENTLY I ASKED ALL OF OUR PROFESSORS to present one of their courses to the rest of the faculty. We concluded each session with interaction about the issues raised. Although there was a diversity in the presentations, a common theme emerged in the discussions: students need to learn how to read.

The professor in the philosophy course was concerned that his students learn how to read Sören Kierkegaard directly and not simply master the secondary sources. The New Testament professor wanted his students to read Luke in a way that was consistent with the intent of the author. In contrast, the literature professor was concerned that her students read the text carefully without placing too much emphasis on interpreting the intent of the writer.

Knowing how to read is not merely a matter of understanding words, sentences, and grammatical structures. It focuses on the interpretive assumptions we bring to a text. It relates to the lenses we use to understand and process the content. If this is true in reading textbooks for college courses, it is absolutely essential when it comes to understanding the Scriptures.

We have seen that Western culture has tipped toward individualism and that the therapeutic enterprise has followed suit. Do we reflect a similar bias as we read the Bible? Do we tend to read it for personal application and individual understanding, or do we understand it as a book written in the context of communities for communities? Do our Western glasses give us an inaccurate perspective on Scripture?

In a recent book that poignantly addresses this topic, Stanley Hauerwas asserts that,

> Most North American Christians assume that they have a right, if not an obligation, to read the Bible. I challenge that assumption. No task is more important than for the church to take the Bible out of the hands of individual Christians in North America. . . . They feel no need to stand under the authority of a truthful community to be told how to read. Instead they assume that they have all the "religious experience" necessary to know what the Bible is all about.[1]

Christian counselors and pastors need to be readers of the Bible. At a basic level, this involves an appreciation and respect for its power and authority as well as an understanding of its content. But it also requires that we approach the Bible with a grid that is in tandem with a communal understanding.

The grid that we bring to the biblical text is influenced to some degree by our understanding of the relationship of conversion to community. In theological language we could ask, What is the relationship between soteriology (that which relates to salvation) and ecclesiology[2] (that which relates to the church)? Any discussion about community needs to be put into this kind of framework.[3]

Some come to the biblical text with the assumption that there is no relationship between conversion and communal involvement. Conversion to Christianity is between God and the individual. Others assume that the church is the mediator that relates the believer to Christ. A third group might see entrance into the church and into Christ as simultaneous, an act that is represented by baptism. These three grids represent three theological streams: the first, Protestantism, the second, Catholicism, and the third, Anabaptism.[4]

Given this theological diversity and our Western preoccupation with the individual, we need to reaffirm the centrality of community in our understanding of Scripture. As Jim Wallis suggests:

> A good test of any theology of conversion is the kind of community it creates. In the biblical descriptions, conversion is from one community to another, or from no community to community. Especially in an age of individualism and personal isolation, community becomes central to any idea of conversion.[5]

Conversion is not simply an individual experience. It is a commitment to discipleship within a faith community. In turn, evangelism becomes a by-product of the church's life. If community relationships are carried out in a way that is consistent with the work of the Holy Spirit, we can expect the corporate body to authenticate the verbal message.[6] While proclamation is necessary, biblical evangelism is not linked with particular techniques and methods or specific times and locations. It is the inevitable outcome of the community living corporately as committed disciples. Community life that reflects love will be a powerful testament to the power of Jesus Christ (see John 17:23), just as a collection of worshiping Christians may result in the conversion of an unbeliever (1 Cor. 14:22–25).

In a recent book that critiques evangelical theology, Stanley Grenz argues that our theology of the church needs to be renewed. Central to that vision are "two themes that we can mine from the Scriptures, our heritage and contemporary thought . . . kingdom and community."[7] While particular groups within evangelicalism have left a theology of community untouched,[8] we need to renew our commitment to its centrality. Only then will we have the proper glasses for reading Scripture.

COMMUNITY AND BIBLICAL ANTHROPOLOGY

How do we tie our understanding of community to our view of humanity (anthropology)? Our first introduction to people in Scripture is the solitary individual, Adam. Viewed from our modern perspective, Adam could easily be construed as an intrapsychic individual. We tend to examine his inner thoughts, feelings, and intents.

However, the Genesis account gives exactly the opposite message. Adam is not described in terms of his own essence and inner being. He is seen first as one who is created "in the image of God" (Gen. 1:27), an affirmation that he did not stand alone as an intrapsychic being but rather as one who was in communion with God. He was in relationship right from the very beginning—in relationship with God. In a fundamental sense, Adam was not an individual—he was in communion with another.

Further, God announced that Adam, in this pre-Fall state, was "alone" (Gen. 2:18). He was not, in the words of Ray Anderson, "a completed human."[9] It is an intriguing position: Man in perfect communion with God was judged, by God, to be less than adequate.

Our notions of humanity have tended to revolve around human-animal comparisons or intrapsychic analyses. We are human because we can think, or because we can reason, or because we make choices. However the Genesis account would suggest that we are human primarily in the relational sense. Humankind was created "in the image of God" and "male and female" (Gen. 1:27). Adam related to God, and he related to the woman. This was fundamental to who he was.[10]

It is unfortunate that Genesis 2:18 is often interpreted in terms of our modern understanding of marriage. It is true that Genesis 2 is about the first marriage: The man is alone, God sends along a woman to be his companion, and they live together. But the chapter is tied primarily to the nature of people. It has profound things to say about anthropology before it says anything about marriage.[11] It is a description of the essence of who we are: people in relationship to God and people in relationship to each other. There will be occasions when this can

be generalized to the human family, but the family of priority
is God's family. In this sense the spiritual family takes precedence over the biological family.

In a recent book that presents these concerns in a persuasive
fashion, Rodney Clapp notes that postmodern Christians need
to make two declarations when it comes to our understanding
of the family:

> The negative declaration: The family is not God's
> most important institution on earth. The family is not
> the social agent that most significantly shapes and
> forms the character of Christians. The family is not
> the primary vehicle of God's grace and salvation for
> a waiting, desperate world. . . . And the positive dec-
> laration: The church is God's most important insti-
> tution on earth. The church is the social agent that
> most significantly shapes and forms the character of
> Christians.[12]

If nothing else, this should be encouraging to single people
who have struggled with the marriage orientation to Genesis.
If Genesis 2:18 is asserting the primacy of marriage rather
than the nature of humanity, then singles could sense that
they are less than human. If God created us all to be married,
then being single would be a blatant denial of who we are.
Sadly, these kinds of sentiments are expressed to singles, and
they can easily feel less than human.

However, such an interpretation does not mesh with at
least three other biblical realities. First of all, if marriage is
part of our created essence, then Jesus would have to be considered less than human given his apparent choice to remain
single. Second, the clear teaching of Paul in 1 Corinthians
7:25–35 would indicate that there may be greater spiritual
devotion in remaining unmarried. The most telling argument
is Jesus' statement about marriage in the eternal state (Matt.
22:23–33; Mark 12:18–34; Luke 20:27–40). It is clear that marriage will not be a viable institution but will cease with death.
Since biological marriage and family are confined by time and
space, they are not tied in to the essence of who we are. In

contrast, our connection with God and the Christian community is central.

This understanding of Scripture may be encouraging for singles, but it also serves as a warning for Christian ministries that build their foundation on the priority of marriage and family. The breakdown of these institutions needs to be decried and everything possible needs to be done to minister effectively; however, it would be a mistake to suggest that the essence of life is marriage and family. This will not only alienate singles, but it may create an inaccurate assumption in the minds of those who are married. Life is not about my spouse and my children. Fundamentally it is tied to my relationship with God and with the Christian community.

Given the communal nature of the Genesis account, we might expect that the rest of the biblical record will be characterized by the same emphasis.

COMMUNITY AND THE HEBREW SCRIPTURES

If community is central, it will obviously be affected by the presence of sin. So it is no surprise that Genesis 3 shows a tension in the relationship between people and God as well as between Adam and Eve. Genesis 4 documents the first case of sibling rivalry, one that resulted in the death of Abel. In Genesis chapters 5, 6, and 7, the increase in the size of the human community is seen in direct proportion to the sin that they committed—sin that resulted ultimately in the flood and the destruction of every living thing that was not inside the ark (Gen. 7:23).

Following the flood, God initiated two agreements: The first (Gen. 9:1–17) with Noah was an "everlasting covenant between God and all living creatures of every kind on the earth" (Gen. 9:16) sealed by a rainbow. The second agreement (Gen. 12:1–9) with Abram was also generalized to people who would follow: "All peoples on earth will be blessed through you" (Gen. 12:3).

What transpired between God and these two individuals was representative of what would transpire between God and many people. Noah and Abram were in relationship with God but were also connected implicitly to a broader human community. So in this early part of Genesis we get a glimpse of God's heart. He cherishes his relationship with individuals but also with a community. A quick overview of the entire canon will reveal such a trend.

The rest of the book of Genesis, for instance, takes us through a fascinating history of key families who had more trauma and stress than you could imagine. This collection of stories has supplied many a Sunday school teacher with interesting lessons. It has provided many an observer with individual examples of faith and sacrifice. However, at the core it demonstrates how God works with a community, showing his care and affection for his people. While there may be heroes and villains, the story is not as much about individual people as it is about the sovereign God in dialogue with a corporate body. Even Joseph acknowledged that all that had transpired was not a testimony to his own personal story but was a statement by God that all that happened was "for good to accomplish what is now being done, the saving of many lives" (Gen. 50:20).

Joseph's conclusion had a prophetic quality to it. The book of Genesis describes the family of Isaac (the Hebrew children) who left Canaan and were royally welcomed into Egypt. The following book, Exodus, describes the Hebrews being brutally forced out of Egypt and traveling to Canaan. In both their coming and going, God's passion to protect his own people is evident. Through the miseries of famine in Genesis and plague in Exodus, God shows his communal mandate to save many lives.

The first fifteen chapters of Exodus focus on the hardships in Egypt and the commencement of the wilderness journey. While Moses receives some prominence in the story, the major focus is on the Israelite community. The concern is not with the autonomous individual but with the people as a corporate entity—God's redeemed people.

Three months after they left Egypt, God had a meeting with Moses (Exod. 19:3). This was not just any meeting, but one that would set a new course for his people. If they were going to be a community and be God's "treasured possession . . . kingdom

of priests and a holy nation" (Exod. 19:5–6), then they needed
to follow God's law. This link became fundamental. A spiritual community that was going to survive and persist would
need to follow God's mandate. A community could not operate independent of law. Its very existence depended on it. Dale
Patrick reminds us:

> Through law, community is established and main-
> tained; without it, people simply could not live
> together. Nor is law merely a practical instrument
> for social integration. It is a repository of religious
> and philosophic concepts and values that give
> coherence and purpose to communal living. Law en-
> shrines and protects what a community holds to be
> sacred and partakes of the sacrality it guards.[13]

There is a subtlety in this, however. The law was not given
to simply provide individuals with a way of operating. It was
not addressed autonomously so that each person followed it
in a privatistic fashion. Since the community had priority
over the individual in an anthropological sense, the law was
anchored to the same assumption.[14] One example will illustrate this distinction.

The fifth commandment in the Ten Commandments encourages the honoring of father and mother "so that you may live
long in the land the LORD your God is giving you" (Exod. 20:12).
It is picked up again in the Deuteronomic code, where the
promise is, "so that you may live long and that it may go well
with you in the land the LORD your God is giving you" (Deut.
5:16). In the Ephesian letter (6:1), Paul cites this promise in his
discussion on the relationship between parents and children.

An individual rendering of the passage would go something
like this: If as a son or daughter you honor your father and
mother, then you will live a long and prosperous life. However, there are many children who have respected, honored,
and revered their parents but have died before they reached
adulthood. Their days were neither long nor prosperous. The
corollary of this is also true. There are many children who have
abused, negated, and invalidated their parents but have lived

fulfilling and enjoyable lives, sometimes living even longer than their parents. These two scenarios would appear to invalidate the individual interpretation of the passage.

What, then, is the appropriate understanding of this commandment? If the community and its fundamental identity are central, then the overall good of the community needs to be in focus. Who will pass on the teaching and values of the community? Parents. However, if parents are not respected and revered throughout the community, then the assimilation of God's truth will suffer. Through a process of poor teaching, the truth will be watered down to such a degree that God's community will start to look like the communities around it. In essence, the community will cease to exist and prosper under God's hand. This is why God is concerned that parents, their children, "and their children after them may fear the LORD your God" (Deut. 6:2).

This theme helps to explain much of the teaching of the Torah (or law) captured in Genesis, Exodus, Leviticus, Numbers, and Deuteronomy. For example, when someone tried to entice a person to follow other gods, the community had to assume some responsibility for the consequences by being involved in the stoning (Deut. 3:6–10). Even the sin of adultery, which could be conceptualized in individual terms, was seen as something that needed to be purged because of its effect on the whole community (Deut. 22:13–24). At the core, God was striving to cleanse his people from sin so they would be a distinctive people, different from all the other nations around them (Deut. 25:17–19). This was facilitated by an understanding that God's law brought consequences—blessing for obedience and cursing for disobedience. To step outside of the community by doing what was right in your own eyes (Judg. 17:6; 21:25) was to miss God's intent.

For much of the rest of Old Testament history the nation sinned and experienced decline or lived righteously and experienced blessing. So the book of Joshua shows victory and conquest, while Judges describes a lack of faithfulness. The book of Ruth reveals righteousness, while the kingdom period of 1 and 2 Samuel, 1 and 2 Kings, and 1 and 2 Chronicles describes a community that spends more time in disarray and sin than it does in holiness and peace. It is only when we read the books of Ezra, Nehemiah, and Esther that we see the nation returning to their homeland to worship the one true God. When they do, it is no surprise that the reading of the law is central to the process of restoration (Neh. 8). Again the pairing of law with community is significant.

As is the case with the individual commandments, one could run this historical period through either an individualistic or a communal grid. A study of the book of Nehemiah is a good example of this. As the culmination of Old Testament history, the book describes a time of communal restoration when the nation returned to its homeland and to its God. It was a time of work, celebration, and worship because God and his people were united again.

A more individualistic approach tends to emphasize the title of the book. Nehemiah becomes the individual who God used in the restoration, and the book is funneled through an understanding of organizational development and behavior. We then can read the book as a presentation of how to be a successful manager or mobilizer. We would be hard pressed to see such interpretations as inherently wrong,[15] but imputing modern notions of leadership and the psychology of motivation is to miss the fact that the book is fundamentally a presentation of how God engages in community building. The emphasis is on God and his people, not on the instrument he chooses to be a catalyst in the process.

Where do the prophetic writings and wisdom literature fit into such a schema? If God does not want an individual, alone, but wants a community or a people for himself, then he is grieved when his people wander away in disobedience. In the Torah, God carefully documented the relationship between behavior and consequences. Both sin and righteousness as causal agents had an effect. Obedience to the law was mandatory if the community was going to survive. When his people did depart from the law, they needed to be warned and called to repent. This is the message of the prophets.

Within the chronology of the Old Testament, the prophets are paired with the historical books. Although they are positioned at the end of many of our English Bibles (Isaiah through to Malachi), they, in fact, are paired with events that took place between the books of 2 Kings and Nehemiah. Since these historical books are enmeshed in a community paradigm, the prophets cannot be factored out of this.

The prophets brought a word from the Lord (Jer. 37:17) to the community concerning their relationship with God. With the exception of Habakkuk, who brought his concerns about the people to the Lord, all the prophets brought the Lord's concerns to the people—not to individuals but to the community. God had made a covenant with his people, and the prophets served to remind the community of the demands of that covenant.

Finally, the prophets consistently referred to the nature of the covenant and the priority of God's law.[16] The prophetic books are not distinct from the law but rather speak on its behalf. The community needed to be reminded of divine expectations. For the community to function as it should, the priority of God's law required assertion.

What, then, of the literature often referred to as "the writings"—Job, Psalms, Proverbs, Ecclesiastes, and Song of Solomon? Again, this body of literature coincides with a particular historical period and cannot be removed from the context of community. While Job may be prior to the period of the patriarchs, the other four books can be located between 1 Samuel and 2 Kings.

However, there is more than just temporal location that puts this collection of books in a community paradigm. First of all, with the exception of the Psalms, the other four books are often seen as representing a wisdom tradition. They present a way of living in community that is consistent with a knowledge of a sovereign God. In a sense, they provide a type of socialization by indicating what is acceptable behavior and what is unacceptable.[17] In so doing, the wisdom literature continues the connection between community and law. In order to operate and survive in a community, law is necessary. It undergirds its identity and vision. However, in this body of literature the presentation of the law is different. It is not the statement of commandments but the articulation of life-related situations that require God's wisdom. There is an earthy, human sense to the presentation. It is communal in that wisdom requires the reader to live in this world, to exist in relationship, to live life in connection with others, but always in the context of Yahweh. There is no vertical-horizontal separation here. When one fears the Lord, the evidence of it is found in community. It is not other-worldly.

The book of Psalms, a collection of poems representing the reflections of a number of writers, is an affirmation of the power and glory of God in relation to his people. It is no surprise, then, that this book served as a hymnbook for Israel. It was a way of expressing, corporately, their worship and devotion to the one God. Being in God's presence with God's people was the ultimate of all that life could offer.

> As a deer longs for flowing streams,
>   so my soul longs for you, O God.
> My soul thirsts for God,
>   for the living God.
> When shall I come and behold
>   the face of God?
> My tears have been my food
>   day and night,
> while people say to me continually,
>   "Where is your God?"
> These things I remember,
>   as I pour out my soul:
> how I went with the throng,
>   and led them in procession to the house of God,
> with glad shouts and songs of thanksgiving,
>   a multitude keeping festival.

(Ps. 42:1–4 NRSV)

COMMUNITY AND THE NEW TESTAMENT

If we assume a unity between the Hebrew Scriptures and the New Testament, then we may expect a continuity of the communal theme. A cursory reading of the New Testament will reveal again God's desire for a holy people.

Each of the four Gospels give a perspective on the life of Jesus. He had a concern for calling individuals-in-community. This is demonstrated by his constant references to the kingdom and to kingdom values (see Matt. 5–7), by his commissioning of a group of twelve men to be his disciples (Matt. 10:1–42), and by his stress on the unity of all believers (John 17:20–26). As was the case in the Old Testament, the continuity of the community was crucial. The proclamation of the apostles and the lifestyle witness of the believers would ensure that this would happen. The salvation of individuals was important but with the ultimate view of a communal body. As Elton Trueblood has noted, "Jesus was deeply concerned for the continuation of his redemptive work after the close of his earthly existence, and his chosen method was the formation of a redemptive society."[18]

While it is true that the Gospel accounts do not discuss the mechanics of the communal body and that Jesus only mentioned the church on two occasions (Matt. 16:18; 18:17), the book of Acts provides an effective transition between the first four books of the New Testament and the twenty-two that follow. In essence, it describes the continued work of Jesus through the apostles and the coming of the Holy Spirit at Pentecost. Again, it is the group of believers who are present (Acts 2:1) and who meet together as a community (Acts 2:42–47) to express that unity. Throughout the rest of the book the community flourishes, and the history of the early church takes shape.

It is in the context of this growth that the twenty-one epistles (Romans through Jude) were written. While they are uniquely tailored to meet particular needs, their overall thrust is the nurture and cultivation of the Christian community.[19] In each epistle there is a strong commitment to the corporate expression of Christ's body and the appropriate ethics that should follow.

So when Paul instructs the Ephesians about integrity of speech, he reminds them that "each of you must put off falsehood and speak truthfully to his neighbor, for we are all members of one body" (Eph. 4:25). The individual application is clear: Each person should endeavor to speak in a way that is consistent with a Christian commitment. However, this is not simply to achieve a personal standard or a privatized ethic. The injunction is addressed to the whole church because membership in the body requires adherence to a communal standard.

As a result, the various terms that are used to describe God's people do not describe the inner dynamics of individuals; rather, they focus on the corporate and communal dimensions. So we read of the people of God, the church of Israel, the commonwealth of Israel, believers, saints, God's household, the family of believers, the body of Christ, fellowship, and disciples.[20]

It is probably the passage in 1 Peter 2:9–10 that is the most poignant in this area. Peter affirms the fact that Christians are "being built into a spiritual house to be a holy priesthood" (1 Pet. 2:5). We do not exist independently or autonomously. We function together to bring God praise. Later in the chapter Peter drives home the same point by using four Old Testament expressions to describe Christians. Interestingly, this again would demonstrate the continuity of the Old and New Testament with regard to God's corporate desires.

The first of these terms is "a chosen people" (1 Pet. 2:9). Connecting with expressions in the Hebrew Scriptures (Deut. 4:20; 7:6), God is seen as the initiator of this relationship where people are adopted into his family. The second and third terms, "a royal priesthood, a holy nation" (1 Pet. 2:9; cf. Exod. 19:5–6), give kingly dignity to this group of people who are set apart for God's use. The fourth term, "a people belonging to God" (1 Pet. 2:9; cf. Isa. 43:20–21), captures the issue of ownership and priority, asserting God's sovereignty in the process.

Peter summarizes this section with a categorical statement: "Once you were not a people, but now you are the people of God" (1 Pet. 2:10). This is noteworthy because it suggests that value and identity are tied up in the community relationship. To be part of God's chosen people is to have significance. In essence, their preconversion state is best described as being noncommunal. They were on their own. They did what was right in their own eyes.

Given Peter's emphasis, it is no surprise that so much of the biblical presentation of conversion is put in communal and relational terms. Salvation is not just something that transpires between God and the individual. As Hosea has captured so beautifully, the move from being an enemy of God to being part of God's family is an affirmation by God that, "I will show my love to the one I called 'Not my loved one.' I will say to those called 'Not my people,' 'You are my people'" (Hos. 2:23).

So when New Testament individuals acknowledged Jesus, they were baptized and formally identified themselves with a group known as Christians. Their link with that visible community became a public statement of their conversion experience. It was not that they had lost their individuality, but they had found it essentially in the context of community. Even the expression of their giftedness was not a statement of their own individual ability but a key component of the overall operation of the body.

It follows that the priesthood of all believers (1 Pet. 2:5, 9) becomes a key paradigm for appropriate functioning in the community. Priests are those who have access to God based on the work of Christ, but priesthood is more than that. It is a mode of relating that permeates the entire body. There is a mutual responsibility to each other, one that is anchored in a new identity found in community.[21] Being a member of the body of Christ provides both the right and the duty to function as a priest to other believers.

This approach makes Paul's presentation of the gospel in the book of Ephesians more understandable. He is careful to talk about what has happened to all Christians who have been redeemed (Eph. 1:1–2:10). He then follows that up with a careful delineation of the nature of the change (2:11–22). Note that the change is not described individually or intrapsychically but is conceptualized as a move away from being "separate from Christ, excluded from citizenship in Israel and foreigners to the covenants of promise" (2:12) into a new relationship where "you are no longer foreigners and aliens, but fellow citizens with God's people and members of God's household" (2:19). This is Paul sounding like Peter. Real conversion is a transition from no community to a true community.

In Revelation a voice resounds from the throne: "See, the home of God is among mortals. He will dwell with them as their God; they will be his peoples, and God himself will be with them" (Rev. 21:3, NRSV). This is not the conclusion of a story where the individual autonomous person has found his or her self-fulfillment but the climax of history where God finally has a people for himself, a community that is holy and righteous.

So What Is the Problem?

Pastors and Christian counselors need to have an interest in reading Scripture and a willingness to expend the energy to understand what it means. However, they need to be aware of the influence of a Western sensibility that turns the Bible into a document provided solely for an individual's personal spiritual walk.

When we claim to be Christian in our helping, there is an implicit assumption that Scripture will have an influence on what we do. But if the Bible is read with an individualistic grid, the role of the community will be missed. Given the power of the communal message in Scripture, this is bound to leave the pastor and the Christian counselor with limited resources when it comes to helping others.

It is clear that many of us, pastors and counselors alike, need to learn to read the Bible accurately.

Summary

How do we read the Bible, and how does this influence our understanding of community? Throughout history there has been great diversity as to how we understand community theologically. This diversity is tied to our understanding of the church, conversion, and their relationship to each other. However, when we come to the anthropological statements of early Genesis, God's desire is clear. To talk of community is to acknowledge the conception of humanity as individuals-in-community.

An overview of the Hebrew Scriptures shows a continuation of that theme. Whether it is the historical sections, the wisdom literature, or the prophetic writings, the communal milieu is central to our understanding of God and his work in the lives of his people. The New Testament demonstrates a similar pattern through the calling of the disciples, to the formation of the church and the injunctions that are given to the community of faith.

Counselors and pastors need to have an appreciation for the communal ethos of Scripture if they are seeking to be Christian in the work they have been called to do.

NOTES

1. Stanley Hauerwas, *Unleashing the Scripture: Freeing the Bible from Captivity to America* (Nashville: Abingdon, 1993), 15.

2. For more detailed discussion on this topic, see Avery Dulles, *Models of the Church* (New York: Image, 1987) or Hans Kung, *The Church* (Garden City, N.Y.: Image, 1976).

3. John R. Loeschen, *The Divine Community: Trinity, Church, and Ethics in Reformation Theologies* (Kirksville, Mo.: Sixteenth Century Journal Publishers, 1981) compares Martin Luther, Menno Simons, and John Calvin and argues that their respective views of the Trinity have had an influence on their view of the church as well as social and political ethics. This is the kind of analysis that is needed in our understanding of Christian community.

4. C. Norman Kraus, *Evangelicalism and Anabaptism* (Kitchener, Ontario: Herald, 1979).

5. Jim Wallis, "Community," *Sojourners* (October 1981): 25.

6. Karl Barth, *Evangelical Theology: An Introduction* (Grand Rapids: Eerdmans, 1979), argues that a theologically interested and informed community becomes a secondary witness (after Christ) to the nature of the gospel, through both their words and their physical witness. S. De Dietrich, *The Witnessing Community: The Biblical Record of God's Purpose* (Philadelphia: Westminster Press, 1958), suggests that a community is not only set apart but is sent to witness.

7. Stanley J. Grenz, *Revisioning Evangelical Theology: A Fresh Agenda for the 21st Century* (Downers Grove, Ill.: InterVarsity, 1993), 180.

8. C. E. Gunton, "The Church on Earth: The Roots of Community," in *On Being the Church: Essays on the Christian Community,* ed. C. E. Gunton and D. W. Hardy (Edinburgh: Clark, 1989), 48–80; H. A. Snyder, *The Community of the King* (Downers Grove, Ill.: InterVarsity, 1977).

9. Ray S. Anderson, *On Being Human: Essays in Theological Anthropology* (Grand Rapids: Eerdmans, 1982), 48.

10. Mary Stewart Van Leeuwen, *Gender and Grace: Love, Work and Parenting in a Changing World* (Downers Grove, Ill.: InterVarsity, 1990), explores this particular topic in some depth.

11. The issues of anthropology and cohumanity may be examined further by consulting the following: Anderson, *On Being Human;* Dietrich Bonhoeffer, *The Communion of Saints: A Dogmatic Inquiry into the Sociology of the Church*

(New York: Harper and Row, 1960); D. Hardy, "Created and Redeemed Sociality," in *On Being the Church: Essays on the Christian Community*, ed. C. E. Gunton and D. W. Hardy (Edinburgh, Scotland: Clark, 1989); and G. E. Wright, *The Biblical Doctrine of Man in Society* (London: SCM Press, 1954).

12. Rodney Clapp, *Families at the Crossroads: Beyond Traditional and Modern Options* (Downers Grove, Ill.: InterVarsity, 1993), 67–68.

13. Dale Patrick, *Old Testament Law* (Atlanta: Knox, 1985), 1.

14. Particularly helpful on this point is the writing of Walter Brueggemann, *The Creative Word: Canon as a Model for Biblical Education* (Philadelphia: Fortress Press, 1982).

15. For examples of approaches that tend to take a more individualistic orientation to the book, see Cyril J. Barber, *Nehemiah and the Dynamics of Effective Leadership* (Neptune, N.J.: Loizeaux, 1984); Ted S. Rendall, *Nehemiah: Laws of Leadership* (Three Hills, Alberta: Prairie, 1980); and John White, *Excellence in Leadership: Reaching Goals with Prayer, Courage and Determination* (Downers Grove, Ill.: InterVarsity, 1986).

16. See Isa. 1:10; Jer. 6:19; Lam. 2:9; Ezek. 22:26; Dan. 9:11; Hos. 4:6; Amos 2:4; Mic. 4:2; Hab. 1:4; Zeph. 3:4; Hag. 2:11; Zech. 7:12; Mal. 2:9.

17. The nature of the socialization process has been divided into *clan wisdom*, where the teaching of the young is informal, or *court school*, where the education is oriented to boys of nobility. See Brueggemann, *Creative Word*, and G. Von Rad, *Wisdom in Israel* (New York: Abingdon, 1972). In either case the communal context is clear.

18. S. R. Sebert and W. G. Ross, eds., *The Meditations of Elton Trueblood* (New York: Harper and Row, 1975), 8.

19. For an excellent description of how the apostle Paul shaped and nurtured a Christian community see Abraham J. Malherbe, *Paul and the Thessalonians: The Philosophic Tradition of Pastoral Care* (Philadelphia: Fortress Press, 1987).

20. A detailed review of these terms does not fit with the intent of this book. The reader is encouraged to utilize a concordance and/or any of the following material: Harold S. Bender, *These Are My People* (Scottdale, Pa.: Herald, 1962); R. T. Bender, *The People of God* (Scottdale, Pa.: Herald, 1971); John Driver, *Community and Commitment* (Kitchener, Ontario: Herald, 1976); C. Norman Kraus, *The Community of the Spirit* (Grand Rapids: Eerdmans, 1974); and G. Lohfink, *Jesus and Community: The Social Dimensions of the Christian Faith* (Philadelphia: Fortress Press, 1984).

21. For further reflection on the priesthood of all believers see Bonhoeffer, *Communion of Saints*; J. R. Burkholder and C. Redekop, *Kingdom, Cross and Community* (Kitchener, Ontario: Herald, 1976); and C. Marney, *Priests to Each Other* (Valley Forge, Pa.: Judson, 1974).

PART II

Practical Implications for Pastors and Private Counselors

Chapter Five

Community and the Counselor

If Christian leaders would listen to what people say about their churches, their feelings of alienation from other believers, and their overall loneliness, they would know the necessity of making the church more compassionate and sensitive.

—George Barna and
William Paul McKay

JIM IS THE SENIOR PASTOR OF A LARGE urban church. In his two seminary counseling courses he was exposed to the various systems of counseling, both Christian and secular. He learned the differences between Adams, Crabb, and Collins, and he became familiar with the issues around the integration of psychology and theology. There was some opportunity to do role-playing and discuss case studies. However, when he left seminary, his understanding of the field was minimal.

For the past ten years Jim's church has grown, with the attendant increase in counseling demands. Early in his ministry he enjoyed meeting with people and counseling, but in recent years the demands of preaching, teaching, and administration have made it impossible to give careful attention to the concerns of individual members. He finds himself referring almost everyone to outside professionals.

Jim believes in the power of the church to bring healing and is committed to the importance of body life, so his tendency to refer reflects pragmatic concerns rather than a particular philosophy of ministry. However, he begins to wonder if pastors should do counseling and whether his problem is tied to his own functioning or is somehow inherent to the role.

Jim's situation reflects a common theme among many pastors and Christian leaders,[1] a theme that is often reinforced by the literature on pastors and counseling. For example, Krebs suggests that "the reasons for my counseling failures are inherent in the pastoral situation and are essentially unavoidable."[2] Pastoral counseling promises cheap growth, does not allow for the resolution of transference issues, creates role confusion, and draws the pastor into misplaced priorities. As a result, the pastor who works with members of the congregation in a counseling capacity is failing to recognize the true nature of their relationship. For Krebs, doing counseling with members of a congregation is synonymous with having your friends or family as clients.

In a similar vein, Rolfe sees pastors as being seduced by the counseling role because it gives them a sense of importance and status. They are drawn into the counselor role and then often begin to dispense help in an aloof manner so that their counseling has a paternalistic quality to it. To offset this tendency, therapeutic help can only come from someone outside the system.[3] In other words, the church as system or the pastor as leader does not have the requisite resources to meet the needs of people with dysfunction of various sorts.

Krebs and Rolfe give a clear response to the questions being raised by Jim: They should not be doing counseling as part of their pastoral role.

This is both a welcome and an irritating conclusion for people who work in Christian communities. It is welcome because it appears to absolve them from responsibility in carrying out a counseling ministry within their own context. On the other hand, it is irritating because they will continue to be exposed to situations requiring counseling whether they are deemed equipped to help or not.

In the face of a recent U.S. survey of over four hundred pastors, this conclusion is even more disturbing.[4] Of this group, 41 percent saw more than twenty-five people in counseling in the past year, with 74 percent of them averaging two to five interviews. A total of 50 percent described their counseling load as having increased in the past year. Clearly, the notion that they should not be doing counseling is not being heeded by the typical pastor. Add to this the fact that only 13 percent felt adequately prepared for their counseling responsibilities, and you have the recipe for psychic tension. On the one hand, there are many people to counsel; on the other, pastors are poorly prepared for carrying out the job.

What is the nature of pastoral ministry in the community of faith? In a recent book, David Benner draws a distinction between

pastoral ministry —which includes preaching, teaching, leading worship, congregational leadership and administration, lay enabling, and pastoral care and counseling;

pastoral care—which includes all the helping contacts between the pastor and the congregation;

pastoral counseling—which is usually initiated by the parishioner around a particular problem.[5]

Often there is a connection between these three spheres. Many pastors have stood in the pulpit on Sunday morning, visited an individual who was hospitalized on Monday, and then followed up with that same person after he or she expressed a particular concern that needed to be addressed in counseling. If we invoke the role confusion critique that is often used against pastors doing counseling, we will miss the fact that significant ministry goes on at all three levels. The individual member of the congregation is taught and encouraged by the sermon, is nurtured and supported by the visit, and is given understanding by the pastoral counseling. There is significant overlap between pastoral ministry, pastoral care, and pastoral counseling.

Because the pastor is a representative of the community and the individual is a member of that community, the ministry emphasis is not on particular gifts resident in the pastor or particular problems resident in the member but rather on the fact that they form part of a community. In fact, one could well agree with Moody when he says that the "whole area of mediation between communal tradition and individual cases forms the content of pastoral theology."[6]

This brings us back to the distinction between *Gesellschaft* (society) and *Gemeinschaft* (community). If pastors conceptualize their work within the former category, then the member will be related to within the framework of individual, autonomous concerns. On the other hand, a pastor who understands ministry within the latter category will recognize that the individual's health and wholeness is tied to his or her relationship with the faith community. Cure will only come about with full connection in the faith community.

So the pastor will make the community a priority in all his or her interventions. At the same time, the pastor, in being linked with the community, will be understood as an exemplar of that community, whether the task is leading worship, preaching a sermon, or offering counsel.

The same cannot be said of private counselors. The very nature of private practice is an explicit removal from communal connectedness. Furthermore, some have argued that many counselors

> seem to have difficulty finding a church in their community where they can participate comfortably and feel that their spiritual, social, and emotional needs are being met. Some feel disenfranchised by the church or alienated from it. Although they openly maintain their personal commitment to Christ and desiring a church home, they have trouble finding one. The problem often begins to emerge in the course of professional training.[7]

This was certainly the case for Brenda. After graduating from a Ph.D. program in clinical psychology, she spent four days a week in private practice and one day in consultation to a local psychiatric hospital. Prior to graduate school she was extensively involved in a local evangelical church. However, as she moved through her program, she began to experience a growing disenchantment with the church. There were a number of reasons for this:

1. Confusion on the part of church members as to why a Christian would be involved in the field of psychology.

2. A tendency on the part of many in the church to spiritualize all problems and negate the value of the social sciences.

3. An increasing awareness that the number of personal problems in the church was in stark contrast to the facade created by the church culture.

4. Frustration over the dichotomy between the superficiality of the public preaching and the private pain of the congregation.

It was not long before Brenda's involvement in the church lessened, and her attendance became sporadic. After a number of years she developed enough frustration with the evangelical church that she had trouble being objective when a client came out of that background. Her counseling began to take on an anti-evangelical edge, and she found support among other therapists who had gone through similar experiences. Not only did they cease to be involved in evangelical churches, but they found their communal connectedness in various accrediting bodies and professional conferences. Their counseling no longer represented an inherent link with the evangelical community. When clients came for counseling, they came to a representative of the professional community. Because Brenda was known within her own church and throughout the denomination, her shift of emphasis did not go unnoticed. In earlier years she received many referrals from the church and would often work together with the leadership on particular cases. But suspicion increased, and a lack of trust created an environment where churches would rarely initiate contact. In the end, the church confirmed Brenda's own conviction: She no longer represented the Christian community.

Guy and Liaboe suggest a number of issues that intensify the sense of isolation for counselors in private practice:

1. Client hours as well as preparation and paperwork build in aloneness.

2. Psychic isolation occurs because the relationship is one way and not for the nurture of the therapist.

3. Private counselors can become distant and interpretive in all relationships, so problems are created in marriage, family, and friendships.

4. Confidentiality protects the sense of isolation to the degree that family and friends cannot be of the same support as is true in other professions.

5. If the church is a referral network, neither counselor nor client will feel completely comfortable in that environment.

They offer a number of solutions:

1. Be aware of this potential danger.
2. Become involved in nonprofessional outside activities.
3. Pursue teaching or research.
4. Involve yourself in supervision and consultation.
5. Limit the number of clients.
6. Develop your relationship with God and other Christians.[8]

At the core Guy and Liaboe argue:

> It may be important to find ways to be involved in one's church without the potential role-confusion to allow for meaningful participation in the richness of Christian community. This may require limiting professional involvement in the church in order to provide adequate opportunities for fellowship with fellow believers without fear of "dual role" problems.[9]

It is clear that the professional role is given primacy in their analysis, while the Christian community is peripheral. A fear of dual-role problems becomes the central focus, and there is only tacit acknowledgment that the Christian community has some inherent value.

The key issue, however, should not be around the protection of professional status. The private counselor needs to represent the Christian community and be accountable to it. As Al Dueck suggests:

> Healing rituals in Western societies are extremely private. That also makes accountability to external communities difficult. . . . As a member of the Christian community the individual healer is a representative of its story. Therapy then is never simply a private practice. It is the individual therapist's responsibility to demonstrate that what transpires in the therapeutic process is consistent with the Christian story. It is the church's responsibility to affirm the healing gifts of a potential therapist, to bless the work of the healer and to faithfully discern and embody its confession.[10]

Here the Christian community moves beyond simply providing the private counselor with opportunities for prayer support, facilities, expense reduction, a forum for expressing ideas, or a place to become revitalized. The Christian community becomes the moral-ethical arena where the counselor works. He or she has a sense of responsibility to both embody a particular mind-set and be accountable to the community for that embodiment. Dueck affirms the primary mandate of the Christian counselor: "To help the church become a liberating structure and a discerning ethical community is the first responsibility of the Christian therapist."[11]

Dueck recognizes the difficulty of putting this into practice given the nature of current counseling approaches. Counselors tend to see themselves in the context of their accrediting body or professional conferences and publications rather than within the context of the Christian community. Given the open-ended nature of accounting to an accrediting body or a professional society, the counselor becomes an independent ethicist with no accountability to a primary community.

I remember experiencing this issue directly when Dwayne, an evangelical elder in a city a number of miles from Toronto, telephoned for some guidance. Tom, a young man in his church, had approached him asking for help in his struggle with homosexuality. He feared the censure of his church, since their only public statement on homosexuality was that it was sin. Dwayne spent an evening listening and trying to understand but in the process recognized that he was not in a position to help. Because of his concern that the intervention of the church leadership might not work, he referred Tom to a local private Christian counselor.

After a number of sessions Tom came back to Dwayne and expressed confusion. The counselor had listened to his story and had affirmed his homosexual identity. He also had communicated his own conviction that Tom would be within the bounds of Scripture if he were to commit himself to a monogamous homosexual relationship. Now Tom was asking Dwayne what he should do. Dwayne, in turn, called me to find out what he should tell Tom.

While I suggested that Tom should be encouraged to work through the situation with the counselor directly, the issues were more complex than the theological concerns related to homosexuality. There was a fundamental gap between the moral-ethical context of the church embodied in Dwayne and reflected in Tom and the moral-ethical context of the private counselor. Dwayne's conclusion was that he would not be referring any more people to that particular counselor. The counselor realized that one of his clients had not come for a number of weeks but was unaware of the nature and scope of the tension. He was not doing his counseling in the context of a particular Christian community, felt no need for specific accountability to this community, and saw no relationship between that church and his own personal ethics. In the absence of communication between these two worlds, it was difficult to arrive at a happy resolution.

For both the pastor and the private counselor, the church community needs to be "the context for our work, the locus of accountability, and the source of our personal ethic."[12]

BEING AN EXEMPLAR

True Christian counselors are in the tradition of commitment, not analytic therapy. They understand that the healing process occurs when the well-being of the individual seeking help is dependent on their full involvement in the community. Counselors also understand that their own role, in the words of Dueck, is "exemplary in that the healer's life reflects the ideals of the culture or community."[13]

The counselor out of the analytic tradition is not concerned with being a communal representative. He or she relies on technical skills and expertise and, in the process, functions as an autonomous individual. In contrast, commitment therapists serve as models or patterns for the community they represent, and in the process they typify the values of that community.

This dual responsibility presupposes an intimacy between the counselor and the community. It requires that he or she is involved in a Christian community. It assumes that there is ongoing communication between the community and the counselor. It presupposes that his or her exemplary role has content that is informed by and directed by the community that is being represented. It calls for a sense of mutual accountability so that both parties have a sense of working together. In the words of Dueck: "It is the function of the sacralist to help both an individual and an entire community carry out their pledges to some communal purpose."[14]

Pastors and parachurch leaders readily agree. They affirm the importance of community. They have long been suspicious of the private practitioner model and have felt slighted by the therapeutic world. However, it is dangerous to presume that the role and function of community has been understood simply because one exists in a community. Many pastors counsel in a way that does not reflect the climate of their congregation. Many parachurch leaders direct and guide in ways that are discrepant from the heartbeat of the community.

HOW CAN PASTORS BE EXEMPLARS OF THEIR COMMUNITIES?

1. *Grasp the culture of the community you represent.* It is often assumed that leaders of Christian communities know the group they are leading. If you are trained to be a pastor, then you obviously understand the nature of the church. If you are leading a parachurch organization, you must know how these organizations function. However, you may miss the subtleties of community culture. No two churches are exactly the same. No two Christian organizations function identically. In fact, there has been a shift in our understanding of these organisms in the past thirty years. Whereas the sixties saw a homogenizing of Christian institutions so that they all had a similar look, the seventies brought a recognition that, in the words of James Wind,

> congregations built words of belief and value of their own, how each fashioned itself out of a particular amalgam of personal stories, denominational heritages, local history and larger cultural events. . . . The discovery of congregational culture poses an interpretive challenge as sizable as that presented by the scriptures themselves.[15]

The work of Melvin Williams is instructive in this area. He wanted to understand Zion Church in Pittsburg, a church composed largely of African-Americans who had moved from the south. How did he determine the congregational culture? He watched and listened! For a period of two years he observed the formal and informal aspects of church life. It was his commitment to watching and listening that helped him understand the culture of that particular church. He even found there was a social ritual each time someone moved, which allowed the church community to rally around the displaced individual.[16]

This careful watching is desperately needed in church and parachurch organizations: Leaders who will watch. Leaders who will listen. Leaders who will seek to come to terms with the nature of the community before they confidently become a sacral example of it. Clearly this does not mean that every new pastor should spend the first few years doing nothing but listening. However, it may suggest that the early part of any leader's ministry needs to be heavier on the attending side than the influencing.

2. ***Understand the moral-ethical framework that is embedded in the community you represent.*** If a pastor is committed to the exemplar model, he or she must speak in a way that is consistent with the Christian community that is represented. It would be inconceivable for a leader to espouse a moral position that is inconsistent with the community mind-set. The reflections of Hauerwas and Willimon are helpful in this regard:

> Christian community, life in the colony, is not primarily about togetherness. It is about the way of Jesus Christ with those whom he calls to himself. It is about disciplining our wants and needs in congruence with a true story, which gives us the resources to lead truthful lives. . . . It is important to recognize that all ethics, even non-Christian ethics, arise out of a tradition that depicts the way the world works, what is real, what is worth having, worth believing. Tradition is a function and a product of community. So all ethics, even non-Christian ethics, make sense only when embodied in sets of social practices that constitute a community.[17]

When a young girl comes to the pastor and raises the issue of abortion, or an older man discusses euthanasia, or a young man talks of his struggle with AIDS, the moral-ethical framework of the Christian community must come into play. Where does the church stand on these issues? What is the Holy Spirit saying at this time, to this church, about these issues? To be a true and accurate representative of the community, these questions need to be answered.

If ethics and morality become embodied in the individual pastor or parachurch leader but are not consistent with the community they represent, there will be tension not just for the counselee but also for the pastor and the community. In fact, individuals who consistently function in ways that are discrepant from the community ethos usually end up leaving that community, not because they are incompetent or lacking in skill, but because of a lack of communal fit. Pastors and parachurch leaders must function in ways that affirm the community.

However, the leader has a role to play in the development of the community ethic. In fact, many leaders will put these kinds of topics on the table for discussion with the leadership in particular and the community in general. The topics will be generated by the listening and the watching. What is the community saying? Where are the hot spots? What are the controversial issues?

When a personnel director in a mission society finds that there are an increasing number of divorced and remarried applicants applying for field placement, he or she has a responsibility to bring that issue to the attention of the mission leadership and the mission family at large. Through a process of study, reflection, and listening, the community will have to grapple with the theological, biblical, and social issues involved in divorce and remarriage. The director may become a facilitator of this process but is constantly working to determine the communal mind. At that point the director is able to function in a way that is consistent with the moral-ethical framework of that Christian community.

3. *Practice accountability to your community so there is interdependence.* It follows quite naturally that accountability and mutual dependence would accompany this commitment to the community's moral-ethical framework. Accountability is, first and foremost, recognizing that the resources for counseling are not resident in the individual helper. When a pastor who believes in the tradition of commitment therapy determines that someone is in need of help, he or she is not interested only in self-management. There is a concerted effort to understand the individual in the context of the community and to be sure that healing involves incorporation into that community. By the same token, the pastor is not performing a function that is independent of his or her own community. There is a responsibility there as well.

This means that the pastor must have a particular understanding of the role of the church. Rieff points this out:

> That the church is, supposedly, in but not wholly
> of this world supplied a critical principle of renewal

which is basic to all Christian therapies of commitment. The Church, as an institution, is vital only inasmuch as its symbolic is detached from the established social order, thus preserving its capacity for being the guardian critic of our inherited moral demand.[18]

In the Christian community, the pastor has the backdrop of a body of believers who play the role of guardian. They observe his or her functioning, not in the sense of a watchdog, but rather as those who are committed to particular moral demands that need to be respected. In turn, they can expect accountability.

How this works itself out will be influenced by the context in which the pastor or leader is counseling. At the very least, there needs to be times of regular accountability where the issues of counseling are discussed and the pulse of the community is taken. This can be done without violating confidentiality through a discussion of subject areas like homosexuality, divorce, remarriage, and alcoholism.

How Can Private Counselors Be Representatives of a Christian Community?

1. *Determine the centrality of the Christian community in your practice.* I am under no illusion in writing this book. Private counselors are not going to close up shop! Strictly speaking, that is not my desire. What I would invite, though, is a careful reflection on the centrality of Christian community in your practice. Again, this does not concern the role of the community in the lives of your clients or counselees. Rather it is focused on the role of the Christian community in your own life as a counselor. For many of us who have been trained within Western individualism, it is difficult to readjust our thinking. We find it more comfortable to talk about the Christian community as it influences our clients. However, as Evans has argued,

> Christian psychologists must think of themselves not merely as the Christians in the world of psychology, but as the psychologists of that community called the church, which always deserves their first loyalty.[19]

For some of you this reflection will necessitate a reassessment of your physical and geographical location. In positioning your office in a neutral site, with no explicit connection with a Christian community, you have made a statement that the counseling is removed from the community ethos.

For others, it may mean a reexamination of your own church involvement and commitment. Possibly you are not seen by any Christian community as their representative because you have not become deeply rooted in any of them.

Some of you may need to take a fresh look at accreditation. In a subtle way it has become a replacement for the Christian community, but it does not have a guiding function in terms of your actual practice.

Those of you who work in Christian agencies may need to look at the communal culture of the agency to determine if it is impacting how you as individual counselors function. At the same time, you may want to ask whether the culture of the agency is inextricably linked with and informed by a church or denominational community.

For all of you it may create a new venue for reading. Much of your reading has been in areas that nurture the autonomous mind-set, with the result that you have difficulty thinking about counseling and therapy through a communal paradigm. This may be particularly true for those of you who are within the evangelical world, with its emphasis on the personal and the individual.

2. *Reflect on your moral-ethical presuppositions and their relationship to the Christian community.* If we assume that counseling cannot be value-free, we need to ask where those values are resident. When you are confronted with issues of abortion, euthanasia, or AIDS, what informs your moral-ethical stance? As we have already seen, pastors and parachurch leaders have a built-in Christian community that provides the venue for communication. Through a sensitive listening to each other and to the Spirit, the community ethic becomes clear.

One of the dangers you run is to move the ethical decisions into your own individualized experience. Out of your own reading, reflection, and experience you develop some notions, establish some positions, and counsel in light of them. In a sense, you are no better off than the client who develops a worldview out of autonomous reflection without feedback from the broader society. As a private counselor you run the risk of positioning ethics within your own personal perspective and ignoring the wisdom of the Christian community.

Those who function in Christian agencies run another risk: namely, the insularity that occurs when ideas are shared only with those in a similar profession within the same organization. When we talk of healing, we need a multidisciplinary focus that moves us out of our own mind-set and exposes us to a community that is a cross section of life. Members of Christian organizations often fall into the illusion that they have a built-in moral-ethical framework because they talk to each other. Unfortunately, this framework has often not been tested by an outside community.

This is particularly important in contemporary culture. Very few issues can be addressed within the framework of a single discipline or cluster of disciplines. Take homosexuality and AIDS, for instance. To argue that the counseling of homosexuals with AIDS, with all the attendant moral-ethical concerns, is the exclusive mandate of the counseling profession is to ignore the contribution of theologians and biblical scholars in the hermeneutical questions, philosophers and ethicists in the social ethics questions, medical personnel in both research and treatment, pastors and church leaders in the communal issues, economists and insurance companies in financial concerns, as well as civil servants and politicians in legislative matters.

3. *Move from a utilitarian to a reciprocal mode in terms of your relationship with the Christian community.* Many private Christian counselors and agencies would not survive without the church. Benefits that may come to the counselor include free or inexpensive space within the church building, a referral network through individual churches or denominations, partial payment for clients who are sent from the church, as well as opportunities for preaching or teaching that provide personal exposure.

The danger is that this arrangement becomes paternalistic. One dispenses benefits while the other receives. There is a lack of mutuality, and the church becomes subservient to the private counseling world. This may explain the resentment that many church leaders feel toward private counseling. They may express it in other terms, but at the core it is tied to the inequity in the relationship. The church can only offer things that facilitate and enhance the world of the counselor: more clients, more money, more exposure.

Some of these same leaders do not understand why they cannot dialogue with counselors in more detail. They are not sure why they are often left out of the healing process. The fact that their pastoral perspective is often ignored does not go unnoticed. When a relationship has a utilitarian perspective, one side can easily become arrogant as the other becomes more subservient. Reciprocity is lost, so meaningful communication cannot occur.

As a private counselor, determine ways in which the church can offer something to you that goes beyond economic concerns. Christian communities want to have meaningful involvement in the lives of their people. They want to be heard and understood. As an equal partner in the healing process, they want to do more than simply support your private practice.

These issues are also relevant for Christian agencies that find themselves calling on the Christian community for funds. Often this exacerbates the issues noted above as churches can feel they are again being forced to support something that is distant. While some of the people in their congregation have benefited from the help offered by the counselor or agency, they, as a collective body, still do not have a sense of being an equal participant. You do not have to know much about fundraising to know that a sense of partnership is a prerequisite for the relinquishing of funds.

COMMUNITY RELATIONSHIPS

If a pastor or a private counselor is to function as an exemplar of a community, it follows that he or she will have relationships within that community. Being a representative of a group of people presupposes contact with those people. If this occurs, it is possible that the counselee or client will be a part of that community. This is obviously the case where pastors are concerned. A person in the congregation may relate to the pastor both as a member of that Christian community and as a counselee who comes for individual help.

However, in spite of the potential that exists for pastors and their congregations, there is often an assumption that so-called professional distance is necessary for proper pastoral relationships. Do not get too close to the congregation because they may not respect your role. If you make friends with parishioners, they may manipulate you. Ironically, this belief undercuts the built-in communal connectedness that pastors are afforded in their role.

This possibility for connection is less likely for private counselors, where the relationship tends to be contained within therapeutic boundaries and there is no contact outside of these. However, I know a number of private counselors who have become friends with their counselees, spending time with them socially outside the boundaries of the therapeutic relationship. I have known other situations where the counselor and the client have been part of the same Christian community and have learned to adapt to the complexity of their roles. Counselors often discuss these relationships quietly and with some sense of awkwardness, but they often affirm that this broader communal connection has in fact enhanced the client's growth.

Both pastors and private counselors experience similar prohibitions. Community relationships for the pastor can be negated because of notions of professional distance. Private counselors who engage in communal relationships with their clients can feel uncomfortable because they are violating therapeutic boundaries and professional ethics.

Part of the communal relationship tension that exists for both groups may tie to gender issues. In the evangelical world in particular, the male perspective dominates the mind-set of many churches and parachurch organizations. Even where there is an openness to females in leadership positions, the overall ethos reflects a male bias. And where are men as far as community relationships are concerned?

For many Western men, autonomy is more important than community, and independence is more important than relationships. If these men are put in positions of leadership, they will have difficulty facilitating a communal spirit and will avoid meaningful relationships. Because so many of our churches and parachurch organizations are influenced by the male psyche, it is possible that our problems with community relationships have more to do with gender than other variables.

> The burden of being somebody is so heavy in our society, and the imperative of dominance so strong, that masks are required as props for those difficult scripts. Primarily it is the male who must carry the weight of these myth-scripts in our culture.[20]

While women's issues are an important topic of concern in the broader culture and the church, men's concerns are receiving increasing attention.[21] Much of this literature focuses on the male problem with communication and relationships. In a book that suggests men have struggles with friendship, David Smith lists six reasons why this might be the case:

1. aversion to showing feelings
2. social interaction tends to be superficial
3. inadequate role models
4. inordinately competitive
5. inability to ask for help
6. incorrect priorities[22]

A similar list is offered by Kolbenschlag:[23]

1. low self-disclosure
2. repression of feelings
3. excessive task and instrumental orientation
4. detached autonomy and narcissism with inability to connect, empathize, and collaborate

5. abstract projection that often overrides reality
6. obsessive need to win and be on top
7. fear of vulnerability or any threat to self-reliance
8. dependency

Kolbenschlag suggests that these qualities typify males who have power in our society. In the short term they allow for the achievement of specific goals, but in the long run this dominance and control makes them insensitive and unempathic with minimal insight into others. Success becomes individualized so that men move ahead by distancing themselves from others.[24] Ironically, this pursuit creates greater neuromuscular tension and stress as well as a lower life expectancy than women.

Reuben Fine suggests that this profile of men develops through a process of enculturation. Men are taught to believe that they are more rational and less emotional than women.

> Often enough, however, the man's rationality is little more than a defense against feeling. One consequence is that men are much more apt to deny their feelings, which leads them to stay away from therapy as "sissy stuff."[25]

And not only do they stay away from therapy:

> Traditionally, men are supposed to be strong and silent, not communicative with their wives or fellow workers. This frequently makes it difficult for them to express themselves.[26]

Since many Western men find autonomy to be more important than community, and since the male perspective dominates the thinking of the evangelical world, the importance of community relationships can easily become devalued.

HOW CAN PASTORS CULTIVATE HEALTHY COMMUNITY RELATIONSHIPS?

1. *Seek warm and caring relationships within your community.* As exemplars of your community, it is crucial that you

develop warm and caring relationships within that community. The term *pastor* denotes that this is the nature of the task:
to shepherd and care for those in the community and in the
process facilitate their growth. In fact, this task may be the most
difficult in pastoral ministry. It is much easier to be preoccu-
pied with the administrative details of the mission society or
the fund-raising demands of the Christian school or the preaching responsibilities of Sunday morning.

To have these kinds of relationships, you will need to be
strongly committed to listening to what is going on inside of
people. Rather than being caught up in appearances and public profile, you will spend time trying to catch the heartbeat of
their inner being. Henri Nouwen's description of pastors who
do not develop these kinds of relationships in the congregation is instructive: "Those who avoid the painful encounter
with the unseen are doomed to live a supercilious, boring and
superficial life."[27]

One of the questions I ask people when they come for private
counseling is: "Why did you not go to your pastor/elders/deacons
for help?" Some of the most frequent answers I have been given
involve communal relationships:

> "He/she does not relate very well."
>
> "He/she seems to have a superficial approach to life."
>
> "I have never talked to him/her about anything in
> depth, but I think he/she would tend to simplify my
> difficulties."

A commitment to communal relationships will allow you to be
an exemplar of your community; even more, it will allow you to
understand individuals to a much greater extent and open up
opportunities for more extensive personal ministry.

Is there something inherent to the pastoral situation that
makes this task impossible? Does the congregation actually want
the pastor to maintain a professional distance? Blackbird and
Wright investigated this question under the rubric of the "pedestal effect."[28] The pedestal effect, as they define it, is the

assumption that there is a built-in difference between the pastor and the congregation so that it becomes difficult for a close relationship to develop between the two. Experimental studies did not substantiate this antifraternization norm, leading the investigators to speculate that this may be a perception problem created by pastors. Pastors bring this to the community and then act accordingly. The congregation, at least in these two studies, saw pastoral friendships as appropriate and desirable.

Is it conceivable that there is nothing inherent to the pastoral situation that makes relationships difficult? Quite possibly the influence of the male bias, with its push toward autonomy, has made communal connections more difficult.

2. *Recognize the power inherent in the pastoral role and the potential danger that this brings to communal relationships.* One of the reasons pastors and parachurch leaders are encouraged to avoid close relationships within the community is because of the potential for romantic and/or sexual involvement.[29] A recent book on this topic suggests that roughly 10 percent of pastors have had sexual intercourse with someone in their congregation, while about one-fourth of pastors engaged in some sexual behavior that they considered to be wrong with a parishioner.[30] While these statistics are not encouraging, they do suggest that the vast majority of people in pastoral ministry do *not* become involved sexually with members of their congregation.

In an attempt to engage yourself in warm and caring relationships, it is important to understand the dynamics involved. Lebacqz and Barton identify the issue as

> the recognition that mutuality is missing in the pastor-parishioner relationship. The pastor has power, and the parishioner is vulnerable. The very freedom of access to parishioners' lives means that pastors are dealing with people who are often extremely vulnerable. The core of professional ethics lies in the recognition of this power imbalance between the pastor and the parishioner. It is this that makes sexual contact problematic.[31]

When leaders fall, the publicity often revolves around concerns about sex or money. The leader (it is usually male in these cases) is depicted as sexually obsessed or financially greedy. If there is a woman involved, she is often portrayed as some sort of sex object. However, closer examination will reveal that these relationships have less to do with money and sex and are more related to a misunderstanding of the nature of power.[32]

When a pastor is in a relationship with a parishioner, there is a lack of mutuality and an inequality in terms of power. This has nothing to do with whether the pastor feels strong, secure, or self-confident. It comes more from the pastoral role. The member of the congregation comes with his or her problems and communicates them in a relationship where there is trust and safety. In contrast, the pastor is not there to talk about his or her own difficulties. These factors put the pastor in a risky role. Listening to the wounds of the individual allows entry into some very personal and vulnerable areas. It is at this point where an abuse of power could result in sexual indiscretion.

There are various ways to respond to the potential danger in getting close to people. Some have opted for a professional distance that precludes closeness and intimacy. Because of a fear of sexual indiscretion, they are emotionally distant from the community. Others have failed to recognize the power dynamics involved in relationships of this nature and become extensively involved with people. Because of naiveté, they do not understand the potential danger of relationships where roles are imbalanced.

To engage in impersonal distance on the one side or naive involvement on the other is to miss what is necessary: Pastors need to become close to the Christian community while recognizing the risks involved. If they are going to be exemplars of the community, they must know others and be known by them. This will involve risks, like any other meaningful relationship.

3. *Admit to your legitimate needs for affirmation and care without imposing on the community to fulfill them.* In an article that outlines the destructive potential of counseling for the pastor, Rolfe argues that pastors can experience stress and seductiveness by dealing with the dysfunction of others. There is a feeling of importance and status in helping people. The

danger is that this can become a problem if the pastor does not have his or her own needs in check. [33]

In a similar vein, Meloy posits that the clergy profession reinforces narcissistic character disorders, which include the following symptoms:

> a grandiose sense of self-importance or uniqueness; preoccupation with fantasies of unlimited success, power, brilliance, beauty, or ideal love; exhibitionism; cool indifference or marked feelings of rage, inferiority, shame, humiliation, or emptiness in response to criticism, indifference of others, or defeat; and interpersonal difficulties characterized by entitlement, exploitativeness, feelings of overidealization and devaluation of others, and a lack of empathy.[34]

A pastor with these tendencies, either in blatant or subtle form, will have a high need for affirmation from others while at the same time having little regard for them. They are often detached or hurt and angry with a very low tolerance for interpersonal confrontation. The pastoral role, where people are always looking up to you, creates incredible stress both for the individual and the congregation.

Both of these articles pick up on a common theme. When pastors are involved with a Christian community, the relational pressures have a personal impact. How they handle these pressures will very much depend on their understanding of their own particular needs. Bouma also acknowledges that male pastors have needs for affirmation, esteem, and care, but they have a tendency to compartmentalize their lives. These legitimate needs tend to be unexpressed in the context of family but are shared inappropriately in the context of the congregation. One of the by-products of this is clergy divorce.[35]

An understanding of this dynamic is crucial for pastors, particularly for those who are male. Being involved relationally in your Christian community is a worthy goal. This can be risky in terms of role, as we have seen, but there are also potential dangers in terms of personal needs. The desire to be accepted and liked is appropriate, within bounds, but the pastor needs to avoid the natural tendency to make inordinate demands on the community.

HOW CAN PRIVATE COUNSELORS DEVELOP HEALTHY COMMUNAL RELATIONSHIPS?

1. *Revisit the dual-relationship issue and its application in your own context.* The AAMFT (American Association of Marriage and Family Therapy) Code of Ethical Principles for Marriage and Family Therapists addresses dual relationships in paragraph 1.2 and 4.1. The wording of this particular accrediting body is consistent with the parameters for most mental health professionals:

> Marriage and family therapists are cognizant of their potentially influential position with respect to clients, and they avoid exploiting the trust and dependence of such persons. Marriage and family therapists therefore make every effort to avoid dual relationships with clients that could impair their professional judgment or increase the risk of exploitation. Examples of such dual relationships include, but are not limited to, business or close personal relationships with clients. Sexual intimacy with former clients for two years following the termination of therapy is prohibited. . . .

> Examples of such dual relationships include, but are not limited to, provision of therapy to students, employees, or supervisees, and business or close personal relationships with students, employees, or supervisees. Sexual intimacy with students or supervisees is prohibited. [36]

Two ethical concerns are being addressed in the code: personal relationships and therapeutic involvement. In the former, the guideline argues for the avoidance of personal relationships with clients, including lack of sexual intimacy, up to a period of two years after termination. In the case of therapeutic involvement, it is considered inappropriate to be involved in a therapeutic relationship concurrent with some other connection, such as teacher-student, employer-employee, or supervisor-supervisee.

A number of reasons are given to support these directives:

1. The potentially influential position of a therapist over a client.

2. The potential of exploiting the trust and dependence of clients.

3. The possibility that a dual relationship could impair professional judgment.

4. The possibility that a dual relationship could increase the risk of exploitation.

Ryder and Hepworth point out that codes of ethics have inevitable weaknesses built into them. Consider the lack of sexual involvement for two years as an illustration: One could argue that this clause is too concrete in that it prohibits an action on one day and then allows it the next day. The code is also nonconsensual, in that you may want to extend the prohibition indefinitely in the case of a client who may become a client again. In the minds of some it may convey the message that sexual relationships inevitably follow therapeutic involvement. Finally, it is somewhat simplistic, in that a therapist who is involved sexually with many clients, but always after two years, is missing the spirit of the code. [37]

Tied with these concerns is the issue of ambiguity in the statements. The phrase "include, but are not limited to" obviously can be interpreted widely. What other relationships are tied to this? How far can we interpret it? Engleberg and Symansky, for example, have suggested that "the answer to such questions rests on a consensus of the opinion of therapists in a given community." [38] This, in combination with use of the term *potentially*, gives a fair degree of latitude for interpretation.

Private counselors need to reflect on the implications of dual-relationship concerns if they are going to grapple with community relationships.

2. *Acknowledge that all relationships are ambiguous.* Ryder and Hepworth express concern that rule systems, like all codes of ethics, run the risk of "moving our field, or some people in

it, more into safe ways of dealing with clients."[39] Counseling is confusing, ambiguous, and risky. To deny that is to make the whole enterprise more distant and technique-centered. In particular, counselors who prize the client-counselor relationship will find that the rules will in fact be more of a problem than a solution.

One of the places where this shows itself most directly is in the supervisor-supervisee relationship. Many graduate students become close to their supervisor and in the process may become friends. An attempt to legislate against such a relationship is to fail to recognize that a "good supervisory relationship might be one that emphasizes ambiguity, contradiction and complexity, and that avoids oversimplifying relationships."[40] Any of us who have supervised students will know that it is impossible to eliminate the complexity in that relationship. Having a student in a formal lecture class, then in a small-group supervision session, may lead to the development of a friendship. How this is worked out requires care and sensitivity, but codes of ethics will not wipe out the possibility of it occurring.

A lack of appreciation for the ambiguity of relationships is to deny one of the central tenets of the therapeutic enterprise. In fact, many of us who do counseling spend a lot of our time encouraging our clients to recognize the risk, confusion, and messiness of relationships. Our task is often to help them branch out and leave the safety of their self-imposed structures. Ironically, it would be easy for a counselor to fall into this trap in community relationships. "I cannot see my counselees in a communal setting. It would be awkward and uncomfortable. It might jeopardize what is happening in the therapeutic relationship. There would be inevitable role confusion." Ryder and Hepworth counsel:

> We, as a profession, learned long ago that paradox and contradiction are central features of human relationships. That knowledge did not end our profession. Instead, we seized on it, and made it one central part of our strength. . . . The last thing we should want is to drive underground all awareness of relationship complications.[41]

Obviously this area needs to be approached with wisdom and discernment. Codes of ethics do have their place in providing limits and boundaries. However, this strength needs to be kept in healthy tension with the reality that many communal relationships bring ambiguity and a lack of clarity. We also need to recognize that these issues have particular application in rural settings where role confusion is heightened for those who are involved in any mental health profession.[42]

3. *Separate dual-relationship concerns form the potential for exploitation.* Lurking behind the concern with dual relationships is the fear of exploitation. Too much closeness could result in the therapist or supervisor receiving undue advantage— an advantage that could be used to damage the client or supervisee. However, do dual relationships necessarily lead to exploitation? Ryder and Hepworth clarify:

> Differences in status and power, not specifically dual relationships, facilitate exploitation. Most of the complications described above pertain to relationships that are unevenly equal, or are moving unevenly in the direction of equality. That is to say, they are moving away from exploitation, not toward it, to the extent that they are moving genuinely toward collegiality and equality. . . . Exploitation involves the deliberate maintenance of differences in status and power, so that those differences can be used (exploited) for the advantage of the more powerful person. From this point of view, if the potential for dual relationships were reduced, status relationships would be maintained more sharply, and the potential for exploitation might be increased rather than reduced.[43]

This line of argument is in sharp contrast to much of what therapists hear regarding dual relationships of various sorts. There is not a cause-and-effect correlation between dual relationships and exploitation. If the latter involves status and power and the former collegiality and equality, then one could argue, along with Ryder and Hepworth, that dual relationships may lessen the possibility of exploitation rather than increase it.

Although we have trouble admitting this, many of us have found that our supervisory and counseling relationships have been enhanced by communal connection with these same individuals. Our relationship started within the framework of supervision or counseling, but its extension to outside involvement was not only helpful for the other person, but it removed the inequality and power that was resident in the formal connection. This, in fact, became key for both of us. We were able to relate in a nonhierarchical fashion with both of us experiencing equal power and respect. While the new mutuality brought risks and ambiguity, this did not undermine its value.

MUTUAL PILGRIMAGE

If pastors and private counselors recognize that the environment for healing is communal and not individual, they will realize that the pressure is taken off the helper to be solely responsible for the therapeutic intervention. This task is shared by the community with the helper conceptualizing himself or herself as one part of the process.

When you are the senior pastor of a church, it is easy to see yourself as totally responsible for the health and well-being of the congregation. Obviously, a sense of responsibility is one of the prices of leadership, but the danger in all these situations is that the leader does not really understand the nature of mutual pilgrimage. The risk is that the community may be implicitly ignored. William Hug reminds us:

> We hear a lot about copilgrimage in pastoral counseling today. It is the notion that we as counselors do not have all the answers. Rather, we seek to share a journey with our clients. Ours is a mutual pilgrimage.[44]

In an evangelical culture where there is a lot of discussion on "servant leadership," it is easy to get the impression that a particular kind of individual can have what it takes to bring hope to the community. This individual has the requisite resources, skills, and gifts for leadership, and he or she brings them to bear on various situations. Unfortunately, what is not understood is that being a servant is a statement on how one views his or her capacity to help. A servant acknowledges with humility and deference that not all the answers are readily available; there is not an abundant supply for all that people need. Rather, the servant is a pilgrim on a journey that has confusion and messiness at every turn. More important, the servant is a fellow pilgrim with others who are also confronting life's ambiguities.

As exemplars, pastors and private counselors are representatives of the moral-ethical framework of the community. As those who are committed to relationships, they are willing to take the risks to move outside their roles or professions and connect with people in the community. However, as a copilgrim there is a more intimate connection with the community.

Pastors and the Need for Mutual Pilgrimage

1. *Make sure your private performance squares with your public performance.* In his book, *The Seven Habits of Highly Effective People*, Stephen Covey suggests that people who influence others need to have a high commitment to understanding them.[45] Whether it is a wife with a husband, a parent with a child, an employer with an employee, a counselor with a counselee, or a pastor with members of the congregation, there is high value in knowing what is going on with the other. However, the key to this knowledge is not technique, where skills and tricks are used in a manipulative way; instead, it is the essence of the person—his or her character. In other words, to be a person who understands others is to focus on *who I am* rather than *what I do*.

This is why some very well trained pastors are seen as having poor relational skills. This is why some mission administrators are not trusted by the missionaries they lead. This is why some directors of parachurch organizations are out of touch with their employees. They have not understood a fundamental issue in dealing with people. As Covey observes:

> If your life runs hot and cold, if you're both caustic
> and kind, and, above all, if your private performance
> doesn't square up with your public performance, it's
> very hard for me to open up with you. Then, as much

as I may want and even need to receive your love
and influence, I don't feel safe enough to expose my
opinions and experiences and tender feelings.[46]

When you are involved in a community as a pastor, you do
not only bring your particular gifts and expertise to bear; you
also expose what you are really like. This is inevitable in a
Christian community. Even if you pull back and stay unin-
volved, this will be read by those who observe. Even if you try
to create an aura or an image, this attempt will form part of
the communal assessment. Personal exposure is guaranteed
when you function in a community.

People experience safety and trust

- when there is consistency in the leader's life,
- when there is congruity between what is said in the pulpit
  and what is said in the home,
- when there is compatibility between the pastor's relationship with his or her spouse and what is said about marriage
  publicly,
- when there is general agreement between the pastor's own
  self-perception and the congregation's impression of him
  or her,
- when the private performance squares with the public
  performance.

I find that pastors often miss the intricacies of this issue.
They have come to believe that backslapping, glad-handing,
and expressions of affirmation are the essence of pastoral care.
Often these pastors are liked or appreciated because they make
some people feel accepted. However, there is a major integrity
issue at stake.

If as a pastor you spend your life engaging in superficial
affirmation of others, you will soon find yourself creating a
congregation where that same superficiality dominates. More
important, people will go elsewhere when they need to deal
with their significant experiences and tender feelings. The
reason? People intuitively respond to someone who lives

with integrity. They know that there is pain and struggle behind your "happy bear" pastoral presence. There has to be;
you are also human. They also know that you are hiding it,
consciously or unconsciously. As a result, you are not a person who can be trusted. And if you cannot be trusted, then
people are not going to open up to you.

To be a copilgrim in the Christian community, the pastoral
leader must live with integrity. There must be congruity in
the public realm. There must be consistency in the private
realm. But most important, there must be harmony between
the public and the private. Members of a Christian community will detect violations of this very quickly and respond
accordingly.

2. *Recognize the relationship between intimacy and self-
disclosure.* The copilgrim metaphor draws the pastor into close
communal relationship, bringing the person-role tension to the
surface. If you are connecting personally within the community, it is impossible not to struggle with the distinction
between role and person. Some pastors, for instance, find it
easy to lose themselves in their role. They develop a particular
style of relating, a pastoral voice, and an overall demeanor that
presumably goes with the role. The congregation is never quite
sure where the pastor is at because the role is the dominating
form of communication.

If integrity is the operative mode, then the person is not
lost in the role; rather, the person becomes instrumental in
how the role is crafted. The pastor's own style, personality,
and character infuse the role so that the pastoral work is a
reflection of the uniqueness of that particular individual.
Within this model no two pastors perform identically because
"who you are" informs the nature of the task. But when the
pastor functions with integrity, it provides a foundation for
the community to feel understood. In the context of self-
disclosure and understanding, the person can open up and
move toward healing.

Self-disclosure is the willingness to "be open, make contact,
and reach out with authenticity."[47] It is a sharing of my personal
feelings and opinions, not just in general, but as they come up
in the context of a relationship. In a sense, it is interaction that

revolves around the theme, "How are we doing together in our relationship? Here's what I am feeling/experiencing." When this level of interaction occurs in a relationship, intimacy is deepened.

In a recent review of over two hundred studies that focused on self-disclosure, Watkins found that self-disclosure on the part of counselors resulted in

1. higher counselor ratings by the counselee,

2. greater self-disclosure by the counselee,

3. more willingness to continue with the counseling.[48]

Building on similar conclusions, Healey suggests that because Judeo-Christian religion is relationship-based, self-disclosure is crucial not only for the community to have a sense of identity and solidarity but because it "ultimately produces intimacy with (or a clearer vision of) God. This intimacy is mediated in most cases by others."[49]

A pastor who understands this dynamic will recognize that communal relationships will be deepened if there is a commitment to self-disclosure. Rather than hiding behind the pastoral role, a willingness to be yourself will not only facilitate intimacy in the community but may provide a context where openness will characterize people's relationships with others and with God.

3. *Elevate the ministry of the community above the expressions of your own giftedness.* One of the ways pastors can distance themselves from the community and negate a co-pilgrimage spirit is to conceptualize their own giftedness as foundational and that of the community as secondary. When this happens, the pastor tends to perceive the community in a utilitarian mode. People are there to facilitate his or her giftedness and profession. They provide the context for the ministry to continue, but they do not have a viable ministry of their own.

When this occurs, giftedness is not seen as communal but as individual. The contributions of the body of Christ are autonomous, with the major expression coming from the pastor. When this happens, the mission's director must have the missionaries so he is able to fulfill his need to do pastoral administration. The parachurch leader must have employees so she can fulfill her need to carry out public ministry. Little thought is given to the ministry of the whole body as a communal expression of God's enabling.

Nouwen captures this well:

> We should never forget that God has called us as a people, and that our individual religious vocations should always be seen as a part of the larger vocation of the community. We cannot use the community as a means to develop or give shape to our individual religious aspirations. As long as we see the community as a support system to help us realize our individual ideals, we are more children of our time than children of God. Our own individual vocation can only be seen as a particular manifestation of the vocation of the community to which we belong.[50]

Pastors who see the community as a support system are bound to separate themselves from that body. It will be impossible for them to engage in the journey of copilgrimage because the community will be far removed.

PRIVATE COUNSELORS AND THE NEED FOR MUTUAL PILGRIMAGE

1. *Recognize the integrity problem built into the counseling process.* One of the themes that comes up often in private counseling is the matter of integrity. Among the statements that clients will make are the following:

> "Do you really care about me, or are you just doing this because it is your job?"

> "Is this genuine for you?"

> "Are you being a counselor in saying that, or do you mean it?"

There are various twists on this theme, but they all come down to the same issue: Do private counselors respond with integrity?

It would be inappropriate to suggest that private counselors, at the level of personal values and ethics, have a problem with integrity. What might be more appropriate is to suggest that the structural process of counseling makes integrity difficult. While counselors may try to level with people in counseling and seek to share their experience, the constraints of the office, the hour, the fee, and the professional nature of the contact mean that full personal contact is difficult. Central in this is the absence of communal connectedness. These clients do not form part of our community, so their knowledge of us as people is limited.

I appreciate the honesty of Kottler on this topic. He says that clients

> may not know what we are really like, but they know
> us at our absolute best. . . . I have always found it
> ironic that clients who pay for my time, people
> whom I would rarely choose as friends, nevertheless
> receive 95 percent of my attention, my focused con-
> centration. . . . I give my best away to people who
> pay for my time.[51]

If Kottler is expressing the true nature of private counseling, and I believe he is, it calls into question whether the private counseling enterprise can really facilitate copilgrimage. If clients do not know what we are really like, then how can we journey together? If this is purely a professional transaction with an exchange of fee and does not reflect friendship, then our sense of togetherness may have an artificial quality to it.

Again I would suggest that private counselors need to revisit the dual relationship issue and determine whether the lack of communal connectedness may be inhibiting the healing process rather than facilitating it. Those of us who have taken the risk with communal exposure have found that counselees were often reassured to see us as we are, rather than at our absolute best. One wonders whether our encouragements to clients regarding masks, facades, and scripts may be worthy of our own consideration.

2. *Accept your own dependency needs and allow yourself to be vulnerable.* Private counselors spend their professional lives helping others. This means they are in relationships where the other is vulnerable and dependent. Clients share their stories, their pain, their difficulty, and in the process the counselor seeks to move these people toward health and healing. As already stated, there is an integrity problem built into this structure because the counselor is in a position where there is little mutuality and reciprocity. This can be offset to some degree by self-disclosure within the confines of the office, but it may not be as effective as communal connectedness with clients.

After a number of years of these kinds of relationships, it is often difficult for counselors to be on the other end of the spectrum. I have talked to counselors who have experienced personal pain and trauma that has resulted in others helping them. This may have been in the form of hospitalization for themselves or a family member or even therapeutic help for some of their own issues. While they appreciated the help and concern, it was not easy to experience the vulnerability and dependence. I know other counselors who have difficulty in simple social situations because they are used to relationships where there is a lack of mutuality and they are in control.

Hedgespeth goes as far as to say that this may be endemic to many in the profession:

> I think that many mental health professionals may have difficulties accepting their dependency needs and allowing themselves to be vulnerable with others. There may be much more comfort in nurturing than in receiving nurturance, particularly when there is external pressure to appear to have it all together.[52]

Communal connection with clients is an issue that probably could be debated, but counselors need to be conscious of the need for general communal relationships where their own dependency needs and vulnerability can filter to the surface. This will not only allow for a greater awareness of what it is like to be a client, but it will put counselors in touch with some of their own dynamics—dynamics that may be blurred when relationships are one-sided.

3. *Acknowledge your own weakness as a key component of the healing process.* Kottler argued that private counselors are at their best when they are with clients. This is in contrast to what they are like in other situations, whether it be home, church, or family. Presumably, "being at your best" precludes weakness. In focusing attention on the client and his or her difficulties, our own weaknesses are kept hidden. How does this fit with copilgrimage? If our counselees are struggling with their own frailties and weaknesses, then our being at our best may in fact negate their struggles rather than lead to a sense of mutuality.

I have often wondered whether the enterprise of counseling and the pressure it puts on counselors to be at their best may in fact intensify some clients' struggles. As they are constantly exposed to someone who they only see in the office, who seems to have things together, and who is not exposed in the context of a community, the standard of health may seem insurmountable. Our desire to protect others from our weaknesses may be instrumental in them not dealing with their own.

For some this facade even continues into the church. In discussing the church as a referral network, Guy and Liaboe suggest that counselors may not want to reveal weakness in that context "due to fear that they will be less willing to refer if they know that you have personal weaknesses."[53] They go as far as to say that for some counselors no church gathering may be comfortable if he or she is receiving referrals from them. Apart from what this says about counselors, it is an interesting statement on what counselees look for in a counselor.

This sense of isolation from the community and the attendant avoidance of our own weaknesses puts private counselors in an awkward situation. Most of us know enough about the self-disclosure literature to know the potential positive effect our weakness will have on others. We also know that one of the major qualities of inexperienced counselors is that they are out of touch with their own strengths and weaknesses and are overwhelmed by the weaknesses that are known.[54] To embrace our own weakness and allow others to observe it is not an indication that we are weak—quite the opposite.

SUMMARY

Pastors and other Christian leaders who are doing counseling within their faith community struggle with the adequacy of their preparation and time allocation. However, they have a built-in advantage because their ministry allows them to function within a community. In contrast, private counselors do not find themselves tied to Christian communities, so there are some structural barriers to overcome.

Both pastors and private counselors need to be exemplars of the communities they represent. In doing this they are not seeking to bring their parishioners or clients into contact with the communities but are seeking to be a representative of it themselves. They also need to engage in community relationships, an aspiration that will not only give them a clearer sense of the nature of their communities but will also allow them to be seen for who they are in the context of helping. Finally, both pastors and private counselors need to understand the power of copilgrimage, where vulnerabilities and weaknesses provide a context of mutuality and reciprocity in the community.

NOTES

1. Again, keep in mind that the term *pastoral* describes the function of many people in Christian communities, both church and parachurch. It is not being used to refer to a particular role or position in a church context.

2. Richard L. Krebs, "Why Pastors Should Not Be Counselors," *The Journal of Pastoral Care* 34 (1980): 229.

3. David J. Rolfe, "The Destructive Potential of Psychological Counseling for Pastor and Parish," *Pastoral Psychology* 34 (1985): 61–68.

4. David G. Benner, *Strategic Pastoral Counseling: A Short-Term Structured Model* (Grand Rapids: Baker Book House, 1992).

5. Ibid., 14–15.

6. Christopher Moody, "Pastors or Counselors?" *Theology* 91 (1988): 387–92.

7. "Integrative Inquiry," *Journal of Psychology and Theology* 19 (1991): 285.

8. James D. Guy and Gary P. Liaboe, "Isolation in Christian Psychotherapeutic Practice," *Journal of Psychology and Theology* 13 (1985): 167–71.

9. Ibid., 170.

10. Al Dueck, "Ethical Contexts of Healing: Ecclesia and Praxis," *Pastoral Psychology* 36 (1987): 53–54.

11. Ibid., 55.

12. Ibid.

13. Al Dueck, "Ethical Contexts of Healing: Character and Ritual," *Pastoral Psychology* 36 (1987): 75.

14. Philip Rieff, *The Triumph of the Therapeutic: Uses of Faith after Freud* (New York: Harper and Row, 1966), 76.

15. James P. Wind, "Leading Congregations, Discovering Congregational Cultures," *The Christian Century* (3–10 February 1993): 105.

16. Melvin Williams, *Community in a Black Pentecostal Church* (Pittsburg: University of Pittsburg, 1974).

17. Stanley Hauerwas and William H. Willimon, *Resident Aliens: Life in the Christian Colony* (Nashville: Abingdon, 1989), 79.

18. Rieff, *Triumph of the Therapeutic*, 250.

19. C. Stephen Evans, *Wisdom and Humanness in Psychology* (Grand Rapids: Baker Book House, 1989), 143.

20. M. Kolbenschlag, *Lost in the Land of Oz: The Search for Identity and Community in American Life* (New York: Harper and Row, 1988), 53.

21. Two recent books of interest: Richard L. Meth et al., *Men in Therapy: The Challenge of Change* (New York: Guilford Press, 1990); and Samuel Osherson, *Wrestling with Love: How Men Struggle with Intimacy with Women, Children, Parents, and Each Other* (New York: Fawcett Columbine, 1992).

22. David Smith, *The Friendless American Male* (Ventura, Calif.: Regal Books, 1984), 13–22.

23. Kolbenschlag, *Land of Oz*, 53.

24. For a description of this in a Christian context, see Herb Stanelle, "The Emotionally Isolated Christian Male," *Social Work and Christianity* 18 (1991): 104–15.

25. Reuben Fine, *Troubled Men: The Psychology, Emotional Conflicts, and Therapy of Men* (San Francisco: Jossey-Bass, 1988), 21.

26. Ibid., 21–22.

27. Henri J. M. Nouwen, *The Wounded Healer* (Garden City, N.Y.: Image, 1972), 37.

28. Tegan Blackbird and Paul H. Wright, "Pastors' Friendships, Part 1: Project Overview and an Exploration of the Pedestal Effect," *Journal of Psychology and Theology* 13 (1985): 274–83; Paul H. Wright and Tegan Blackbird, "Pastors' Friendships, Part 2: The Impact of Congregational Norms," *Journal of Psychology and Theology* 14 (1986): 29–41.

29. See Peter Rutter, *Sex in the Forbidden Zone* (New York: Ballantine Books, 1989).

30. Karen Lebacqz and Ronald G. Barton, *Sex in the Parish* (Louisville: Westminster/John Knox, 1991).

31. Ibid., 102.

32. See Marilyn R. Peterson, *At Personal Risk: Boundary Violations in Professional-Client Relationships* (New York: Norton, 1992).

33. Rolfe, "Destructive Potential," 61–68.

34. J. Reid Meloy, "Narcissistic Psychopathology and the Clergy," *Pastoral Psychology* 35 (1986): 51.

35. M. Bouma, *Divorce in the Parsonage* (Minneapolis: Bethany House, 1979).

36. "Code of Ethical Principles for Marriage and Family Therapists," *American Association for Marriage and Family Therapy* (Washington, D.C., 1988), 1, 4.

37. Robert Ryder and Jeri Hepworth, "AAMFT Ethical Code: 'Dual Relationships,'" *Journal of Marital and Family Therapy* 16 (1990): 127–32.

38. S. Engelberg and J. Symansky, "Ethics and the Law," *Family Therapy Networker* 13 (1989): 31.

39. Ryder and Hepworth, "Ethical Code," 129.

40. Ibid., 130.

41. Ibid., 131.

42. Melanie C. Geyer, "Dual Role Relationships and Christian Counseling," *Journal of Psychology and Theology* 22 (1994): 187–95, draws some important parallels between the tensions faced by Christian counselors in church settings and those problems that arise in the context of rural mental health.

43. Ryder and Hepworth, "Ethical Code," 130.

44. William F. Hug, "Beyond Therapy and Technique: Reflections on the Process of Becoming," in *Pastoral Counseling*, ed. Barry K. Estadt, Melvin Blanchette, and John R. Compton (Englewood Cliffs, N.J.: Prentice-Hall, 1983), 80.

45. Stephen R. Covey, *The Seven Habits of Highly Effective People: Restoring the Character Ethic* (New York: Simon and Schuster, 1989).

46. Ibid., 238.

47. George Stricker and Martin Fisher, eds., *Self-Disclosure in the Therapeutic Relationship* (New York: Plenum, 1990), vii.

48. C. Edward Watkins, "The Effects of Counselor Self-Disclosure: A Research Review," *The Counseling Psychologist* 18 (1990): 477–500.

49. Bede J. Healey "Self-Disclosure in Religious Spiritual Direction: Antecedents and Parallels to Self-Disclosure in Psychotherapy," in Stricker and Fisher, *Self-Disclosure*, 17–27.

50. Henri J. M. Nouwen, *Clowning in Rome: Reflections on Solitude, Celibacy, Prayer, and Contemplation* (Garden City, N.Y.: Image, 1979), 22.

51. Jeffrey A. Kottler, *On Being a Therapist* (San Franciso: Jossey-Bass, 1986) 17, 21.

52. Joanne Hedgespeth, "Integrative Inquiry: Response 2," *Journal of Psychology and Theology* 19 (1991): 288.

53. Guy and Liaboe, "Isolation," 169.

54. Mary O'Leary Wiley and Philip B. Ray, "Counseling Supervision by Developmental Level," *Journal of Counseling Psychology* 33 (1986): 439–45.

Chapter Six

Community and the Counseling Context

This interest in spirituality is, in many ways, like that of our ancestors. But the deep ties with community that sustained people in their faith and in their lives over the centuries, argue many social observers, may now be on the verge of collapse.
—Robert Wuthnow

SARAH AND JEREMY HAVE BEEN MARRIED for six years. To all external appearances they are "the perfect couple." They are successful in business, active socially, and quite involved in the church. However, for the past two years the marriage has been rocky. Jeremy had an affair with his administrative assistant, and although it ended, the strain on Sarah continues. Around the same time the affair ended, Jeremy began to be verbally abusive and on a number of occasions has pushed Sarah. She is at a loss to know where to turn because she wants to protect his reputation in the church community, where he is highly respected for his administrative and financial skills. The pastor is a strong supporter of Jeremy, and they often spend time together on the golf course. In fact, Sarah worries that Jeremy has developed such an aura at the church that no one would believe her if she did open up.

As a result, Sundays are very difficult for Sarah. After a Saturday evening of abuse and disrespect, she watches Jeremy perform beautifully the next morning. He is warm and friendly, and his wit endears him to everyone. Her resentment runs high, and she wonders how he can be so two-faced. At times she confronts him with this, but he laughs it off and says he is not as bad as she makes him out to be. If she suggests they reach out for help from the pastor or a counselor, Jeremy gets extremely angry and the abuse intensifies.

Last month the pastor gave a series of sermons on marriage. Sarah was looking forward to that series with the hope that it would have an impact on Jeremy and result in some change. Instead, the pastor made some derogatory remarks on the feminist movement and its unhealthy influence on Christian women, and he indicated that the main problem with marriage today is the fact that men are not taking their leadership responsibilities seriously. Women were presented as appendages of men, and there were numerous chauvinistic remarks interspersed throughout the sessions.

When the series was over, Jeremy quoted liberally from the pastor's remarks, and Sarah was shocked to find that his abusive behavior became more entrenched as he sought to, in his words, "take his leadership responsibilities more seriously." This was the last straw for Sarah. She decided to get help.

A number of things are confusing for Sarah. Her deep-seated conviction that she has to protect Jeremy and their marital situation from the church community is strong. On the other hand, it is frustrating her that this kind of facade might continue if she does not tell the truth and let the church know.

She also struggles with the church's role in all this, particularly the involvement of the pastor. Are people really oblivious to what is going on? What is it about this church that seems to allow people to function behind layers and veneers so that problems are denied and minimized?

Her pain in the abusive marriage seems to be facilitated by the church liturgy. Human suffering is almost negated. Earthly issues are elevated to such a lofty spiritual level that she feels disconnected with God and the community of faith. When marriage is discussed, she feels disempowered and discouraged.

Sarah can privatize the pain and keep it inside, but there is a communal context for her struggles, and this context needs to be understood if appropriate help is going to occur. For this reason, confidentiality becomes an important subject. Furthermore, the questionable ethics in this situation go beyond Jeremy's marital unfaithfulness. Sin is also resident in the social structure of the church community. Finally, the church liturgy provides a context where the pain is intensified. The body of Christ is not a place of healing and safety.

CONFIDENTIALITY

One of the most helpful ways to understand the intricacies and importance of confidentiality is to examine the theme of secrets. The information we retain within, whether it is about ourselves or others, forms part of who we are. There is a constant pull to share the secrets, on the one hand, and hold them in on the other. Frederick Buechner summarizes this well:

> I have come to believe that by and large the human family all has the same secrets, which are both very telling and very important to tell. They are telling in the sense that they tell what is perhaps the central paradox of our condition—that what we hunger for perhaps more than anything else is to be known in our full humanness, and yet that is often what we also fear more than anything else.[1]

Sarah has a secret. Her husband has been unfaithful and abusive. This secret has been kept from everyone. Those who have bought into the facade at the church do not know the secret. She would like them to know, partially because she is tired of the charade and also because she believes that it might result in help. In telling, however, it will reveal the true state of things. The marriage will be unmasked, and both of them will be exposed in all their humanness. This creates fear for Sarah.

Paul Tournier views this as an important stage in the process of development.[2] In having secrets and keeping them to yourself you maintain a sense of individuality. You are distinct from others because you have information that they do not have.[3] Unlike young children who tell their parents practically everything, a sense of self develops when we develop an ability to keep our own secrets. However, to move into the next stage—personhood—there is a need to willfully share with others. Tournier writes:

> One cannot become a person without first being an individual, without freeing himself from the clan, from parental domination, without becoming aware of his own individuality, which has a right to secrecy. But if one remains at this stage, one remains an individual, rather than a person. By opening out, by telling one's secrets—but freely this time—one becomes personally linked with those to whom he reveals them, and becomes fully a person thereby.[4]

This is why the breaking of a confidence can be so devastating. To tell your own secrets is a key part of development. When someone does it on your behalf, they have robbed you in ways that cannot be measured. Sadly, these situations drive some people inside themselves so they never choose to share their secrets again. Tournier goes on to explain:

> The disclosure of a secret is a betrayal, a violation of the person. The very process which could have been so valuable for the formation of the individual is going to block the evolution of the person if he fails because of indiscreetness. Whoever has been betrayed once, in that way, when he had given himself in complete frankness and honesty, becomes distrustful for a long time, at times for his entire life.[5]

In sharing secrets with others there is not only the development of personhood, but there are also dynamics related to loyalty, power, boundaries, and alliances.[6] Let's say, for example, that Sarah went to her best friend, Melody, and told her the whole situation. For Sarah this might relieve some tension and let her experience the care of someone else. However, Melody is now in an awkward position. She has information that

1. intensifies the loyalty between her and Sarah,
2. gives her increased power because she is in possession of information that no one else has,
3. creates a boundary in her relationship with Jeremy of which he is unaware,
4. provides an alliance with Sarah that gives them a bond distinguishing them from others.

As Melody reflects on the situation, she realizes that Jeremy's behavior is unacceptable and that her withholding of the information is preventing him from receiving appropriate help. On the other hand, she, like Sarah, wants to protect him from the church community so his reputation is not tarnished. If she tells, that will break the alliance that has been developed with Sarah—a conversation that took place "in confidence." And who would she tell? It may be too risky to let anyone in the church know about the affair and the abuse.

Implicit in much of the concern about confidentiality is a concern for the individual. Since it is crucial for the development of personhood, people should not be betrayed by others. A rather extreme example is presented by Michael Kottow, a medical doctor who argues that confidentiality should never be breached within the context of medical practice because "the autonomy of patients and the sovereignty of the medical profession are all better served."[7]

To illustrate this position, Kottow discusses the case of a bus driver coming to a physician and finding out he has epilepsy. He argues that confidentiality precludes disclosure to the employer.

> If this results in the bus driver continuing to work under precarious conditions it means that the company has not established an efficient medical service

to check its drivers and is negligent. Physicians are to declare themselves explicitly and unmistakably loyal to those who engage their services.[8]

When confidentiality is obligatory, the fact that the bus driver could injure others becomes secondary; the autonomous individual takes priority over the community.

Christian counselors and pastors do not have the liberty to prize confidentiality and the autonomous individual to the exclusion of a communal sensibility. They are in a constant state of trying to be loyal to both. In fact, one of the reasons counselors experience ethical dilemmas is because they often work in contexts where the "institutional value systems may be quite different from those of the counseling profession itself."[9]

Take, for example, the typical undergraduate college campus. Faculty counselors are called upon to be both a part of the community, in terms of teaching, administration, and social connection, as well as provide counseling services to individuals. Often these are compatible tasks, but there are times when they create tension. On many occasions I have sat in faculty meetings on our own campus where we were deciding who would graduate. Since I had been in a counseling relationship with a number of the prospective graduates, I was privy to personal information. At times I was unclear whether it was my responsibility to share this information for the greater good or to withhold it so the student was protected. Were the needs of the individual student and my commitment to confidentiality more important than my communal responsibility as a faculty member? To give positive or negative information was to breach confidentiality, and to withhold it, in the words of Grayson and Cauley,

> may mark therapists as unhelpful, priggish, or snobbish-elitists who feel that no one else is qualified to know what they know. Holding secrets is not a good way to gain popularity or generate referrals.[10]

Similar ethical difficulties confront pastors who are dealing with individual members of the congregation. Noyce, for instance, presents the situation of a fifteen-year-old girl who comes to the pastor and indicates she is pregnant. What is his responsibility? Is it to her as an individual? To her parents? To the church at large?

> One of our most difficult dilemmas arises from the multivalenced quality of the ministry contract. By adults, for example, the minister may be seen as teacher and steward of the traditional mores, "in loco parentis." Yet the minister hopes to be an accessible friend and confessor and spiritual director of adolescents who are in transit toward a separate adulthood of their own, away from parents. Does this mean the pastor colludes with a fifteen-year-old girl in keeping her pregnancy secret from her parents, who are also parishioners?[11]

The pastor does not have the option of thinking only of the autonomous individual. Communities are affected by the behavior of individuals. The pastor's commitment to the teenage girl cannot blur his responsibility to the parents and to the broader church community. Rauch has summarized the delicate balance that is required:

> Faithfulness to one person must be balanced by faithfulness to other individuals, to the Christian community, and to the Lord. It is not enough to be faithful to one and faithless to the rest. Knowing how to balance faithfulness to all is a matter of teaching the Lord's mind on the right circles for information.[12]

We need to draw those circles in such a way that the community is given its rightful place. Institutions need to hold to a value system that seeks to prize the individual but in the process be faithful to the broader community. One's approach to confidentiality will reflect the true nature of the value system. Jay Haley provides a helpful analysis to illustrate this point:

When a counselor and a counselee meet there is an exchange of information. How much information should be exchanged?

In large measure this depends on what is valued most highly. If the counselor is intent on having the client move toward independence, it "can be argued that individuation and total sharing of information are incompatible. The act of concealment between therapist and client defines a boundary between them and so individuates them."[13]

Often in marriage counseling one partner will tell the counselor something that he or she does not want the spouse to know. This could take place on the telephone, quietly at the end of a session, or in a note. If the counselor decides not to tell the spouse, the counselor is drawing a line between the marriage partners. If the counselor tells, then he or she is acknowledging that the two marriage partners are one. Haley suggests that the "act of concealing or revealing information is not only an ethical one but a definition of marriage."[14] In other words, how the counselor handles information reflects an understanding of the boundaries between the counselor and the client as well as between the individual partners in the marriage.

So if Sarah decides to go to her pastor for counseling, what are the limits on confidentiality? If he decides to keep everything she says in confidence, he runs the risk of being unable to deal with Jeremy. If he spills everything, he may alienate Sarah and make it virtually impossible to get close enough to Jeremy to be of any assistance. If he decides, with Sarah's permission, to draw in others in leadership and then work slowly toward restoring Jeremy to genuine involvement in the community, he will demonstrate his commitment to the broader body and not just to individuals within it.

If Sarah decides to go to a private counselor, what are the boundaries of the circles of information and on what basis are these going to be drawn? If the counselor facilitates a sanctioned retreat, we might expect that all information will be kept confidential since the individual is paramount. The church will have no role to play in the healing process and no responsibility to bear in Jeremy's difficulties. On the other hand, if the counselor seeks, with Sarah's permission, to involve the church leadership, then confidentiality is sacrificed for the sake of a system that is seen to have higher value.

In light of all this, what are some of the issues that pastors and private counselors need to consider?

How Do Pastors Relate to Confidentiality?

1. *Define the limits of confidentiality for the church or parachurch context.* Leaders of church and parachurch organizations need to have a well-thought-out position on confidentiality. This might start with a discussion of some relevant literature as well as interaction around particular cases. For example, if you are in this kind of context, what would you do with the information that Sarah could bring to you? Would you go to Jeremy immediately? Would you go to other leaders in the faith community? Would you consult your colleagues? These questions are better addressed ahead of time in mock situations rather than dealing with the intricacies of real cases.

It is valuable if this position is community-owned and understood. If I am in your Christian community, I need to have some idea what will happen to the information I communicate. Will it go to others in leadership? Will it go to your spouse? If I request confidentiality, will that be respected? In essence, the issue of community expectations needs to be addressed. If people are not sure what you will do with their secrets, they might assume the worst and not reveal them.

The communication of such a policy can be done in various ways. Pastoral leaders find it easiest to communicate their philosophy of confidentiality when they are dealing with a situation personally. This is more direct, but it runs the risk of not communicating clearly to the entire community. Another option is a public gathering, such as a staff or congregational meeting, where the leaders can describe how they understand the issue. Depending on the context, written policies allow the community to hear a consistent message.

Most good definitions of confidentiality include exceptions. What will these be in your context? The "danger to self or other" exception that characterizes most of professional counseling still requires some discernment and judgment. In the context of Christian communities, we also need to ask the moral-ethical questions. So in the case of Jeremy's affair, how would your community handle confidentiality? Would you as a leader be required to go to the rest of the leadership, or even the entire community, or would this be something between the two of you? When does your moral-ethical responsibility to the entire community become more important than your relationship with Jeremy? Wiest and Smith identify the difficulty:

> The defenders of absolute confidentiality hold, implicitly or explicitly, that the loss involved in the breaking of confidentiality will always outweigh losses entailed by maintaining it. But there is no factual evidence that enables us to make such a judgment for all possible situations. Exceptions are not easy to decide. They must be decided on the merits of each particular case and honest differences of judgment must be allowed.[15]

When you are working within a Christian community, you have an ethical responsibility to that community to be a person of virtue and integrity. Professional ethics requires that these traits are demonstrated in a commitment to trusteeship—a recognition that you are entrusted with something of value, namely information about people whom you serve.[16] To have thought through the dynamics of confidentiality and sought community ownership of the same is to provide that community with solid leadership.

2. *Recognize the dangers of the pastoral role.* By its very nature the pastoral role runs some risks when it comes to confidentiality. Steve Levicoff asserts that "even in the church, where we are admonished to have pure hearts, we often end up with big mouths. . . . I haven't seen a church yet in which a person's problems, if known, are not subject to gossip."[17]

Wiest and Smith take this one step further in their comment on clergy:

> Clergy have said of themselves that as a group they may have a more than average inclination to gossip. While we have no scientific studies to confirm this, personalities who are attracted to this profession enjoy human contact and are often ready

talkers. Chatty conversation may easily drift into
gossip. Genuine interest in other human beings may
cause us to talk gratuitously about other persons
with no harm intended.[18]

Within the evangelical subculture, information can be dis-
closed for purposes of preaching illustrations, prayer concerns,
or genuine compassion, but this can easily cross the line into a
breach of confidentiality. I have seen too many situations where
sharing was carried out, either in person or in print, with the
other's best interests at heart, but it turned out to be quite
harmful not only to the individual but to the community. Pastors and Christian leaders need to be aware of this danger
within the community.

Another important issue related to the pastoral role is that of
the nature and scope of privileged communication. In essence,
privileged communication is synonymous with confidentiality
except that the former is codified within the law.

Clergy privileged communications are those disclo-
sures from clients to clergy, by word or writing, that
are exempted from being offered as evidence in
court. Simply, the laws of privileged communications allow clergy to refuse to repeat what clients
have divulged to them when asked to testify.[19]

Ronald Bullis acknowledges that there are differences between various geographical areas but suggests the following
five principles apply to the admissibility of a claim of privileged communication:

1. It must have been intended to be kept secret.

2. The clergy needs to be understood as hearing this kind
   of communication in the context of official duties.

3. The governing body to which the clergy accounts must
   require that the information be kept confidential.

4. The counselee or parishioner must not have indicated
   that others can know.

5. If the information contains information regarding child abuse or potential injury to others, then it is no longer privileged.[20]

While these principles are geared primarily to the United States, they do have application in Canada. However, Michael Code, a specialist in constitutional law, suggests that in Canada there "are very, very few examples of the state ever attempting to compel a priest to testify against a parishioner."[21]

In an excellent review of the subject of Christian counseling and the law, Levicoff discusses the quandary that pastors can get into in the case of child abuse.[22] There is a moral and legal responsibility to report if such a situation is described to the clergy. On the other hand, he or she has the dynamics of the counseling relationship to be concerned about as well as the well-being of the church community.[23] It is clear that pastors are often caught in ethical dilemmas around confidentiality because of their pastoral role.

3. *Facilitate community awareness with permission.* The protection of individuals through adherence to confidentiality is important. But a pastor or Christian leader committed to a communal sensibility will recognize that this is not the supreme value.

> The professional holds responsibility for even larger social purposes than heroic adherence to carefully stated codes. He or she must occasionally exercise moral judgment that goes beyond the rule-book. The sometimes weighty task of taking on that kind of responsibility helps distinguish the professional from the technician.[24]

For the sake of genuine care and compassion, others in the community may need to know what is happening with an individual. A woman in a Christian community where I was involved asked if her husband's battle with AIDS could be kept confidential until she was ready to deal with it publicly. When she was at that point, the community of faith was able to supply practical support as well as prayer and emotional nurture.

She withheld her permission to share at the beginning and then granted it later on.

It is easy for pastors and Christian leaders to get drawn into the *information as power* syndrome. If you know a lot about a member of your Christian community, it can give you a sense of control and dominance. No one else knows what you know. Apart from the dangers of this self-serving motivation, it is limiting for the individual and for the community. Individuals within a Christian community need to know they are supported by more than just a solitary person. Christian communities need an authentic experience of what it is like to be exposed to the difficulties of others. Otherwise the community becomes one that is superficial. Scott Peck notes some of the characteristics of this kind of pseudocommunity. Members of these communities are pleasant and avoid conflict, withhold truth about themselves, have a conscious desire not to offend, deny individual differences, and speak in blanket statements.[25]

When a Christian community is built on these characteristics, it is obviously misnamed; clearly it is not a community. Pseudocommunities are those that keep problems hidden, avoid the truth, and act as if everything is fine. The antidote to this is not to throw confidentiality away and spill all problems to the entire community. However, if permission is granted by the individual, a pastor will find that the community's awareness will provide people with a true experience of what it means to be in community. It will also facilitate the nurture and support of others so that the person experiences communal support.

HOW CAN PRIVATE COUNSELORS DEAL WITH CONFIDENTIALITY?

1. *Identify boundaries as they relate to Christian communities.* Before a private counselor sees a counselee in his or her office, the counselor needs to identify the nature of informational boundaries that will be utilized. If the private practitioner conceptualizes counseling as a sanctioned retreat, then this will not be an issue. However, if there is a commitment to the centrality of the Christian community in the counseling process, boundaries need to include the community.

Haley rightly argues that when

> one views a therapist as gatekeeper of informa-
> tion between segments of society, a more general
> issue than therapy is involved. Implicit in this
> view is the idea that revealing or concealing in-
> formation at a boundary between groups creates
> a boundary between groups. To not reveal to
> parents what their child has said is to draw a
> boundary between parents and child and define
> them as two separate groups. Information and
> boundaries are synonymous.[26]

A similar analysis could be done by looking at the private counseling process and the Christian community. If Sarah comes to an independent practitioner and that person believes the information should be kept from Sarah's church, a boundary has been drawn between Sarah and her community. I believe Haley is right in his analysis that the "act of giving and withholding information across a boundary is an act of forming and dissolving coalitions." By implication, the counselor has power because by "actuality or illusion, he should be defined as the one who allows or prevents information to pass."[27]

By being the gatekeeper of information, the private practitioner has the power to create a boundary between the counseling context and the Christian community. In so doing, a coalition between the counselor and the counselee is created. There is a free exchange of information between them, but there is an absence of coalition between the counselee and the Christian community. It should not go unnoticed that the dynamic that is operative for the counselor is power.

> The more an individual or group gives a therapist
> information it wishes concealed, the more power and
> status the therapist is given. Thus the ethical issues
> involved in the control of information are an essen-
> tial aspect of therapy and so cannot be avoided or
> minimized.[28]

Counselors who consider themselves to be Christian need to facilitate coalitions between clients and their Christian communities. One of the major methods for doing this is by an appropriate understanding of information exchange between the counselee and the Christian community and between the counselor and the Christian community. To use confidentiality as a barrier to a communal approach is to negate the value of the community in the healing process. More important, it is to exert power and status that puts the counselor above the Christian community.

2. *Encourage the client to broaden boundaries.* Assuming that the private counselor has thought through the issue of boundaries as they apply to Christian communities, it is important to bring that conceptual understanding to work with the client. The reality of the counseling process is such that many people come for private counseling precisely for that reason: They want it to be private. However, this puts the counselor in a quandary.

I have listened to stories of spouse abuse, drug addiction, sexual dysfunction, homosexuality, alcoholism, abortion, transsexualism, and adultery in the context of private counseling, and I have struggled with how to respond to the individual's community connection. By the same token, I have seen private counselees go through the painful but exciting process of healing, forgiveness, and growth and have wished that their community could rejoice with them. Most counselees are not a danger to themselves or others, but there may be other reasons why a broadening of boundaries may be beneficial.

If counselors begin to think communally, it will not be long before their private clients will understand the importance of communal connection. Through the counseling process there is ample opportunity to discuss the importance of information exchange between the individual and his or her Christian community. Through support and coaching, the private counselor can help the person work through the process of who should be told, the reason for the revelation, and the best way to carry it out. There is no guarantee that this intervention will work or that the Christian community will always respond appropriately. However, that only puts it in the same class as all other therapeutic interventions.

If a counselee comes with a sanctioned retreat mind-set, the conversion to expanded boundaries is not easy. Often it becomes tied to their own therapeutic issues. I have noticed, for example, that some private clients seek this kind of help as a flight from community. They are jaded with their community experiences and seek out a safe place in a counselor's office. A move back to the pain and chaos of community will not be easy, but ultimately it is often a necessary component of their own development.

3. *Work directly with the leadership of Christian communities.* In counseling we are usually seeking to empower the counselee to function without having to depend on us as counselors. As a result, it is always best to facilitate the expansion of boundaries by the client. However, there may be situations when the private counselor needs to connect with the community's leadership.

One of the best ways to cement the link between the private counseling world and the world of the church and the parachurch is to have greater contact. My experience is similar to many other private practitioners: When we work with the Christian community we are not only helping our client by receiving more information or facilitating greater support, we are also communicating a message that we are in this together. But in order to do this, our approach to confidentiality needs to be clearly understood.

Some Christian leaders will telephone the counselor and essentially demand information about clients. This is intrusive and not in the best interests of the counselor, the counselee, or the Christian community. Citing confidentiality as the reason why such information cannot be given is appropriate in these circumstances. There may be situations, however, where it would be of help to connect directly with the community leadership. As is the case with all breaches of confidentiality, this needs to be done with permission and with a full understanding of the rationale for such interaction.

This connection does not always require details or particular case material. For example, I have found it helpful to talk to pastors about various counseling issues. If and when they send someone from their church, they have some understanding of my approach. At times during the counseling it has been helpful to reconnect, again with permission, to update the pastor or to make a particular request. Clients who have a sense that their support base is much broader than the private counseling express appreciation for this connection.

This dynamic also becomes operative when you receive a referral through a parachurch organization. They have a vested interest in what is happening with the individual, and the counseling may even have employment implications. Again, in these cases it is helpful to work with the leadership of the community so the counselee is receiving a consistent message. Defining the nature and extent of confidentiality is extremely important in these situations so the client and the parachurch organization are clear on where the information boundaries stop and start.

SIN IN SOCIAL STRUCTURES

A second aspect of the counseling context relates to sin in social structures. Because of our tendency to conceptualize sin in individualistic terms, it is difficult for evangelicals to deal with sin in social structures. Sin becomes that which is intrapsychic rather than that which is resident within the community. By the same token, Christian counselors often look for pathology in individuals and human relationships rather than in social structures. To do this is to miss a fundamental reality. Richard Foster observes:

> Organizations and whole nations are often defined and controlled by particular concepts and ideologies. There is a prevailing mood or spirit that gives unity and direction to whole groups of people. These moods are not created in a vacuum, but are closely tied to very genuine spiritual realities. Hence, when we speak of "the spirit of a group" we are perhaps saying more than we know.[29]

In a recent book, Scott Peck discusses "the poverty of our consciousness of organizations and systems."[30] Because organizational structures are invisible and more abstract, it is easier to focus our attention on individuals. By the same token, our responsibility in dealing with systemic problems is diffused with the hope that someone else will deal with them. This distancing from the organizational understanding typifies our culture and makes examination of social structures extremely difficult.

After presenting this argument in one particular seminar, Peck received quite a negative reaction.

> As physicians and nurses, pastors, psychotherapists, and social workers, they are not only accustomed to assisting others with their issues of sin, guilt, and forgiveness but have actually been trained to be sensitive to others and conscious of their needs. Yet when confronted with their involvement in diseased organizations, they were uninterested, petulant, and missed the point.[31]

It was Peck's expectation that this kind of organizational analysis would be accepted in the church context but not in the business world. As it has turned out, his interest in facilitating community building has been welcomed in business and not in the church. While there are exceptions to this rule, he has found that only 10 percent of the members of many congregations are willing to commit themselves to this kind of pursuit. He believes that people do not want the

> painful work of emotionally stretching at church that community requires . . . [since church] is not where people's lives are on the line, but their workplace is. . . .
>
> Most want church to be pseudocommunity, and despite any protestations to the contrary, they have no real desire to see the boat, and their lives, rocked in the least. The minority who do invest their volunteer time more extensively in the church often do so

out of their own leadership needs—that is, they use
the church as a sphere of influence in which they can,
at times, play very personal power games. The few
who make attempts to actualize the church as a place
of the Kingdom of God on earth may find themselves
silenced by the congregation with an enormously
powerful, subtle effectiveness.[32]

Whether Peck's approach to community building is negated
in the church for the reasons cited is probably subject to debate. However, we do need to be asking whether the church's
lack of interest in community is a manifestation of corporate
sin. Is it possible that the lack of corporate consciousness is an
insidious disease that is infecting communities of faith? Peck's
conclusion that "God has possibly left the church and gone into
business"[33] seems to become a form of accommodation to a
problem that needs resolution.

In order to understand sin in social structures, we need to
have a three-fold commitment:

1. There must be a belief in the existence of a corporate
   structure that goes beyond an understanding of individuals. While we may acknowledge the presence of
   problems in individuals, they are not confined to that
   sphere alone. Rather, problems find major expression in
   the communal.

2. We need to recognize that it is much easier to isolate difficulties in individuals rather than communities. By
   definition the latter are more heterogeneous, more nebu-
   lous, more covert.

3. We need to recognize that spiritual powers have an impact beyond the individual. Sin does have corporate
   manifestations.

These three points are emphasized in Philip Hallie's notion
of institutional cruelty. For him cruelty involves a relationship
where one partner is active and powerful while the other is
passive and powerless. When it becomes institutional it

usually grinds its victims not in those dramatic inci-
dents we read about in most histories, but with the
sanction of day-to-day customs and a large appara-
tus of catch-words and justifications. It grinds them
slowly, smoothly, and exceeding small. And the
grinder, the victimizer, is usually a faceless establishment, not a single person into whose eyes we can
stare with a personal curiosity.[34]

If you have experienced this kind of cruelty, you understand
its subtlety. The community has a way of being that negates
the individuals within it. People feel victimized by something
much greater than themselves. Cruelty then exerts its greatest
influence in keeping itself faceless. There is no one to share
with, no one to confront. The establishment exerts its power
by preventing any correction. In this it demonstrates its arrogance and sinfulness and, ultimately, its demonic quality.

The case of Jeremy and Sarah illustrates this expression of
sin in the social structure of the church. Under the leadership
of the pastor, Sarah has experienced alienation and distancing. She has felt compelled to hide her difficulties. Jeremy is
able to function behind a facade, and no one is able to pen-
etrate the layers to provide the help he needs. Support for
Sarah and correction for Jeremy are impossible because of a
strong commitment to impression management. Looking
good has become the antidote to being well.

Three recent developments in the evangelical world are attempts to address these concerns and provide understanding
into the nature of the problem. The first comes from the work
of Neil Anderson, who is the founder and president of Freedom in Christ Ministries. Through writing and seminars he
is encouraging churches to look at the problem of spiritual
bondage at a corporate level. The second development is the
proliferation of literature on the topic of spiritual abuse.[35]
There appears to be an increasing emphasis in this area, and
it has direct links to a communal understanding. Finally, a
trilogy of books by Walter Wink[36] has focused on the role of
principalities and powers in the lives of both individuals and
social structures.

In reaction to their belief that it is not discussed in churches because it does not fit our doctrine of sin, Anderson and Mylander encourage churches to go through a detailed process to deal with corporate sin. Citing the examples of the churches noted in the first two chapters of Revelation, they call for the renunciation of sins like forsaking your first love, tolerating false teaching, overlooking non-Christian beliefs and practices, tolerating sexual immorality among some of our members, and disobedience to God's Word. Anderson and Mylander argue that a "pattern of sinfulness within the group life of the church calls for corporate action on the part of its leaders in order to deal with it." [37]

The spiritual abuse literature comes at the problem in a slightly different way. Essentially, abusive churches misuse spiritual authority; use fear, guilt, and threats; see themselves as special; foster rigidity; discourage questions; and make leaving painful.[38] Furthermore, the abusive system is characterized by power-posturing, performance preoccupation, unspoken rules, and lack of balance.[39] The result is obvious: The community is tainted by sin. Often the leader is identified as being the source of the problem. Ken Blue suggests that spiritual abuse "happens when a leader with spiritual authority uses that authority to coerce, control or exploit a follower, thus causing spiritual wounds."[40]

Walter Wink suggests we need to keep a healthy tension between evil that is individual and that which is corporate. While it is true that there are oppressive structures in society, a belief that these are capable of victimizing us completely "denies human capacities for self-transcendence." On the other hand, to locate all difficulty in personal psychopathology is to "isolate people from the social matrix, without which human existence is impossible." Wink has no question that the

> social demonic is the spirit exuded by a corporate structure that has turned its back on its divine vocation as a creature of God and has made its own goals the highest good. The demonic is not then merely the consequences that follow in the wake of

self-idolizing institutions; it is also the spirit that insinuates itself into those whose compliance the institution requires in order to further its absolutizing schemes.[41]

How Can Pastors Deal with Sin in Social Structures?

1. *Call the community to communal repentance.* Pastors run the risk of giving exclusive emphasis to individual sin. When this happens, parishioners are compelled to focus on their own individual responsibility. If they are sinning in a particular area, they are forced to deal with it and repent. However, if they are not sinning in a particular area, they may feel they have no responsibility to deal with sin at all. They might even feel a little pride because they are not guilty.

A communal view of sin means that pastoral ministry focuses on *we* and *us*. Rather than starting with the assumption that individuals in the congregation are sinning, we need to begin with the idea that the whole body participates in some sins. Bonhoeffer is right when he asks individual Christians:

> When does sin ever occur in the community that he must not examine and blame himself for his own unfaithfulness in prayer and intercession, his lack of brotherly service, of fraternal reproof and encouragement, indeed, for his own personal sin and spiritual laxity, by which he has done injury to himself, the fellowship, and the brethren?[42]

This was the major thrust of Paul's ministry to the Corinthian church in the presence of sexual sin in the community (1 Cor. 5:1–13). The behavior of the individual was secondary compared to the response of the community of faith. After admonishing them to deal with this sin communally, he moved into the imagery of the yeast and the dough. Paul made it clear that sin is not just an entity resident within individuals but something that can spread to the whole body. Sexual sin is a violation of God's standard, but the response of the Corinthian church also missed the mark.

If pastors were to recapture the communal sensibility of the Hebrew Scriptures, we might find more instruction in corporate repentance. In essence, this is what the prophets did: They brought God's message to the people as a collective body. Having set God's standard before the people, the prophets demanded repentance.

> Because of their strong idea of sin, they preach much about repentance. They spell out in considerable detail what is involved in turning to God. The prophets are "covenant enforcement mediators" whose task is to remind the people of God of what it meant to be the people of God (Ex. 19:5–6) in light of his wonderful mercy and grace.[43]

When you are given opportunities to communicate publicly, think about sin in a communal sense. This inclusivity will not only allow you to admit to your own tendency to sin, but you will be able to call the congregation, as a community of faith, to repentance. While the contemporary context may be different, the words of the Old Testament writer need to be heard in more of our churches:

> If my people, who are called by my name, will humble themselves and pray and seek my face and turn from their wicked ways, then will I hear from heaven and will forgive their sin and will heal their land (2 Chron. 7:14).

2. *Take the suffering of individuals seriously.* When a community does not take the suffering of individuals seriously, it slips into one of the more subtle demonstrations of its sinfulness. Bonhoeffer has described this well when he says that the "sin of respectable people reveals itself in a flight from responsibility."[44] If we lead communities and give an implicit message that suffering is not only unacceptable but is to be denied, we have provided those we lead with an invitation to die. We become a community that is respectable but one that does not take the responsibility of ministering to brokenness very seriously.

Whitehead and Whitehead have offered three ways in which communities demonstrate their lack of care for the suffering of individuals:

1. *Ignore.* The community operates out of its own sense of embarrassment and discomfort, hoping that if they ignore the pain it will go away.

2. *Distract.* The individual is distracted, so the pain is removed from the community.

3. *Blame.* The person is held responsible and blamed for what is happening. [45]

All three serve to remove the pain from the context of the community and put it back within the realm of the individual.

How does your community respond when it becomes aware that one of its members has been sexually abused and is going for intensive counseling? What is the reaction when someone loses a parent to death after a long illness? How are infertile couples treated in the context of the community? The examples are endless, but the bottom line is clear. The community that understands its role as the facilitator of growth seeks to keep the individuals and their pain within the context of the community. The suffering is not construed as reflecting inappropriate behavior. However, if the situation warrants it, they are spoken to in a caring and challenging way.

> Recognizing that it cannot itself resolve the crisis, the community is aware that it can assist and encourage the movement toward resolution. . . . Adult growth, psychological and religious, happens best in community. Others teach us how to love and work well; our loved ones and fellow believers protect us during periods of crisis and assure us that we will survive.[46]

People in churches and parachurch organizations have a sixth sense on this issue. They can pick up the messages very easily. If pastors never talk about suffering explicitly and do not acknowledge it as part of the human condition, people will take their pain outside the community and seek resolution elsewhere. Furthermore, the lack of sensitivity in this area will probably translate into other violations in handling those who are weak and helpless. Pastors then run the risk of failing to understand the primacy of social justice. Ellison comments:

> That is why the sad plight of the widow, orphan and stranger is so often stressed. God had entrusted the care of the weak and helpless into the hands of them that bore rule and judged (generally synonymous terms), and so injustice and the perversion of justice were peculiarly affronts to God.[47]

3. *Guard against institutional cruelty.* Because the notion of cruelty is so often linked with individuals, it may be difficult for pastors to even understand that cruelty can be demonstrated in an institutional context. But with Hallie we need to understand that

> this kind of harm-doing happens with machine-like efficiency; it moves slowly, uneventfully, like a quiet, well-oiled mechanism. In fact, it functions so smoothly that both the people who control it and the people who suffer in it often do not know that there is any other way for life to go.[48]

I remember becoming involved in a Christian community that had been experiencing institutional cruelty for a number of years. As I listened, it became clear that many felt victimized by the community and a generalized accommodation had crept in so this state of affairs was accepted. Frustration was part of this package because there was no one to react against. Confusion also dominated because the previous leadership had moved on but the problem seemed to persist. I was amazed how the phrase *institutional cruelty* provided a label for people to name their experience. As is true with many areas of life, the ability to label it provided understanding and brought people toward resolution. In fact, the community adopted the phrase, and it functioned as a form of accountability from that point on (i.e., "Isn't this another example of institutional cruelty?").

We need to reflect on our own church or parachurch context. What is the feel, the aura, the spirit of the place? Is there a cultural malaise that allows the community to disempower people, to discourage them, to render them victims? We need to recognize that this will be hard to put into words. Often our understanding of this kind of cruelty is more sensual and intuitive than cognitive and conceptual. When we use the phrase *institutional cruelty* in our thinking and in our conversation, the concept becomes embedded not just in our own understanding but also in that of the community. One of the most powerful ways to guard against institutional cruelty is to use that label when it occurs.

To walk this path is to follow in the historical path of leaders who have taken biblical justice seriously. As J. B. Smith elaborates:

> In many instances the social structures of a given society actually oppress people in need by denying them access to or opportunity for a better way of life. Christ calls us to stand against policies that discriminate on the basis of race, creed, sex, or color; governments that deny basic human rights; countries that oppress their people; and societies that inhibit the betterment of certain classes. The Social Justice Tradition has always worked for justice in all human relations and social structures. It is our responsibility as we care for our neighbors.[49]

How Can Private Counselors Deal with Sin in Social Structures?

1. *Develop an understanding of sin in social structures.* What is true for pastors is also true for private counselors. Johnson writes:

> It is in the area of the impact of sin upon social structures that most Christian helpers seem least

knowledgeable or experienced. We have not come
to understand the essential relationship between
interpersonal relationships and social structural
dysfunctions.[50]

He goes on to explain that social structural dysfunction is
"the impairment of social structures by sin, thus truncating
their ability to provide abundant life for all members who
share the same society."[51] In other words, when sin affects a
community, it becomes a place where people experience
discouragement and despondency rather than vitality and
vigor.

Those of us trained within the disciplines of psychology and
psychiatry may have more difficulty with this issue than social workers. At least in the latter case there is a consistent
acknowledgment that social systems do play a significant role
in shaping individual lives. For there

is no way in which the psychiatrist can deal with
behavior that is partly generated by a social system
without either strengthening or altering that system. Every encounter with a psychiatrist, therefore,
has political implications.[52]

Private counselors need to reflect on this critique in more
detail, particularly in light of the literature that suggests pastoral counselors have a tendency to be concerned with the
inner processes of individuals rather than broader systemic
analyses.[53] Encouraging this reflection is not an invitation
to explore family systems in the classical sense, but rather to
bring our theological sensitivities to communal structures.
In so doing we allow for the possibility that sin is not a
privatized matter.

How can this be done? It may require reading some of the
literature noted in this chapter. It may also require a more careful examination of the biblical material noted earlier in the
book. Finally, it may require a reexamination of the presuppositions upon which our views of sin are built. It is quite likely
that the influence of Western culture has produced a truncated

viewpoint. A lack of understanding of the influence of evil powers in corporate structures is going to make the therapeutic process extremely difficult.

> Any attempt to transform a social system without addressing both its spirituality and its outer forms is doomed to failure. Only by confronting the spirituality of an institution and its concretions can the total entity be transformed, and that requires a kind of spiritual discernment and praxis that the materialistic ethos in which we live knows nothing about.[54]

2. *Facilitate community intervention.* If you agree with the assumption that sin exists in social structures, it is fairly easy to agree with Dueck's conclusion that the "sanctioned retreat, underestimates the influence and importance of existing social forces and moral contexts."[55] By putting the client in a sociocultural context that is removed from a communal, moral-ethical framework, there is a tendency to let individual change take precedence over social change. How should private counselors respond to this tension?

When you see clients in private counseling, examine the role of the social-moral community out of which they come. Is it sinful in the way it is operating? Can you help people to understand that their problems are tied to the system rather than fully their own responsibility? Can the emphasis for change be shared by the individual and the community? "Unfortunately, many Christian counselors are so entrapped by a reductionistic view of therapy that social change always defers to individual change."[56]

The therapeutic task, then, becomes one of empowerment and facilitation. Rather than clients being exposed to strategies that will help adjustment or accommodation, they may need to be supported as they try to deal with the system and counteract the community sensibility. I have seen this strategy work well in situations where people are being victimized by mission societies, churches, denominations, and parachurch organizations. With a shift of focus from personal sin to communal sin, the responsibility is placed in the right sphere.

Private counselors need to anticipate resistance to this line of analysis, particularly if a community has referred the person for help. If the community and the leadership within it have already identified the problem in individualistic terms, a social structure analysis may be met with disbelief. "After all, we have sent her to you because she has a problem and we cannot help her. Why would you suggest we are part of the problem?" As is the case with institutional cruelty, it is hard to fight against this mind-set, but the task of counselors is to support clients as they attempt to overcome this covert victimization.

> We are accustomed to viewing institutions as sterile, neutral structures that have nothing to do with the spiritual life. . . . We must seek out the "spirit" that energizes the unjust law or the unjust corporate structure and seek to defeat it in the power of Christ.[57]

3. *Grapple with social injustice.* What is the relationship between counseling and social change? Kenneth Leech asserts:

> If the individual is viewed in isolation from the social structure, or if "society" is seen simply as a neutral backcloth for individual problems, then the accusation of reinforcing social injustice is a correct one. Counseling then becomes a substitute for social change, a way of encouraging adjustment and so reducing discontent.[58]

In other words, the whole structure of counseling with its traditional emphasis on individual change may be reinforcing social injustice. This is a strong indictment, but when you reflect on the work of private counseling, Leech may be on to something. Think of all the times we have sat in our offices and listened to the pain of individual Christians who have been victimized by Christian communities: the struggle of women who have been crushed because of the power structure of the culture, and the anguish of racial minorities who have been seen as second-class citizens. What can we do except listen to these people and help them adjust to their suffering?

There is another option. Private counselors who are exposed to the effects of social injustice on a daily basis need to speak out more forcibly. We need to use speaking and writing opportunities to condemn the perpetuation of injustice that we are exposed to in our offices. We need to address the sins that are contained in the social structures of the culture. In doing this, we follow the command of King Lemuel in Proverbs 31:8–9: "Speak up for those who cannot speak up for themselves, for the rights of all who are destitute. Speak up and judge fairly; defend the rights of the poor and needy."

Such a response is not motivated by self-interest but rather, as Johnson explains, there is

> contained here a clear calling to "prophetic ministry" in which Christian helping professionals, and indeed all Christians, willingly condemn the sins of our society. This condemnation is carried out by participating actively in advocacy for social policy goals which usher in social structural change akin to those of the kingdom of God. . . . The challenges of macro-level helping strategies are formidable and call for professional involvements that are unfamiliar and for which there has often not been educational preparation.[59]

COMMUNITY LITURGY

What is the role of community liturgy in the healing process? All Christian communities have a liturgy, or a prescribed ritual for public worship. Some traditions are characterized by explicit and overt forms for worship, such as an invocation, a reading from the prayer book, or the corporate recitation of the Apostles' Creed. A more implicit or covert liturgy characterizes other communities of faith, but most of the members are aware of its existence. They know when the rules have been transgressed! Whether it is explicit or implicit, all church liturgy communicates a particular feel and aura and, at times, a set of expectations. Crabb and Allender point out:

> In some churches, members must be constantly cheerful, positive, and in a good mood. In others, a struggling humility is admired. Sometimes the right layer consists of spending a certain amount of time with God in a specified way. Sometimes it's carrying a church-sanctioned, specially embossed prayer notebook. . . . In these situations the fellowship becomes chained to a set of expectations that must be met if acceptance is to be granted.[60]

There is a variation in the liturgical climate of churches. Some churches appear cold and formal; others are life-giving and invigorating. Some approach worship in a reflective, meditative framework; others are expressive and active. But whatever the tone, there is always a *message* lurking beneath it, a message that is not stated but is abundantly clear to those who attend.

The situation with Sarah illustrates the clarity of the communal message. She was experiencing pain in her marriage, and the culture of the church seemed to emphasize her pain. When the pastor referred to suffering in marriage, the issues were trivialized behind jargon and spiritual platitudes. Her sense of being disempowered and discouraged was facilitated by the spirit of the church. Significantly, she experienced this in the normal course of the church carrying out its mandate. The focus did not have to be on marriage for her to feel like she was on the periphery.

The reverse however, is also true. I was raised in a Christian home, was nurtured in an evangelical church, and made a personal commitment to Christ as an early adolescent. My personal experience of conversion did not have depth. I had never experienced a communal liturgy that had deeply affirmed my conversion to Christ, in spite of regular church attendance and involvement. My sense of being accepted by Christ was clouded by thoughts that I was still guilty. My knowledge of the truth did not seem to convert into my inner being. That changed, however, approximately fifteen years after my conversion.

My wife and I attended a conference in a Methodist church in New Jersey when I was in my late twenties. It was my first experience in this tradition, and I found all the elements of the service came together in a unique way. At one particular meeting the visiting preacher spoke on the three references to the term *Christian* in the New Testament (Acts 11:26, 26:28; 1 Peter 4:16). I have only vague recollections of the content of the message, but I do remember becoming powerfully aware that I was a Christian. It was a very strange experience because this was a fact that I had affirmed for years and a truth that I had believed. At that moment, however, it took on new meaning. The service closed with the singing of Horatio Spafford's old hymn "It is Well with My Soul." I wept as I sang.

At the time I was unaware of all the components that contributed to my fresh appreciation of conversion, but on reflection I have come to understand that my own brokenness and confusion were penetrated by God through the communal liturgy. The way the worship was conducted, the particular direction of the sermon, the music, and the climate in that faith community came together in a unique, life-changing way. Interestingly, the communal liturgy had impact despite the fact that we knew only one other person in the church. The communal expression was not premised on personal friendship, but I realized I was really a Christian by being in-community. Anderson echoes this experience:

> Community takes place, and personhood is enacted and re-enacted; it is reaffirmed, supported, and reinforced. The liturgical events which are intrinsic to community are rituals or reinforcement for human personhood. Community is more than a social event, it is the re-enactment of the personhood of Christ himself (his body), and the manifestation of his own service (*latreia*). This ongoing ministry of Christ through his humanity continues through the human community as his body. This is the ontological grounding of the church as the people of God.[61]

This view of the church is unusual for many evangelicals. Church has become a social event, a place to meet friends, an opportunity to hear sermons. However, if we understand the church as a place where liturgy supports and reinforces the presence of the body of Christ, then we begin to get a glimpse of what it means to be truly human. When the church meets, it is not a proclamation that individuals are in a private relationship with God. Rather, it is an affirmation that the people of God have come together to reflect the reality of the body of Christ. My experience in that Methodist church affirmed this truth in a powerful way. True personhood is found in community.

In what way does liturgy facilitate community? At a very basic level that worship service brought my consciousness of the divine into harmony with a sense of my own humanity. In earlier days I had believed the sentiment expressed in the chorus: Coming into the house of God to worship requires that you "forget about yourself and concentrate on Him and worship Him."[62] While I do not question the sincerity of that sentiment, it sets up an odd dichotomy between my own consciousness and my sense of the divine. In fact, it is in the connectedness between my sense of the transcendent and my sense of self that true worship is expressed. This was Peter's experience kneeling in the boat in front of Jesus as he and his friends struggled to pull in the great catch of fish. He saw the power of the transcendent expressed in Jesus and immediately became conscious of his own frailty and could only cry out, "Go away from me, Lord; I am a sinful man!" (Luke 5:8).

This blending of the transcendent and the human is important to an understanding of true worship. There is a tendency to conceptualize worship as otherworldly rather than something that is tied to my experience on earth. If we see the gospel as a message of reconciliation, however, the brokenness of our relationships with others and with God will be meshed with our understanding of his forgiveness and grace. In fact,

> by virtue of participation in Christian worship, these personal stories of relationship and separation are critiqued and clarified by the story of Jesus Christ,

who provides that meaningfulness and truthfulness which people seek and for which they hope.[63]

This point was driven home to me at a conference I attended a few years ago. Exodus International was established to facilitate help and healing for those who were struggling with homosexuality, and many of those who attended this particular Exodus Conference came out of that background and lifestyle. Brokenness was a key theme, and it was moving to watch how the consciousness of this reality led to great expressions of praise and worship. The singing was like nothing I have ever heard! Again the pairing of the human and the transcendent in the context of worship was contagious. As the community celebrated, they affirmed that they were the people of God. It was no surprise that a group of people who had experienced pain and turmoil in their sexuality were able to express their worship with intense celebration and joy. Maybe Bonhoeffer was onto something when he said that "unison singing, difficult as it is, is less of a musical than a spiritual matter."[64]

I suspect the issues around the viability of the seeker-targeted or seeker-sensitive churches could be further clarified if the role of liturgy was discussed more explicitly. One of the dangers of the evangelistic obsession seen in some churches is that the people of God are not understood as the visible expression of God's work on the earth. In an attempt to be sensitive to seekers, the corporate liturgy can easily be given a secondary place and preaching that has evangelism as its primary goal can dominate. I agree with Douglas Webster when he suggests that the "alternative to both the traditional church and the market-driven church is a Christ-centered household of faith—a community of sojourners who are in the world but not of the world."[65]

Worship is fundamental to the identity of the community. As Gerald Noyce appropriately argues,

> Our peoplehood (1 Peter 2:10) is established in the God-relation that is nourished in worship—an event in which the God-relation is proclaimed and acted

out. When the event is sidetracked, for whatever reason, or when worship becomes so routine as to lose
its sense of holy eventfulness, the community's identity is in jeopardy.[66]

At times the evangelism-worship tension is cast in an
either/or framework. Churches begin to specialize in one to
the exclusion of the other. However, Robert Webber provides
a model that seeks to incorporate the two.[67] He suggests that
liturgical evangelism is not only consistent with church history but with the biblical record.

Liturgical evangelism in the early church asserts
that conversion into Christ takes place through the
church. The church, far from being a mere aggregate
of human persons, is, from the standpoint of evangelism, the mother in whose womb God's children
are born, the mother who offers her breast for nurture and sustenance.[68]

Rather than the church giving up its focus on worship, biblical preaching, or prayer, and turning itself into a body that
simply tries to facilitate conversions, the church continues to
do what it is called to do. It is to instruct people in discipleship, prepare them in spiritual formation, stimulate them to
be baptized, and integrate them into the life of the church
through communion. When the *outsider*, the *seeker*, or the *non-
Christian* are brought face-to-face with the church in action, a
process will begin that will result in conversion and in full
participation in the community. Evangelism, then, is the by-
product of the church liturgy. When the people of God are
functioning as a community, they draw others to Christ.

I have been in churches where some members are concerned about the preaching of the gospel. Often the gospel
is defined in a very narrow way and does not involve the
whole counsel of God. More often than not the presentation
of the gospel is seen in a cognitive, nonrelational framework,
and it has an individualistic thrust. The primary focus is on
the number of conversions. What Webber is presenting is a

refreshing antidote to this tendency. The church needs to engage in corporate worship and vibrant discipleship. In so doing, the gospel will be lived out in-community, and it will mirror the pattern Paul outlined in his letter to the Corinthians.

> If, therefore, the whole church comes together and all speak in tongues, and outsiders or unbelievers enter, will they not say that you are out of your mind? But if all prophesy, an unbeliever or outsider who enters is reproved by all and called to account by all. After the secrets of the unbeliever's heart are disclosed, that person will bow down before God and worship him, declaring, "God is really among you" (1 Cor.: 14:23–25 NRSV).

If the community has a priority in worship, then preaching will be influenced by the same sensibility. It will not be alienating or distancing. It will not be individualistic in its primary thrust. It will not simply be the presentation of a solitary individual. It will be consistent with the communal paradigm of Scripture both in its content and in its aura. The congregation will have a sense that they are part of God's community because the preaching has that as its focus. When this happens, preaching becomes the

> careful and sensitive articulation of what is happening in the community so that those who listen can say: "You say what I suspected, you express what I vaguely felt, you bring to the fore what I fearfully kept in the back of my mind. Yes, yes—you say who we are, you recognize our condition."[69]

This approach to preaching moves it out of a framework where the solitary individual is the only one listening to God. In contrast, the preacher, as a member of the community, is expressing what God is saying to the whole. The practice of obedience through an understanding of God's truth is the responsibility of the entire community. Preaching then "refers to the silent dialogue which should be developing between the preacher and his hearers."[70] This dialogue involves a whole community, as Nouwen explains:

> The question is not simply, "Where does God lead me as an individual person who tries to do his will?" More basic and more significant is the question, "Where does God lead us as a people?" This question requires that we pay careful attention to God's guidance in our life together and that together we search for a creative response.[71]

It is easy to separate the fields of counseling and pastoral care out from worship, evangelism, and preaching. However, Webber's thesis, noted earlier, would suggest that liturgy has the potential to integrate all aspects of church life. In other words, the community that seeks to function in ways that are consistent with its essence will find that its various components are integrated into the whole body, including the pastoral care. This latter point cannot be emphasized enough. "Pastoral care has to be congruent with the preaching, worship, and education that are part of congregational life."[72] When that happens, individuals within that body will find their true personhood, since that is only achieved in the context of community.

> Thus, the rituals of community which express the reality of the ministry of Christ ought to lead to wholeness of personhood as a goal. Not that these rituals in themselves can cure or eliminate every pathological cause of psychical or physical disorder, but they ought to support rather than hinder such healing. Community and its liturgical functions must be viewed as integrative rather than disintegrative experiences.[73]

How does all of this apply to Sarah? Her experience at the church has not facilitated wholeness. This does not mean that all the services should have been linked to marital unfaithfulness. Nor does it suggest that the worship needs to contain marriage allusions at various points. Rather, Sarah's experience in the liturgy of the church needs to provide a context for her growth and healing. More than that, it needs to give Jeremy a communal context where his immorality could be linked with the power of God's grace and forgiveness. If this happens, Sarah and Jeremy will not have been "cured," but their human experience will not be removed from their experience in the context of Christian liturgy.

What Issues do Pastors Need to Consider Regarding Community Liturgy?

1. *Be aware of the power of language.* One of the major ways in which pastors show their lack of understanding of community liturgy is in the use of language. I have listened to worship leaders, preachers, and pastors who have strung together an endless list of clichés and Christian catchphrases with intonations that have been linked with the so-called pastor's voice. VanderMey exclaims: "At best, it is sweet piety in humble uniform," but it also runs the risk of reflecting "pseudopiety and a venal form of empty rhetoric."[74]

Apart from the irritation of repetition in such jargon, there is a lack of the human and the earthy. This is where the inappropriate use of language becomes so important in community liturgy. Language in worship needs to be "inviting, involving and challenging . . . a language of both human experience and Christian experience."[75] Since language shapes our experience and gives us an understanding of it, people need to experience the Christian community as a place where their life experiences are understood and acknowledged. Only then will they be open to the influence of the Holy Spirit.

When leading worship, exalt God and encourage people to direct their passions toward him with language they are familiar with and understand. Use Scripture, but in so doing do not hide your own experiences and thoughts behind it so that your voice is not heard. Be known as a person who communicates with integrity. In leading the people of God, they will notice your hunger for God along with your understanding of human experience. It is in your use of language where people will determine whether your relationship with God and your familiarity with pain and suffering reflect either a depth of experience or shallowness and superficiality. In this Christian leaders create a contagious atmosphere for the rest of the community.

> Such language—stock phrases, bromides, clichés, truisms, lingo, jargon—allows us to acknowledge the experience of life's open moments without having to experience the raw pain or joy of it ourselves.[76]

2. *Preach with communal sensitivity.* I remember being involved in a counseling relationship with Betty. She was struggling with the childhood memories of her Christian father's sexual advances towards her. As a committed Christian, she wanted to deal with these experiences and the accompanying feelings of anger, bitterness, and lack of forgiveness, so she sought out counseling with the ultimate view of resolving the problems. In one particular session she came in quite disturbed because on the previous Sunday the pastor had said from the pulpit, "None of you should be going for counseling. All we need is the Bible. Trust God, and he will show you what is right."

William had a similar experience listening to a sermon. He had been struggling with a manic-depressive disorder for a number of years. Most of the investigations indicated it was due to chemical issues, although there were some psychological factors involved as well. One Sunday morning William sat in church and heard the pastor say, "The Lord can heal manic-depressives if they are willing to forgive."

In both of these instances the pastors did not understand the relationship between private pain and public proclamation. Betty was experiencing the trauma of incest, but that was missed in the preaching from someone who apparently had done very little study in the field of Christian counseling. William had suffered through the highs and lows of a manic-depressive disorder, but his suffering was compounded by the preacher's insensitivity and apparent lack of knowledge.

When people are in pain they often feel alone and isolated. That is where some of their deepest pain comes from: their sense of going through this without communal connectedness. Often their need for care is combined with a need for greater understanding. In other words, they need teaching and instruction. Betty knows she is struggling, but she needs the light of Scripture to be shed in her darkness. William knows that God is to be found somewhere in the middle of his confusion. The preaching needs to affirm the spiritual aspirations in both of them. Without even knowing the details of individual situations, the pastor needs to preach "with great patience and careful instruction" (2 Tim. 4:2). In doing this the community will become a place where people will sense that the Word of God is not used as a weapon against their pain but as a medicine to ease it.

For preaching to have this quality, the pastor needs to understand the human condition. If community is facilitated by the pastor being an exemplar, by engaging in community relationships, and by participating in mutual pilgrimage, then preaching is one of the key domains where these qualities will be noted, either by their presence or absence. Frederick Buechner captures this well:

> Most evangelical preaching that I have heard is seamless, hard sell, and heavily exhortatory. Men in business suits get up and proclaim the faith with the dynamic persuasiveness of insurance salesmen. . . . They give me the sense of being official, public, godly utterances which the preacher stands behind but as a human being somehow does not stand in. . . . At their best they bring many strengths with them into the pulpit but rarely, as I listened to them anyway, their real lives.[77]

Many pastors and preachers have drawn a distinction between preaching and counseling:

"I am not a counselor. I just preach."

"We hear too much about counseling these days and not enough about preaching."

"I much prefer to meet with people one on one than to stand in the pulpit. I think I can be of more help there."

At times I fear we are oversimplifying something that is much more complex. If we understand the relationship between private pain and public proclamation, we will do everything we can to make sure that people experience care and communal connection in both venues. Give people the opportunity to experience the warmth of pastoral contact and the careful instruction of pulpit preaching. This will go a long way to help them deal with the pain that inevitably comes with being human.

3. *Emphasize the importance of communion.* What does communion have to do with counseling? People who need counseling are broken intrapsychically and interpersonally. In their brokenness they need hope and wholeness. They need to find a safe place where problems are put in perspective, where they are framed in ways that are reassuring and life-giving. This tension between brokenness and hope is at the core of all counseling problems. If this is true, what better place to bring my human experience than the communion table? In doing so I will not have my problems solved, since that is not the purpose of such a gathering, nor will I find specific answers to all my questions. However, in bringing my frailty I will find faithfulness, and in bringing my brokenness I will find the Man of Sorrows. The sadness of my world and experience will be brought into contact with the joy and celebration of the grace of God. And all of this in a communal context! Avery Dulles explains:

> It is anomalous for the Eucharist to be celebrated in solitude. . . . Sacraments therefore have a dialogic structure. They take place in a mutual interaction that permits the people together to achieve a spiritual breakthrough that they could not achieve in isolation. A sacrament therefore is a socially constituted or communal symbol of the presence of grace coming to fulfillment.[78]

Unfortunately, many evangelicals do not take communion seriously. Some churches practice it infrequently, and when it does occur it is tacked onto the end of a preaching service, giving a clear message on the relative importance of these two functions. Other churches continue to practice the Lord's Supper on a weekly basis, but it has lost much of its meaning or impact in the body of Christ. While weekly repetition is noteworthy, the power and mystery have been lost.

This is a tragic state of affairs for a number of reasons: The communion service provides an opportunity for "a confession of the covenant bond which makes the Community the People of God." Furthermore, in communion the Christian community "confesses and shares in the spiritual benefits which the historical sacrificial death of Christ has provided." In the richness of these symbols the Christian community "witnesses to and becomes a 'corporate personality'."[79] What a powerful combination!

Communion is not only a remembrance of what Christ has done, but it reflects our covenant relationship with God and symbolizes our corporate identity as the people of God. It is not surprising that "seeing bread broken and wine poured out with this particular significance is fundamental for the encouragement of the people of God."[80] When communion is practiced with understanding, encouragement is inevitable.

How does your community view communion? Is it taken seriously? Is it understood as one of the rich symbols in the Christian tradition? Have you studied the significance of communion biblically, in church history, and in your own tradition? Has preaching replaced communion as the key component of your community liturgy? Is there creative thought and energy put into the planning and execution of the service? Have you developed ways to emphasize the remembrance side of this sacrament? Do people experience community in the context of your communion services? Do people in your tradition experience encouragement through this service? Do these questions even get raised in your community?

How Should Community Liturgy Impact Private Counselors?

1. *Bridge the gap between community liturgy and the counseling context.* In his very helpful book on the relationship of psychotherapy to spirituality, David Benner suggests that

spiritual considerations are almost inevitable in all counseling. However, psychotherapy

> is not a good place to talk about God, prayer, scrip-
> tural interpretation, or theology. It is, however, an
> excellent place for people to talk about their experi-
> ences with God or the meanings of other aspects of
> their spiritual lives. [81]

The crucial issue here is around the two words, *experience* and
meaning. Benner believes it is not the task of the therapist to talk
about the objective issues related to theology and biblical data.
These belong more appropriately in the realm of the spiritual
guide. The therapist, in contrast, should seek to understand the
counselee's perspective on various spiritual matters. Since this
perspective is understood through psychological processes, and
that is the area in which psychotherapists are trained, they
should confine themselves to this endeavor.

Apart from the viability of Benner's distinctions, we need
to ask where counselees develop meaning when it comes to
spirituality. Benner argues that these things are "mediated by
the same internal psychological processes."[82] But what is the
context in which these develop? Is it not in the communal setting? Can we know what people have experienced spiritually
without a detailed understanding of their communal background?

I have found that when so-called spiritual issues come up
in counseling, people are often referring to specific Christian
communities. I remember talking to Rachel, a bright and articulate woman who was involved in missionary work. She
brought guilt and drivenness to her spiritual activities, so
much so that she wore herself out with her commitment to
Christian service. Her experience of God in her work was
negative and authoritarian, and it elicited perfectionism. Ex-
plorations around family dynamics proved fruitless until we
started talking about her early church experience. She was
raised in a strict, ultraconservative environment that employed
guilt as a motivator for all Christian activity. There was little
mention of God's grace or forgiveness and a complete absence

of joy in ministry. As we talked about Rachel's communal experience, it was clear that the meaning she brought to spiritual issues was heavily influenced by that particular church. In order to move on, she needed to bring those concerns to the surface. My task was to seek to conceptualize her intrapsychic issues in a corporate framework. This approach alleviated much of her guilt, since she had been taking sole responsibility for her current difficulty.

Have you understood the power of community liturgy in shaping spiritual meaning and experience? Do you talk about the counselee's experience with community liturgy? Does this form part of your intake interview? Is the dialogue between these two worlds a regular part of the counseling process?

If there is a significant overlap between spiritual direction and the pursuit of psychological health, then private counselors need to explore ways to bridge this gap. As Kenneth Leech has argued:

> It is essential to stress this, for the individual who tries to exercise a ministry of personal guidance from the perimeters of the corporate Christian life is pursuing a course which is highly dangerous both to himself and to those who are subject to his influence.[83]

2. *Emphasize the importance of community in the realization of forgiveness.* The topic of forgiveness is central in therapeutic work. Whether it is related to the counselee's approach to historical pain or current relational difficulty, forgiveness is a concern to many counselees. This is particularly relevant within the context of Christian counseling since our faith is so intertwined with and dependent on our understanding of forgiveness. James Emerson describes this understanding as "realized forgiveness," which is an "awareness of forgiveness to such a degree that a person is free from the guilt he feels" and is able to experience "the freedom to be a new creature and a new creator."[84]

Most counselees' problems with forgiveness do not reside in their cognitive understanding nor in their desire to experience it. Often they have never experienced forgiveness in a full and intimate sense. However, this is confusing for people. If they have accepted the forgiveness of Christ and understood that this is a biblical reality, why do they not feel it? Emerson makes it clear that "to be grasped properly, 'realized forgiveness' must be understood in both social and individual terms."[85] In other words, it is not enough to simply know that you have experienced forgiveness because of the sacrifice of Christ. It must be experienced communally. Forgiveness may be as much a description of the milieu in which we live as it is an intrapsychic transaction.

Forgiveness, then, needs to be mediated in the context of a community. People need to feel forgiven in-relationship. They need to know that others accept them in spite of their failures and foibles. Maybe this is why some of our counselees struggle with our dialogue around forgiveness. An individual counselor may provide a context for the appropriation of forgiveness, but the sanctioned retreat may not communicate with the same power as does the church community. When counselees leave our offices, they need to go back to a situation where forgiveness is realized, where they experience the grace of God in relationship. In light of this we need to realize that "a therapist may be tremendously helpful; but the person being helped will never achieve what he could achieve in answer to his quest for wholeness, apart from some visible expression of God's forgiveness."[86]

Obviously, not all churches understand that the mediation of forgiveness is part of their mandate. It is possible that a private counselor could discuss this with a client only to find that there is ignorance or unwillingness on the part of their church community. I have found, however, that an emphasis in this area requires a fundamental commitment that a Christian community does provide a context for the realization of forgiveness. Not all aspects of community liturgy may provide mediation for forgiveness, but there may be some. It may be as simple as discussing a client's understanding of his or her experience with communion. Through powerful symbols this service often forces reflection on the nature of brokenness and the power of forgiveness.

Like individuals, communities are not perfect, but God continues to mediate his grace through his people. For those of us who may have lost faith in this belief, Emerson encourages us to remember that the church "is important not because it succeeds or fails, but because it is the one fellowship that is concerned about the totality of 'realized forgiveness.'"[87] How this will work itself out in each counseling situation will vary from case to case, but a commitment to it is crucial for the counselor who is seeking to be Christian.

> "Realized forgiveness" is the heart of the gospel. Why? Because the church knew in that first century, as it ought to know now, that when forgiveness is real, then the church is not only relevant, but through it God is heard.[88]

3. *Explore the humanizing qualities of counseling and liturgy.* For most private counselors a purported relationship between the therapeutic enterprise and community liturgy is an unusual suggestion. We have tended to think of them as distinct and separate. However, some of the literature has suggested that they share one major thing in common. James Empereur argues that both worship and therapy have a humanizing function in that they provide greater self-understanding and provide vision for other possibilities. In therapy, humanization results in clarification around dysfunctionality, fragmentation, and past inhibition. In worship we are made aware of the fact that all of life is in need of redemption and restoration.[89] Given our training and expertise, areas that relate to the humanizing of individuals should be of interest to us.

Empereur believes that language should be a significant bridge to join these two worlds. From the sphere of counseling we know that language serves a number of purposes. It provides insight, stimulates understanding, and develops new relationships. By the same token the rituals in worship and the language that goes with them allow for similar development. In both worlds the context is social and interactive. It is in dialogue that both worship and counseling find their human essence.

Commenting on Empereur's work, Michael Aune suggests that the rituals of community liturgy, like those of counseling, do not necessarily result in a problem-solving orientation. When I am involved in a communion service, I do not experience significant solutions to problems or difficulties. Rather, rituals need to be seen "not as aspiring to solve social or cultural problems but rather to change or alter the participants' perceptions of those problems." [90] Like counseling, worship at times provides perspective without providing answers. The human quest, at least on the earth, is one of understanding but not complete resolution.

What might this mean for private counselors? Further examination of the relationship between community liturgy and counseling would be beneficial. This could occur in a more theoretical fashion through research on the role of ritual in the development of the individual. It might also involve reflection on the place of language in both liturgy and counseling. As has already been emphasized in an earlier chapter, it may require that private counselors have a personal experience of communal liturgy so they can understand it in more depth. Ideally this should help counselors have a greater appreciation for the power of symbol and ritual to humanize. Ultimately, private counselors may find that the humanizing components of worship and the communal sensibility contained therein might provide some intriguing implications for the counseling enterprise.

SUMMARY

If healing takes place in a communal context, then a number of issues are relevant to understanding that context. Although pastors and private counselors have unique relationships with Christian communities, they both need to deal with confidentiality, sin in social structures, and community liturgy.

Why is confidentiality important? If pain is not going to be privatized, there need to be boundaries on the sharing of information with some indication as to how these are going to be defined. Our approach to boundaries will communicate implicitly how we understand the nature of community.

Communities are moral-ethical structures that can violate biblical standards as easily as individuals. Often the sin of social structures is a contributing factor to the suffering of individuals. The sin not only needs to be named, but pastors and private counselors need to work against it as much as possible.

Community liturgy has the potential to affirm the individual-in-community by providing a context where the people of God can affirm their fundamental identity. Pastors need to consciously facilitate this through worship and preaching. Private counselors also have a responsibility to provide a bridge between the counseling context and the community liturgy.

NOTES

1. Frederick Buechner, *Telling Secrets* (New York: HarperCollins, 1991), 2.
2. Paul Tournier, *Secrets* (Atlanta: John Knox, 1965).
3. In a recent book on the late President Richard Nixon, Tom Wicker traces Nixon's demise to his obsession with secrecy. Tom Wicker, *One of Us: Richard Nixon and the American Dream* (New York: Random House, 1991).
4. Tournier, *Secrets*, 30.
5. Ibid., 35–36.
6. For helpful material on the role of these variables in family therapy, see Mark A. Karpel and Eric S. Strauss, *Family Evaluation* (New York: Gardner Press, 1983).
7. Michael H. Kottow, "Medical Confidentiality: An Intransigent and Absolute Obligation," *Journal of Medical Ethics* 12 (1986): 119, 121.
8. Ibid., 121.
9. Rickey L. George and Therese S. Cristiani, *Counseling Theory and Practice*, 3d ed. (Englewood Cliffs, N.J.: Prentice-Hall, 1990), 268.
10. Paul A. Grayson and Kate Cauley, eds., *College Psychotherapy* (New York: Guilford Press, 1989), 4.
11. Gaylord Noyce, *Pastoral Ethics: Professional Responsibilities of the Clergy* (Nashville: Abingdon, 1988), 90.
12. Gerry Rauch, "Confidentiality: Just Between You and Me and . . . ?" *Pastoral Renewal* 46 (1984): 39.
13. Jay Haley, *Problem-Solving Therapy* (San Francisco: Jossey-Bass, 1987), 221.
14. Ibid.
15. Walter E. Wiest and Elwyn A. Smith, *Ethics in Ministry: A Guide for the Professional* (Minneapolis: Augsburg Fortress, 1990), 51.
16. Karen Lebacqz, *Professional Ethics* (Nashville: Abingdon, 1985).
17. Steve Levicoff, *Christian Counseling and the Law* (Chicago: Moody, 1991), 99–100.
18. Wiest and Smith, *Ethics in Ministry*, 53.
19. Ronald K. Bullis, "When Confessional Walls Have Ears: The Changing Clergy Privileged Communications Law," *Pastoral Psychology* 39 (1990): 76.

20. Ibid., 77–79.

21. Michael Code, "Guarantees of Freedom of Religion Affecting the Law of Confidentiality," in *Constitutional Issues in Religion and the Law* (Toronto: Social Planning Council of Metropolitan Toronto, 1988): 14, 20.

22. Levicoff, *Christian Counseling*, 119–27.

23. For some helpful material on this particular topic, see Jeffrey J. Hauagaard and N. Dickon Reppucci, *The Sexual Abuse of Children: A Comprehensive Guide to Current Knowledge and Intervention Strategies* (San Francisco: Jossey-Bass, 1988); Paul J. Isley and Peter Isley, "The Sexual Abuse of Male Children by Church Personnel: Intervention and Prevention," *Pastoral Psychology* 39 (1990): 85–99.

24. Noyce, *Pastoral Ethics*, 94–95.

25. M. Scott Peck, *The Different Drum: Community-Making and Peace* (New York: Touchstone, 1987).

26. Haley, *Problem-Solving Therapy*, 239.

27. Ibid., 240.

28. Ibid.

29. Richard J. Foster, *Money, Sex and Power: The Challenge of the Disciplined Life* (New York: Harper and Row, 1985), 182.

30. M. Scott Peck, *A World Waiting to be Born: Civility Rediscovered* (New York: Bantam, 1993), 30.

31. Ibid., 32.

32. Ibid., 352.

33. Ibid., 353.

34. Philip Hallie, *The Paradox of Cruelty* (Middletown, Conn.: Wesleyan University, 1969), 63.

35. Four recent examples of this literature include Ken Blue, *Healing Spiritual Abuse: How to Break Free from Bad Church Experiences* (Downers Grove, Ill.: InterVarsity, 1993); Ronald M. Enroth, *Churches that Abuse* (Grand Rapids: Zondervan, 1992); David Johnson and Jeff VanVonderen, *The Subtle Power of Spiritual Abuse* (Minneapolis: Bethany House, 1991); and Dale Ryan and Juanita Ryan, *Recovering from Spiritual Abuse* (Downers Grove, Ill.: InterVarsity, 1992).

36. Walter Wink, *Naming the Powers: The Language of Power in the New Testament* (Philadelphia: Fortress Press, 1984); *Unmasking the Powers: The Invisible Forces that Determine Human Existence* (Philadelphia: Fortress Press, 1986); and *Engaging the Powers: Discernment and Resistance in a World of Domination* (Minneapolis: Augsburg Fortress, 1992).

37. Neil T. Anderson and Charles Mylander, *Setting Your Church Free: A Biblical Plan to Help Your Church* (Ventura, Calif.: Regal Books, 1994), 212.

38. Enroth, *Churches that Abuse*, 75–186.

39. Johnson and VanVondern, *Spiritual Abuse*, 63–71.

40. Blue, *Healing Spiritual Abuse*, 12.

41. Wink, *Unmasking the Powers*, 42–43.

42. Dietrich Bonhoeffer, *Life Together* (New York: Harper and Row, 1954), 103.

43. Donald A. Leggett, *Loving God and Disturbing Men: Preaching from the Prophets* (Burlington, Ontario: Welch, 1990), 25.

44. Bonhoeffer, *Life Together*, 11.

45. Evelyn Eaton Whitehead and James D. Whitehead, *Christian Life Patterns: The Psychological Challenges and Religious Invitations of Adult Life* (Garden City, N.Y.: Image, 1979).

46. Ibid., 44, 233.

47. H. L. Ellison, *The Old Testament Prophets: Studies in the Hebrew Prophets* (Grand Rapids: Zondervan, 1978), 31.

48. Hallie, *Paradox of Cruelty*, 98.

49. James Bryan Smith, *A Spiritual Formation Workbook: Small Group Resources for Nurturing Christian Growth* (San Francisco: Harper, 1993), 43.

50. Timothy J. Johnson, "Empowerment as a Christian Helping Strategy: Bridging the Chasm Between Client and Institutional Oppression," *Social Work and Christianity* 17 (1990): 67.

51. Ibid., 67.

52. S. L. Halleck, *The Politics of Therapy* (New York: Harper, 1971), 36.

53. H. Steven Scudder, "Social Work and Pastoral Counseling Perspectives: An Exploratory Comparative Analysis," *Social Work and Christianity* 17 (1990): 37–51.

54. Wink, *Engaging the Powers*, 10.

55. Al Dueck, "Ethical Contexts of Healing: Peoplehood and Righteousness," *Pastoral Psychology* 35 (1987): 239–53.

56. Charles R. Ridley, "Cross-Cultural Counseling in Theological Context," *Journal of Psychology and Theology* 14 (1986): 294.

57. Foster, *Money, Sex, and Power*, 183.

58. Kenneth Leech, *Soul Friend: The Practice of Christian Spirituality* (New York: Harper and Row, 1977), 104.

59. Johnson, "Empowerment," 75–76.

60. Lawrence J. Crabb, Jr., and Dan B. Allender, *Encouragement: The Key to Caring* (Grand Rapids: Zondervan, 1984), 36.

61. Ray S. Anderson, *On Being Human: Essays in Theological Anthropology* (Grand Rapids: Eerdmans, 1982), 183.

62. Bruce Ballinger, "We Have Come Into His House," (Beverly Hills, Calif.: All Nations Music/Sound III, Inc., 1976). Used by permission.

63. Michael B. Aune, "'But Only Say the Word': Another Look at Christian Worship as Therapeutic," *Pastoral Psychology* 41 (1993): 148.

64. Bonhoeffer, *Life Together*, 60.

65. Douglas D. Webster, *Selling Jesus: What's Wrong with Marketing the Church* (Downers Grove, Ill.: InterVarsity, 1992), 140.

66. Gaylord Noyce, *The Minister as Moral Counselor* (Nashville: Abingdon, 1989), 159.

67. Robert E. Webber, *Liturgical Evangelism: Worship as Outreach and Nurture* (Harrisburg, Pa.: Morehouse, 1986).

68. Ibid., 6.

69. Henri J. M. Nouwen, *The Wounded Healer: Ministry in Contemporary Society* (Garden City, N. Y.: Image, 1972), 39.

70. John R. W. Stott, *I Believe in Preaching* (London: Hodder and Stoughton, 1982), 60.

71. Henri J. M. Nouwen, *Making All Things New: An Invitation to the Spiritual Life* (San Francisco: Harper and Row, 1981), 87–88.

72. Noyce, *Moral Counselor*, 74.

73. Anderson, *On Being Human*, 184.

74. Randall J. VanderMey, *God Talk: The Triteness and Truth in Christian Cliches* (Downers Grove, Ill.: InterVarsity, 1993), 15.

75. Aune, "Say the Word," 149.

76. VanderMey, *God Talk*, 14.

77. Buechner, *Telling Secrets*, 84.

78. Avery Dulles, *Models of the Church* (New York: Image, 1987), 67.

79. Russell Philip Shedd, *Man in Community: A Study of St. Paul's Application of Old Testament and Early Jewish Conceptions of Human Solidarity* (London: Epworth, 1958), 191, 194.

80. D. Prior, *Creating Community: An Every-Member Approach to Ministry in the Local Church* (Colorado Springs: NavPress, 1992), 115.

81. David G. Benner, *Psychotherapy and the Spiritual Quest* (Grand Rapids: Baker Book House, 1988), 156–57.

82. Ibid., 157–58.

83. Leech, *Soul Friend*, 121.

84. James G. Emerson, Jr., *The Dynamics of Forgiveness* (Philadelphia: Westminster Press, 1964), 21.

85. Ibid., 165.

86. Ibid., 167.

87. Ibid.

88. Ibid., 188.

89. James L. Empereur, "Liturgy as Humanizing or as Therapeutic," in *Exploring the Sacred* (Washington, D.C.: The Pastoral Press, 1986), 85–96.

90. Aune, "Say the Word," 152.

Chapter Seven

Community and the Counselee

The ambiguity of human life always requires that there be distinctions between good and bad, in one form or another. The great change is that a good man used to be the one who cares for others, as opposed to the one who cares exclusively for himself. Now the good man is the one who knows how to care for himself, as opposed to the man who does not.

—Allan Bloom

GARY WAS ONE OF MY FIRST CLIENTS at the university counseling center. Dressed in typical midseventies student garb of jeans and a loose-fitting shirt, he greeted me with enthusiasm and did not portray what I would have expected from a prospective counselee. He was confident, positive, and almost giddy. We proceeded down the hall to my office, and after receiving permission to turn on the video tape, I began to listen to his story.

He was gay—that was all I heard. I am sure that this was not the whole message, because he talked at great length about many things. But that was all I heard. He was gay.

Let me backtrack a little: I was raised in a home and a church that espoused the tenets of evangelical Christianity. At a young age I learned that certain attitudes and behaviors reflected righteousness, while others reflected sin. Homosexuality? I had heard very little about it, but anything I had heard was put on the sin side of the equation. Homosexuality was a sin, and homosexuals were sinners. End of story.

However, it was not the end of the story. There sitting in front of me was a homosexual. I am sure I had sat across from many homosexuals prior to that moment, but this was the first in terms of self-awareness. And Gary had not come for help with his homosexuality but was reaching out for help because he wanted some conflict-resolution strategies.

My supervisor made it clear that the moral-ethical concerns regarding homosexuality are not part of a therapist's concern. It was my task to listen to Gary, understand him, and facilitate his own understanding. He was an individual with his own rights and choices, and his desire to follow a gay lifestyle was his to make, not mine to question.

Given that I was a neophyte in the field and I was being mentored by an experienced supervisor, I decided to take his advice and in the process I learned a lot! I learned that my moral-ethical stance on homosexuality was informed to some degree by Scripture but was influenced heavily by bigotry, hatred, and profound ignorance. I came to recognize that my own heterosexual arrogance needed to be allocated to the sin side of the equation as well and that sexual orientation should not be a deterrent to seeing people as fully human, created in the image of God, and deserving of respect.

However, I was still plagued by the issue of morality and ethics in the counseling relationship. My supervisor had made it clear that good therapists do not get involved in these concerns. I was to be the scientific practitioner. I was to understand Gary's actions, not judge them. I was to predict behavior, not assess its relative goodness or moral viability. I was to affirm Gary's self-determination and offer a morally neutral environment. But as a Christian, I have to be concerned with morality and ethics. Since life is not morally neutral, I need to focus on the goodness or evil found in my behavior and that of others. While individuals can make their own choices, that does not preclude an assessment of the relative goodness of those choices.

While a concern for goodness requires kindness and gentleness, truth should not be replaced by warm relationships. Christians are not asked to make a decision between truth and love. Paul told the church at Ephesus that Christian maturity is demonstrated by "speaking the truth in love" (Eph. 4:15). This is not simply an affirmation of my own opinion or viewpoint. As the Sanhedrin phrased it many years ago: "Every Judge who judges a judgement of truth, true to the truth of the matter, causes the glory of God to dwell in Israel."[1]

MORALITY

In a review of counseling and psychotherapy textbooks in the early 1980s, Grant found that the vast majority of the books had no references to morality, either on the part of the counselor or the counselee.[2] With this dearth it is no surprise, in the words of Mary Nicholas, that counselors

> often feel constrained from discussing patients' moral failures and from recognizing and admiring their virtues because they are afraid of committing the unpardonable "sin" of having a moral opinion or, worse yet, making a value judgment in the presence of their patients.[3]

However, it is inevitable that moral-ethical issues will be raised in counseling.

"Should I continue with the affair?"

"How do I understand the loss of my wife in a tragic car accident?"

"What do I do when I find out that my father is suicidal?"

"Should I put my mother in a nursing home?"

"How do I forgive my alcoholic son?"

These questions are concerned with the way things should be, with a sense of right and wrong. Beneath each of the questions is a fundamental query: What is the good in this situation?

The priority of this question should not be missed by those who are interested in counseling that is Christian. In their classic book on the history of pastoral care, Clebsch and Jaekle suggest there are four forms of pastoral care: healing, guiding, sustaining, and reconciling.[4] Throughout church history one of these has dominated as a major mode of care because of particular cultural concerns. In primitive Christianity, for example, *sustaining* was the key strategy because of a belief that the end was near. On the other hand, the third century saw an interest in pastoral care that was oriented toward *reconciliation* because of the intense persecution being experienced by the church. The underlying dynamic in all of this is clear: the process of care is a form of socialization in that it provides people with values, norms, and moral-ethical structures for dealing with life. Healing always relates to "what is the good"—to what way life should be ordered.

The *should* of counseling became a concern for O. Hobart Mowrer in the 1960s in reaction to the cultural milieu that had influenced the field up to that point. With the rise of psychoanalytic therapy in the 1920s and nondirective counseling in the 1950s, the focus of help became talking-oriented so that people would have better self-understanding. Lacking in this approach was a concern for the moral-ethical dimensions of life and the role sin played in the etiology of personal problems. Mowrer believed that therapeutic interventions of the future would "take guilt, confession, and expiation seriously and [would] involve programs of action rather than mere groping for insight."[5] Again, it is not enough to simply deal with the way things *are*; counselors need to be concerned with the way things *should be*.

Based on his direct exposure to Mowrer through an intensive summer internship in two psychiatric facilities, as well as his conviction that Christian counseling needed to return to a biblical foundation, Jay Adams produced his first book, *Competent to Counsel*, in 1970. Offering a form of applied Calvinism, Adams argued,

> Apart from those who had organic problems, like brain damage, the people I met in the two institutions in Illinois were there because of their own failure to meet life's problems. To put it simply, they were there because of their unforgiven and unaltered

sinful behavior. Secondly, the whole experience drove me back to the Bible to ask once again, "What do the Scriptures say about such people and the solution to their problems?"[6]

While Jay Adams's approach has generated a considerable amount of controversy in the field of Christian counseling over the past twenty-five years, his desire to focus on the moral-ethical dimensions of care is to be applauded. In doing so he is consistent with an ongoing concern in the history of pastoral care: Morality cannot be separated from care.

In a recent book that focuses on moral issues in psychotherapy, Mary Nicholas recognizes that goodness and morality are usually framed within the confines of spirituality and philosophy, but she argues that they can be understood from the standpoint of secular psychotherapy. For her, there are at least four reasons why moral distinctions should be made in the context of therapy:

1. Therapists cannot be all that neutral anyway. . . .
2. While they may fear being judged, patients will not trust a therapist who condones all their behavior. . . .
3. To suspend such opinions is to create a lie in the therapeutic relationship, which, in essence, invalidates the entire treatment. . . .
4. Sometimes moral issues are at the heart of the dilemmas clients bring to therapy, even though they may not realize it.[7]

I agree with Don Browning when he asserts that "there is a moral context to all acts of care."[8] Dealing with people in a counseling relationship is not just to deal with "the way things are." Obviously this has its place. We need to be empathic and warm so people experience acceptance and understanding. But counselors who desire to be Christian are always struggling through "the way things should be." This is not as simple as allocating certain behaviors to the sin side of the equation. It requires discernment, wisdom, and a willingness to grapple with the moral ambiguities of life. When a counselee asks, "Should I put my mother in a nursing home?" she wants intervention that reflects the way thing are, but she also assumes there are some answers for the way things should be.

MORALITY AND COMMUNITY

One of the major effects of a noncommunal orientation is that morality becomes personalized and privatized. Support for particular behaviors or attitudes is resident in the individual, and the greater communal or cultural good becomes incidental. Even in the business sector a commitment to morality is perceived as more than an individual decision. In a recent article, Lynn Paine explains:

> Rarely do the character flaws of a lone actor fully explain corporate misconduct. More typically, unethical business practice involves the tacit, if not explicit, cooperation of others and reflects the values, attitudes, beliefs, language, and behavioral patterns that define an organization's operating culture. Ethics, then, is as much an organizational as a personal issue.[9]

I remember meeting with Shawn, a theological student who told me that his spiritual life was enhanced when he took drugs. LSD gave him a deeper awareness of God and his work in the world. The fact that his involvement in the drug culture was not only illegal but immoral was unimportant. Before God he had decided that this was right, and he was pursuing this course of action with conviction. While Shawn was aware that the broader Christian community would not condone his actions, his conviction was enshrined in an individualistic framework. His conscience became the final arbiter in this moral-ethical decision. He had determined it was right; therefore it was right.

When morality is moved into the private sphere, the Christian community simply becomes a venue for connection and belonging. We use the community to feel accepted and nurtured.

It becomes a place where we receive interpersonal support but no moral input. It is not that ethical concerns are jettisoned by people like Shawn; they are simply allocated to the personal sphere and removed from the communal. Stanley Hauweras and William Willimon summarize:

> So all ethics, even non-Christian ethics, make sense only when embodied in sets of social practices that constitute a community. Such communities support a sense of right and wrong. Yet most modern ethics begin from the Enlightenment presupposition of the isolated, heroic self, the allegedly rational individual who stands alone and decides and chooses. The goal of this ethic is to detach the individual from his or her tradition, parents, stories, community, and history, and thereby allow him or her to stand alone, to decide, to choose, and to act alone.[10]

If morality is taken seriously, pastors and counselors need to understand the role of discipline, confession, and fees. *Discipline* bridges the gap between the sinfulness of humanity and God's desire for righteousness. *Confession* does not receive much attention in Protestant circles, but it may need to be revived if Christian communities are going to take their ethical responsibilities seriously. Finally, a misunderstood area in the counseling profession is that of *fees*. How do we understand fee structures in Christian counseling, and how do we bring a moral-ethical framework to bear on our understanding of monetary issues?

DISCIPLINE

Angelo had been a member of the local evangelical church in his town for many years. Although he showed little commitment to any specific program, he attended most Sunday mornings and periodically on Sunday nights. A friendly sort of man, he was liked by most in the church and was seen as a good person. However, the congregation was unaware of Angelo's long-standing addiction to alcohol. This was his secret, and he, along with his family, worked very hard to hide it from the church.

In an attempt to take another stab at resolving the problem, he and his wife consulted their family physician and decided that a confession to the leadership of the church would be an important component of the healing process. They decided they wanted to stop the charade and the dishonesty and function with integrity. Somehow they thought the leadership of the church would be able not only to understand the struggle but help facilitate some solutions. The meeting was set up, and with fear and hope, Angelo told his story.

The response of the leadership was guarded, and they told him that they would have no option but to excommunicate him from the church. Since alcoholism is a sin, and sin cannot be taken lightly in the Christian community, they would have to remove him on the basis of 1 Corinthians 5. The membership of the church was informed that he had confessed to alcoholism and was being removed from the church. The church was asked to pray for him and reminded that their contact with him was to be severely limited since this is part of Paul's injunction, "With such a man do not even eat" (1 Cor. 5:11).

Angelo and his wife had thought that confession to the leadership would facilitate healing, yet now they felt cut off and alienated, and were no further ahead in resolving the problem. Some of the leaders had said they would pray for Angelo, and the congregation was invited to do the same, but that was it. There was no communal connection, no relational contact, and nothing about alcoholism at all except the public pronouncement that it was sin.

How did I find out about Angelo's situation? Jacob told me the story in a private counseling setting. He was involved in a sordid life of immorality and self-destruction, while at the same time maintaining a Christian image at his church. He was known for his biblical knowledge, wise and discerning counsel, and strong commitment to evangelical Christianity. He came for counseling because he could see the self-destructiveness in his lifestyle, and he wanted to break out of the unhealthy pattern. As we talked about his community of faith and their knowledge or lack of knowledge about his lifestyle, he made it clear that he would not be saying anything to anyone. Why? Jacob went to the same church as Angelo. He had watched with dismay when Angelo was disciplined, and he knew that Angelo was worse off in the end. Jacob feared the isolation, so he had no interest in confessing to the leadership.

The cases of Angelo and Jacob raise a number of concerns that both pastors and private counselors need to address if they are going to engage in healing that is purportedly Christian. First, we need to recognize that the church is not simply a venue for social connection and belonging but is a place for moral-ethical grounding. When parishioners become part of a faith community, they should be nurtured in what is right, discerning, and good. The church's explicit expectation that Angelo not pursue his addiction to alcohol and Jacob's expectation that the faith community would not condone his duplicity are not misguided. The problem is the way those expectations are being expressed.

While recognizing an aspiration to purity, we need to acknowledge that the church is comprised of people who, in the words of Samuel Southard, "enter the kingdom of God through admission of failure in personal experience, and who gather to consider God's future for their broken lives."[11] The church should not be a showpiece where people are always at their best. Rather, it is a collection of broken people who are seeking to incorporate the grace of God into the messiness of life.

How can we both aspire to standards of holiness and righteousness and recognize that the church is filled with those who sin? This is precisely where discipline fits in. While the church is a place where doctrine is preached and the sacraments are administered, it is also the place where the body of Christ functions as a community that cares and nurtures. How does it care and nurture? Marlin Jeschke emphasizes the priority of discipline:

> In discipline, as in the presentation of the good news to the non-Christian, a person is presented the opportunity of being liberated from the power of sin in all its forms by coming under the rule of Christ and walking in His way.[12]

At the heart of discipline is a concern for education, for discipleship, for bringing a person's life into harmony with biblical truth. This starts with self-discipline. Through the encouragement of the community of faith, an individual needs to demonstrate the fruit of the Spirit known as self-control (Gal. 5:23). There will be times, though, when someone sins against us and we need to "go and point out the fault when the two of you are alone" (Matt. 18:15 NRSV; see also Gal. 6:1). If this strategy is not effective, then the biblical injunction is to "take one or two others along with you" (Matt. 18:16 NRSV). Failing appropriate resolution at this level, the instruction is to "tell it to the church" (Matt. 18:17 NRSV; see also 1 Cor. 5:1–13). Unfortunately, this last step is often the only one that people think of when they hear the term *discipline*, but it is presented as the last resort in a chronological sequence of interventions that are communal and relational.

While the implementation of these various stages is difficult and often ignored by modern evangelical churches, it is crucial that we understand that these steps are a critical part of church ministry. Discipline is at the core of what the church should be about. John White summarizes it well:

> We have in the Western world no more than a series of syndicated Christian organizations and clubs, misnamed churches and denominations . . . for certainly any real attempt to regulate the lives of their members is noticeably absent. We cover up. We act with discretion. We are concerned with our public image and our public relations. Our reputation, rather than our testimony, is supremely important to us; so we keep our house reasonably tidy. But the firm, loving discipline of sinning members, so conspicuous in the New Testament, is almost entirely missing. We are the Church of Private People with Private Lives.[13]

J. Carl Laney agrees that the "church without discipline is a church without purity, power, and progress."[14]

We have already argued that morality is problematic in Western culture because of an individualistic emphasis.

Discipline also becomes difficult because, to use White's words, we "are the Church of Private People with Private Lives." It is clear that the modern evangelical world needs to take discipline seriously both through careful study and wise implementation.[15]

HOW CAN PASTORS EFFECTIVELY DISCIPLINE?

1. *Learn to distinguish caring instruction from legalistic rules.* When we hear the term *discipline,* there is a tendency to think of heavy-handed expulsion from the community with an attendant lack of care and compassion. Given this kind of stereotype, it is not surprising that church and parachurch leaders have difficulty providing leadership in this area. As Karl Menninger has suggested, pastors

> fear the public reproach of having reverted (as some extremists have) to threats of fire-and-brimstone damnation. They dread this accusation so much that they don't speak out even what they believe should be heard and heeded by the man in the pew. [16]

The presence of inaccurate stereotypes and public reproach are reinforced by our Western sensibility. As John White and Ken Blue argue:

> Our individualism (as well as our sinfulness) militates against exercising corrective discipline. To be members of the people of God means that our physical and spiritual well-being becomes our brother's business and his well-being becomes ours. But such attitudes are so alien to the Western church that when we do opt for biblical discipline, we will be criticized.[17]

The literature on spiritual abuse has intensified our fear of discipline even further. Discipline has become a form of oppression with a legalistic rule orientation that does not facilitate people in their growth. It even becomes difficult to encourage people to go and resolve their difficulties one-on-one.

Somehow we feel this is too directive and encourages too much interference in the lives of others. And such interference may result in others experiencing a form of abuse.

So how are pastors to cope with this attitude? Fundamentally, we need to separate caring instruction from legalistic rules. Paul Gilchrist provides some helpful input in this regard. Focusing on the term *torah,* he suggests that the primary concept of law in Scripture is teaching and instruction oriented rather than legislation and regulation centered.

> Christ and Paul clearly understood the covenantal definition of torah as authoritative instruction for a people in covenant relationship, rather than as a legal code to be used as a sledgehammer which kills. [18]

Do you teach the congregation about the importance of discipline? Are people in your community aware of the importance of the various forms of discipline? Do you do it in a way that affirms their covenant relationship with God so that their motivation is based on love and desire rather than guilt and obligation? Do you use the Bible as a sledgehammer so that people feel wounded or as a light and a lamp so people experience instruction and care? Do you model the importance of discipline in your own interaction with others in the faith community?

Finally, we need to recognize that a commitment to caring instruction does not come simply from distant proclamation. As John White and Ken Blue suggest:

> Corrective church discipline is also thwarted by the belief that Spirit-inspired preaching of Scripture will by itself produce holy congregations. Congregations can wallow comfortably in familiar rhetoric while hearts are hardened to the Spirit's pleading.[19]

Pastors need to be part of their community, both as exemplars and as those who are in-relationship, so the proclamation of truth is lived out in the body of believers. As James Houston said candidly:

Sometimes . . . the best expositors and communicators are hopeless in spiritual conversation and guidance on a personal basis, and can only offer "talk" and guidance at long range. But as long as we assume that "talk" automatically leads to living the gospel, there will be spiritual leakage.[20]

2. *Make remediation a key component of discipline.* There was a fundamental flaw in the discipline that Angelo experienced when he admitted to alcoholism. While the church aspired to righteous standards and called all its members to live with purity, the leadership missed a fundamental component of discipline. Whether it is in the context of one-on-one confrontation, a visit by two or three, or full corporate discipline, remediation needs to be prominent in the process. In this case Angelo was not only removed from communal connection, but his problem with alcoholism was untouched. As John White and Ken Blue affirm:

Restoration thus opens the door to reconciliation. The former rebel becomes a friend again. The fallen become comrades in arms with the fighters. The once wounded resume their roles as integral members of a healthy community. The goal of their reconciliation is achieved along with that of their restoration to holy living.[21]

The incident related in 1 Corinthians 5 is only part of the biblical narrative. The end of the story is found in 2 Corinthians 2:5–8:

If anyone has caused grief, he has not so much grieved me as he has grieved all of you, to some extent—not to put it too severely. The punishment inflicted on him by the majority is sufficient for him. Now instead, you ought to forgive and comfort him, so that he will not be overwhelmed by excessive sorrow. I urge you, therefore, to reaffirm your love for him.

Note the responsibility of the community in the restoration of someone who has fallen. The word *comfort* is the Greek word *parakaleo*, which can mean "console, help, urge, assist, encourage or aid." Restoration is not merely a matter of attendance at church services. Assuming that repentance has occurred and there is a desire to assimilate into the community, the sinner needs to be forgiven and helped.

Whether Angelo was put out of the church, spoken to by a small group, or confronted individually, the community bore a responsibility to help him deal with his alcoholism. This might entail connection with a counselor, a small group support system, or residential treatment. It may even require particular members of the community to meet with him for dialogue, prayer, and instruction. To fail to provide remediation for Angelo is to ignore the causes of his alcoholism. To discipline the sexually immoral person without understanding the etiology of the problem is to facilitate further problems in the future. To excommunicate the greedy person without discerning his or her inner struggles is to put a Band-Aid on an open wound. Discipline that does not take remediation into consideration is giving an invitation for a repetition of the same action.

In discussing this point as it applies to sexually abusive clergy, Gerald Blanchard provides an appropriate strategy:

> Because it cannot be regarded (or dismissed) as a mere lapse in judgment, admonishment, reprimand, censure, or dismissal are not adequate remedies. Effective remediation requires a resolute and decisive intervention followed by a contracting process that insures the implementation of comprehensive treatment protocols. Along with a stern approach, there is the requisite need to treat wounded colleagues as we would any other distressed person—with forbearance, compassion, fairness, and dignity.[22]

3. *Identify the place of confidentiality and legal concerns.* Since discipline involves the activities of an individual in the context of a community, we must return to the subject of

confidentiality and boundaries of information. When does a church have a right to judge the behavior of one of its members either in personal conversation or in the corporate setting? Pastors who are called on to facilitate discipline in their community of faith need to grapple with these questions, particularly in the litigious culture in which we live.

In his excellent book, *Christian Counseling and the Law*, Steve Levicoff suggests that a key issue in discipline is the invasion of privacy. This could take the form of "intrusion upon a person's seclusion or solitude or into his or her private affairs" or "public disclosure of embarrassing private facts about a person." The key in disciplinary matters is that "members coming into the church should be informed of the church's policies regarding disciplinary matters. Thus, their implied consent to the procedures will be given in an informed manner."[23] In other words, be sure that the faith community knows the policy on discipline and invasion of privacy. The church has every right within the law to administer discipline if this provision is met.

In a comprehensive article that summarizes the legalities of church discipline in Canada, Terrance Carter provides a number of specifics that will help the pastor in dealing with disciplinary questions. His counsel in the Canadian context parallels Levicoff's concerns in the United States. Some of the specifics that pastors need to note are as follows:

1. To ensure that the church has an authoritative basis for implementing church discipline, its constitution should clearly set out the biblical references for discipline and dispute resolution amongst its members. . . .

2. If there are policy statements of the church concerning conduct of life-style requirements that are legitimate expectations imposed on church members, those policies must be set out . . . in the church constitution. . . .

3. A prospective member should be required to subscribe in writing for membership to confirm his or her voluntary decision to become part of the

local church and be subject to the authority of the church leadership. . . .

4. Throughout the disciplinary proceedings, the confidentiality of information given to church leaders must be respected. As such, only those persons involved in the disciplinary proceedings should be apprised of the information that is divulged in confidence by the person being disciplined. In the event that the church leadership decides that an announcement concerning the discipline of a member needs to be made to the church, such announcement should be directed to the members of the church and should be given orally from a prepared text. To avoid a claim for breach of privacy, any statement pertaining to the discipline of a member at a public worship service should be avoided. Instead, the matter should be dealt with at a meeting of members only.[24]

It is important to note Carter's affirmation that we can talk about discipline publicly. In doing so, however, he indicates that we need to ask ourselves an important question:

Does the information need to be disseminated to assure other members that the integrity of the collective ministry of the church is being maintained and can it be reasonably concluded that such information will not unduly embarrass or prejudice the reputation of a member? For example, in the case of adultery, a statement that a member has been found to be in an adulterous relationship would be appropriate but the details of the relationship would not be.[25]

Pastors who are committed to a biblical approach to church discipline would be strongly advised to obtain legal advice in their own geographical location. In doing so, they will be able to function within the community of faith in a way that demonstrates an understanding of broader judicial concerns.

How Can Private Counselors Use Discipline?

1. *Do not jettison moral concerns due to a fear of being moralistic.* On several occasions in the past twenty years I have worked with a number of transsexuals. In some situations the individuals had not gone through complete gender reassignment, while in others they had experienced surgery. For Christians who are experiencing this particular problem, the moral-ethical dilemma is overwhelming. How do they deal with their identity struggles? How do they explain this to friends and family? How do they cope with the cause of their difficulty? How do they deal with the biblical and theological themes around the image of God, sexuality, the body, and gender? How do they function postoperatively in social and church situations?

What is the private counselor called to do in this situation? A counselor with a privatized approach to ethics would simply focus on the mind-set and worldview of the client so that his or her own self-actualization is paramount. As Dueck has rightly argued, this perspective on being moralistic "is usually defined as rigidity, literalism, biblicism, legalism, and authoritarianism."[26] Unfortunately, these are the only two options for some private counselors. They either adopt an individualized ethic or else engage in a form of authoritarian legalism. As Dueck argues, a misunderstanding about the nature of moralism has led some to conclude that "moralism implicitly assumes that when conservative religious values are expressed it is an imposition, but when modernity is the context, it is enlightenment."[27]

I remember being involved in a situation where a transsexual pursued not only medical and psychiatric intervention but also Christian counseling. This was further supplemented by communal intervention from her denominational leaders, who dealt with the biblical, theological, ethical, and moral components of her difficulty and the implications of all this for the churches within that denomination. All the leaders expressed a deep conviction to reflect on the moral-ethical concerns inherent to her situation. She was not alienated through rigidity and authoritarianism; rather, she experienced affection and understanding from a community that was willing to confront the moral issues directly. Their commitment to being moral did not lead to them becoming moralistic.

Too often in Christian counseling there is a polarization between rampant individualism that nurtures a personal ethic and hostile moralism that leaves people feeling bruised and misunderstood. The retention of moral concerns in the context of communal thinking is the antidote to both of these extremes.

2. *Affirm the true nature of the church in its mandate to discipline.* Most of the books on discipline begin with an overview that demonstrates its prevalence throughout church history and then contrasts this with its absence in modern evangelical culture. Many reasons are given for this shift, but J. Carl Laney has suggested that in "many churches, counseling has now replaced discipline."[28] How does this happen? People are taking their personal and communal struggles outside the church, moving into the sanctioned retreat, and receiving help in that context. Often, although not always, the faith community is an innocent (or guilty in some cases) bystander that has no involvement in the process of restoration.

In order for private counselors to affirm the true nature of the church in its mandate to discipline, there must be a biblical and theological conviction that can only come through careful study and reflection. However, it also involves an understanding of the nature of impulse control and a recognition that therapeutic intervention is only part of the resolution.

A number of years ago I was invited, along with three others, to go with a friend to see her counselor. We were all part of her faith community, and she wanted us to participate in the healing process by providing her with communal accountability and prayer. She recognized that some of her interpersonal reactions needed to be monitored and confronted, and both she and her counselor thought the community could play a role. The message was clear that her personal struggles could not be handled autonomously. She needed the discipline and nurture of the Christian community to function.

This approach raises the question of how people control their impulses, tendencies, and proclivities. Do they have the inherent ability to do this, or do they need the support of a broader community? It was this issue that led Philip Slater to point out that in stable societies "the control of human impulses is usually a collective responsibility," and because of this "the group is always near at hand to stop him or shame him or punish him should he forget himself." In contrast, in "more fluid, changing societies we are more apt to find controls that are internalized—that do not depend to so great an extent on control and enforcement by external agents."[29] Private counselors need to understand that the church, with its mandate to provide discipline for its members, provides collective responsibility for the well-being of individuals.

This admission will also produce an awareness that therapeutic involvement is only part of the resolution when people are struggling with moral-ethical issues. In his discussion on sexual addiction among clergy, Mark Laaser makes it clear that to "call clergy sexual misconduct sexual addiction is also not to deny that it is sinful, immoral, or in some cases criminal behavior."[30] This is really the opposite of what pastors need to hear. As has already been noted, pastors can forget that immorality needs to be understood in a broader context than simply as sin, especially if they are going to facilitate restoration. Private counselors need to recognize that some therapeutic issues involve sin and immorality. When this happens, the church needs to become an equal partner in the remediation.

3. *Develop a position on confidentiality and work with the church.* If the church is going to be an equal partner, then the topic of confidentiality must be addressed. In chapter 6, private counselors were encouraged to identify boundaries as they relate to Christian communities, encourage the client to broaden boundaries, and work directly with the leadership of Christian communities. With these principles as a backdrop, the discipline question can be addressed.

First and foremost, private counselors need to exercise discernment. A commitment to discipline does not require counselors to connect with the church every time someone comes to see them. Not only would this be ill-advised for the counselee, it would communicate a message to potential counselees that would probably preclude their involvement in counseling. They would be so frightened of what the counselor might do that they would not want to take the chance.

So cautions concerning the sanctioned retreat should not be construed as a complete dismantling of the walls in the counselor's office. However, on the other side, we need to keep the discipline question in tension with the traditional approaches to confidentiality. Take the following two positions as illustrations.

In an article on legal and ethical issues in lay counseling Becker is clear:

> Confession to appropriate church leaders should be encouraged so that healing within the church body can occur, but betraying the confidentiality of the therapeutic relationship for the sake of church discipline should be avoided.[31]

Jay Adams holds an opposing view on the relationship between discipline and confidentiality:

> Frequently it is the practice of Bible-believing Christians to give assurances of absolute confidentiality, never realizing that they are following a policy that originated in the Middle Ages and that is unbiblical and contrary to Scripture (there is not a scrap of evidence in the Bible for this practice). . . . Both individuals and counselors must be aware of the all-important fact that absolute confidentiality prohibits the proper exercise of church discipline.[32]

How can this conundrum be addressed? Can one be loyal to the principles of discipline in the church and retain the longstanding tradition of confidentiality in the counseling relationship? Steve Levicoff suggests that counselors need to obtain acknowledgment of informed consent at the beginning of the counseling relationship. This would provide the counselor with the opportunity to disclose information to particular people for a specific reason. For Levicoff this would cover the traditional danger to self and others criteria "or—in the case of church discipline—unrepented sin."[33] He goes on to describe an adulterous affair where the person continues in this relationship even after they have received counseling over a period of time. In that situation the guidelines of Matthew 18:15–17 would be invoked.

There are three ways in which private counselors can provide informed consent. One way is to simply state: "What goes on between the two of us is in strictest confidence. If I sense there is any reason why I should be disclosing some of the information that you relay to me outside of this office, I will talk with you first." This message provides reassurance that the counseling is in confidence, but it also indicates that confidence does not mean no disclosure will ever take place. It does, however, let the client know that this will not happen outside his or her awareness.

The second method is a form that is signed by the client at the beginning of the relationship. In his book on lay counseling, Siang-Yang Tan provides an example of such a form that includes a statement on confidentiality:

> The confidentiality that you share with your lay counselor will be carefully guarded. However, it is required by California law that all counselors have a duty to warn the appropriate individuals if the counselee intends to take harmful, dangerous, or criminal actions against themselves or someone around them. Counselors are also mandated to report any incidences of "reasonably suspected child abuse" (physical or sexual), elderly abuse, or suicide attempts to the Department of Social Services and/or the Police Department.[34]

The third method is simply a variation of the second. Rather than having the counselee sign a form at the beginning, the counselor would share his or her personal position on confidentiality or that of the agency and then record that this has occurred in the counseling notes. This could be retained on record.

A commitment to discipline in the context of the church will necessitate the private counselor moving beyond the traditional "danger to self and others" standard. Immoral actions that continue after a significant period of counseling may need to be brought outside the counseling relationship. What this will mean in each situation is difficult to articulate, so private counselors may find it helpful to use the first or third strategy above. It is difficult to articulate unrepentant attitudes and particular immoral behaviors in a written form.

CONFESSION

A second aspect of community and the counselee is tied to confession. For morality to be taken seriously so that counselees experience communal discipline, confession needs to become an important facet of the process of discipline.[35] The first recorded question in Scripture is significant in this regard. After having realized that they had disobeyed God's command in the Garden, the man and the woman covered themselves with fig leaves and tried to avoid God's eye by hiding among the trees. His question, "Where are you?" (Gen. 3:9), did not reflect the fact that God did not know where they were. Obviously, the Creator of the fig leaves and the trees would be able to locate his own creatures! What it did signify was the early beginnings of the human tendency to try to cover impurity and disobedience and God's desire to have his people function with moral integrity.

How does confession relate to our understanding of counseling? Richard Butman argues:

> Both confession and individually oriented therapy, then, are intimate, one-to-one interpersonal relationships with the aim of reducing subjective distress and restoring emotional and/or spiritual health. In contrast, however, confession stresses conscious motivation and recall, whereas more depth-oriented approaches to therapy aim at finding out whether or not unconscious dynamics might be influencing current functioning.[36]

He goes on to suggest that psychotherapy is not as "concerned with the confession of a moral offense, but rather looks for the causes of problems."[37] Here again the therapeutic side is positioned as distinct from ethical concerns. The *why* of behavior is separated from its moral value. The field of counseling can focus on one and bypass the other. For those concerned with community concerns, this is not an acceptable solution.

Among the many references to confession in biblical literature, the following emphasize its importance.

- Its presence is linked with general well-being:

  No one who conceals transgressions will prosper, but one who confesses and forsakes them will obtain mercy (Prov. 28:13 NRSV).

- Confession is a way to bring healing:

  Therefore confess your sins to each other and pray for each other so that you may be healed (James 5:16).

- Its absence often is played out in the presence of physical and emotional turmoil:

  When I kept silent, my bones wasted away through my groaning all day long. For day and night your hand was heavy upon me; my strength was sapped as in the heat of summer. Then I acknowledged my sin to you and did not cover up my iniquity (Ps. 32:3–5).

The biblical material has a primary emphasis that should not be ignored. God is aware of our proclivities to sin. He knows our natural inclination to fail and fall short of holy standards. And while the Scriptures condemn sin, there is also a strong emphasis on the concealment of sin. To refuse to deal with our sin is to create problems not just in terms of our relationship with God but also in our general functioning. From the earliest example in the Garden, hiding our sin from ourselves and others compounds an already serious problem.

At an unconscious level, this is what motivated Angelo to go the leadership of his church. He knew that his problem with alcoholism was hiding behind his own personally constructed "fig leaves" of propriety, impression management, and an evangelical facade. Over a period of time, Angelo's problem of alcoholism was compounded by his struggle with the communal charade. The hiding became as much of a problem as the original difficulty. Confession was an obvious antidote.

It is no surprise, then, that the early church made confession and self-disclosure a key part of their liturgy.[38] It became a foundation for the appropriation of forgiveness and mercy. At the time of the Nicene Creed in A.D. 325, however, Emperor Constantine moved public corporate confession into the private realm, and by the thirteenth century people were expected to confess to a priest once a year. During the Reformation, Martin Luther reacted against the compulsory nature of private confession and argued that people could make daily confession to God, public confession of sin through the liturgy, and personal confession to another Christian. The requirement of a priest for private confession was no longer necessary because of a renewed commitment to the priesthood of all believers; each had the opportunity to hear the confession of the other. The Roman Catholic tradition, in contrast, continued with the designated priest as an intermediary for private confession.

In his outline of these historical developments, Dietrich Bonhoeffer has suggested that two trends have taken place that have moved confession into a less prominent place. First of all, a pietistic emphasis has resulted in confession becoming more and more private. Second, psychotherapy has become a secular version of confession—a replacement for what was once a deeply religious concern. As a result of these two influences, confession has lost its communal emphasis and its visibility in the church.[39] What does the weakening of confession do to the church? It forces people to be secret carriers. The church becomes a place where hiding is the operative strategy and moral integrity is absent.

When Gordon MacDonald turned over a two-by-six board and found a large collection of bugs underneath, he thought of the church and its tendency to facilitate hiding:

As I watched them scurry for cover, I thought of what might be called the underside of the church: those numberless people who walk into sanctuaries all over the world carrying their secrets behind bright clothing and forced smiles. They sing the songs, pray the prayers, listen to the sermons. And all the while the secrets fester within the private world causing either a constantly broken heart or a hardened heart. They come in fear of their secrets being exposed, and they quite likely go in fear that they will have to live this way for the rest of their lives. Believe me, the underside of the church is there, listening and watching to find out whether there is anyone with whom their secret might be safe if revealed.[40]

Confession is a way to break out of this secret-carrying. When individuals are able to admit to their own frailty and sin, there is a sense of community because there is a lessening of the individual struggle. I am not struggling alone. I am doing it in-community with a brother or sister. When the wall is broken down, I can be restored to the people of God. I need to hide no longer. I can live with moral integrity in front of others because I have experienced the reality of mercy and forgiveness in the body. In essence, confession has become a way of being restored back into community.[41]

Before looking at the implications of confession for pastors, a word of caution. Confession is a multifaceted issue that has great potential for good. However, there are latent dangers. Some churches have spiritual exhibitionists who tell all at inappropriate times. They only serve to make the community feel awkward and uncomfortable. Some communities have obsessively oriented people who are stricken by oversensitive consciences. Often their confession is not for the purpose of restoration but an attempt to both atone for their own sins and appease their own conscience. Finally, some evangelical Christians have forgotten that the highest virtue is love, not honesty. To tell all is no guarantee that the confession is motivated by love. While affirming the biblical emphasis on confession and the many benefits that can be derived in the community, we should not be oblivious to the potential dangers.

PASTORS AND THE NEED FOR CONFESSION

1. *Acknowledge the dangers of a pious community.* One of the questions that private Christian counselors are asked frequently is, Do you get depressed always having to talk to people who are struggling? I would suspect that most of us who have done private counseling would say that a bigger frustration than the pain of individuals is the existence of so many pious communities. As Dietrich Bonhoeffer describes so poignantly, the "pious fellowship permits no one to be a sinner. So everybody must conceal his sin from himself and from the fellowship."[42]

In pious communities there is a lack of integrity. The whole atmosphere is not conducive to confession because the communal message is clear: We do not talk about sin and frailty. There is an insidious nature to this mind-set in some evangelical churches where this facade is fostered by an obsession with theological and doctrinal accuracy. The prayers, hymns, and sermons are scrutinized for their biblical accuracy, but the private lives of the members are fraught with sin and immorality. Unfortunately, the structure of the church allows individuals to maintain a compartmentalization that separates spiritual rhetoric from the realities of personal lifestyle.

In an interesting study that focuses on how churches handle adolescent rebellion, Cathryn Hill suggests that teenagers go through a normal developmental process of rebellion. This time of questioning and doubt is normal and does not necessarily reflect a lack of faith. In fact, this time of reaction may be an integral part of their growth into a more personalized and vital faith. She suggests that churches need to allow these issues to come to the surface and be confessed openly by the teens. At the same time, the community should not be striving for complete compliance, which may cause the rebellion to go underground.

> If . . . this stage of questioning and experimentation
> is labeled by the milieu as potentially growth-

producing, indeed even desirable in the formation of mature faith, then the adolescent can experience freedom to complete the internalization or "owning" process, perhaps without the same intensity of rebellious behavior.[43]

In order for this kind of ministry to go on in Christian communities, there has to be an atmosphere that facilitates confession. Teenagers who are in rebellion need to feel the freedom to open up. Fathers who are abusing their children need to be able to level with the leadership or a trusted friend. Individuals like Angelo, who are struggling with private addictions, need to have an environment where the facade can be dropped. Christian communities that pretend and hide behind game-playing are nurturing a form of piety that lacks in depth, and most importantly, lacks in truth. As Gordon MacDonald describes so clearly:

> But why secrets? The answer has to do with truth. We acquire secrets when we do not wish to face or reveal the truth. We do a subtle thing when we play with the truth, but we do it all the time. So much so that few people think seriously about how much the systems in which we live constantly manipulate the truth.[44]

2. *Take the sins of others seriously.* Ryan had been the treasurer of the church for three years. To all external appearances he was an exemplary Christian, and he seemed to be managing the finances with integrity. However, the secretary noticed a discrepancy in the books and brought it to the attention of the parish priest. Upon further investigation, they realized that Ryan had been funneling a portion of the church funds into a personal account. Over the following months, Ryan met with the finance committee of the church and with a counselor within the denomination. The finance committee spent most of their time trying to account for all the funds. The counselor focused on Ryan's family background and the motivation that elicited his misdemeanor.

While these components of his behavior are important and require emphasis, no one was dealing with the behavior from the perspective of morality. In the interest of accounting for the money and explaining his motivation, sin was not a viable issue. In saying this I am not advocating a high-handed, arrogant negation of Ryan through unbearable punishment. Rather, we need to recognize, in the words of Clifford Williams, that:

> the first requirement for accepting God's mercy is that we see ourselves as needing mercy.... This is the reason that mercy is severe—seeing ourselves as we really are is extraordinarily painful.[45]

To take sin seriously is to understand individuals not just in their relationship with God but also in their communal connection. Taking the sin of others seriously means that we have a genuine care for what is happening in others' lives. It also means we understand the subtlety in sin and its ability to facilitate self-deception. The writer of the Hebrews made this clear:

> Take care, brothers and sisters, that none of you may have an evil, unbelieving heart that turns away from the living God. But exhort one another every day, as long as it is called "today," so that none of you may be hardened by the deceitfulness of sin. For we have become partners of Christ (Heb. 3:12–14 NRSV).

For pastors in church and parachurch organizations, there is a need to renew our commitment to take sin seriously. While the explanation for behavior is an important dynamic in understanding why something has happened, this does not preclude careful analysis around the insidiousness of sin. To do this is to affirm the priority of morality as well as the centrality of community. Bonhoeffer's summary is apt:

> In confession the break-through to community takes place. Sin demands to have a man by himself. It withdraws him from the community. The more isolated a person is, the more destructive will be the

power of sin over him, and the more deeply he becomes involved in it, the more disastrous is his isolation. Sin wants to remain unknown. It shuns the light. In the darkness of the unexpressed it poisons the whole being of a person .[46]

3. *Facilitate confession in the community*. Given the dangers in a pious community and the need to take the sin of others seriously, how can pastors facilitate confession? First of all, we need to recognize that the facilitation of confession is part of the role of the Christian leader. All Christians need to listen to the confession of others, but leaders need to understand that their modeling of listening to confession will be an example to others. As John White asks so poignantly:

> What are deacons and elders for? What are officers of Christian organizations for? Is the function of a Christian leader to lead singing, make announcements and write thank you letters to visiting speakers? We are all playing Christian club games while men and women around us are tormented by sin, too timid to bare their bosoms, too ashamed to ask our help.[47]

Often in leadership it is easy to slip into the hierarchical top-down approach where we are asking others to engage in behavior we are unwilling to participate in ourselves. We need to be people who make confession as well. In personal conversation and public speaking, pastors need to get used to saying, "I'm sorry," with a genuineness that reflects true repentance from sin. Henri Nouwen expresses it well:

> What discipline is required for the future leader to overcome the temptation of individual heroism? I would like to propose the discipline of confession and forgiveness. Just as the future leaders must be mystics deeply steeped in contemplative prayer, so also must they be persons always willing to confess their own brokenness and ask for forgiveness from those to whom they minister. . . . Often I have the impression

that priests and ministers are the least-confessing people in the Christian community.[48]

We also need to engage in meaningful conversations with others. I have noticed that some pastors like to keep conversations at a somewhat superficial "God is good and so are you" level. This style of interaction tends to entrench those who are in hiding. There is no natural opportunity for them to reveal the darkness that has enveloped their sin.

I remember talking to a young man at a restaurant one night. We were in the same community and had gone out for an evening of what I thought would be pleasant conversation. As we began to talk in detail about how both of us were doing, he began to drop the facade and revealed a double life that was sordid and sinful. His confession was a by-product of conversation and not something that either of us had pursued intentionally.

We also need to recognize that the climate created by our preaching and teaching will either facilitate or squelch confession. I am intrigued by the amount of sharing that goes on after some public presentations and the absence of it in others. I visited a church for two Sunday services and preached on the story of the woman taken in adultery from John 8. A few weeks after the service I received a letter from a teenager in the church who said that he had been obsessed with masturbation for some time and did not know who to talk to. After hearing the way I had talked about sexual sin so openly from the pulpit, he thought that I would be a good person to contact. The striking aspect of this situation was the fact that I had given explicit lectures on masturbation in the past and very few had come forward to talk. Somehow the climate created in the John 8 sermon had encouraged someone to open up.

I appreciate the response of Karl Menninger when asked how Protestant ministers can facilitate confession in the congregation. He indicates that we need to be explicit and clear in our inquiries:

> What have you done this week to hurt your neighbor, your sister, your wife? What have you done to hurt yourself? What have you done to hurt this church

or the ideals for which it stands? What have you done to hurt this city, this land on which we live? What have you done this week against the interests of the next generation? What have you left undone for the suffering, damaged, polluted, exploited earth and its hungry, miserable, exploited population?[49]

How Should Private Counselors Approach Confession?

1. *Recognize the self-deception in sin.* As noted earlier, there has been a historical shift in confession from the public to the private and a concomitant shift from confession as a religious exercise to confession as a therapeutic activity. This means that many Christians are employing the sanctioned retreat to deal with issues of sin. They talk with their counselor in private about moral concerns. This is not all bad. Many of us have helped people work through confession, repentance, and appropriate restoration to the community. However, in all this we need to remember that self-deception is inherent to sin.

Because the apostle Paul experienced extensive criticism in his public ministry, we often find him explaining himself and his attitude to the gospel. On one particular occasion described in the early part of the first letter to the Corinthian church, he indicates that he is not overly concerned about the temporary judgment of others: "Indeed, I do not even judge myself. My conscience is clear, but that does not make me innocent. It is the Lord who judges me" (1 Cor. 4:3–4). He recognizes that personal introspection and self-examination are not sufficient to make a final judgment. Our own motives and intentions are sufficiently mixed and influenced by sin that we cannot come to a definitive conclusion. In this argument Paul echoes the words of Jeremiah many years before: "The heart is deceitful about all things and beyond cure. Who can understand it?" (Jer. 17:9).

If this contention is true, then private counselors need to be aware of the danger of being a facilitator of self-examination. Counselees who are grappling with sin and their need to confess it are not capable of dealing with this alone. As James Houston argues:

> If sin is self-deceiving, then I need a soul friend to give me insights into the ways I am deceived, or insensitive, or hardened by sin within me. I cannot do it alone. Self-examination can only take me so far. I need others to help expose and help me understand where sin would deceive and confuse me.[50]

Although private counselors do provide an outside perspective, they are not sufficient to help decipher all the intricacies of sin. This is the task of the Word of God, which is mediated by the fully functioning Christian community.

2. *Acknowledge the pain of keeping secrets in community.* Four years after we were married, my wife and I realized that we were experiencing infertility. As for many couples, this awareness did not arrive overnight but slowly came to the surface through consultation with various medical practitioners and many months of waiting for a child. During that time we were in a church where young couples were on the receiving end of one-liners about "filling the Sunday School" or "having their quiver full." Wedding receptions usually had jokes about the number of children that would inevitably come to the newlyweds. The community message was clear: Normal, spiritual couples have many biological children, and they have them by choice. Without imputing any intent to the community that propagated this message, we chose not to talk about our problem. When the jokes were told, we laughed. When the one-liners were given, we shot back with another one. In the early years of the struggle, it was the only way we knew to cope with the internal pain. We felt we had to carry the secret alone.

There is considerable pain when you live with secrets in a Christian community. If this is true for an issue like infertility, where there is no explicit sin involved, the absence of confession brings much more acute pain when sin is present. As Gordon MacDonald indicates, "Large amounts of energy once funneled toward creativity and vital living get siphoned off in the constant planning and implementing of elaborate schemes to cover tracks."[51] In fact, what happens is that the pressure to cover up becomes so absorbing that the original problem is compounded considerably.

Private counselors run the risk of intensifying this pain. By inviting counselees into a sanctioned retreat where secrets are revealed in private, there is a danger that this process could, in itself, force more hiding and less transparency in the Christian community. People could feel that their revelations in counseling are sufficient and that there is no need to deal with the communal implications of their behavior. A private counselor who falls into this trap fails to realize the pain of keeping secrets in community and in so doing creates pain in the context of healing. Gordon MacDonald's comments are instructive in this regard:

> Insight then, as I wish to use the term, is the act of constantly aligning our two worlds, private and public, with the truth. Secret carrying, on the other hand, is the act of stretching the two worlds further and further apart.[52]

If we are going to facilitate insight and integrity in the lives of our counselees, they need to understand the dangers of dividing life up into compartments. If the private is not synonymous with the public, they are forced to be secret-carriers, and in the process confession is negated and sin is not resolved. As was mentioned earlier, there are latent dangers in confession, and private counselors must be wise in discerning whether they should either encourage or discourage this process.

3. *Encourage counselees to confess sin.* One of the dangers in any profession is that the professional may have a particular understanding of the way things should be and those he or she serves may have a very different perspective. Because of the power inherent in the individuals providing the service, they can easily miss what their clients actually want and need. This is certainly true in the field of counseling. We need to carefully answer the questions:

What do counselees want?

What do counselors think counselees want?

In a study that focused on these two questions, Everett Worthington and his colleagues found an interesting difference between client and therapist perceptions of confession:

> Clients seemed to perceive needs to confess their sins to others and to God and to forgive others and God more frequently than counselors intended to promote these behaviors. This might suggest that clients might be receptive to more direct stimulation of confession and forgiveness than even Christian therapists credit them with.[53]

What might this mean for private counselors? It will definitely mean that explanations for various behaviors should not be used to the exclusion of moral-ethical assessment. By implication, counselees will be given explicit opportunities to confess sin and seek forgiveness in the context of counseling. However, it will also result in private counselors encouraging counselees to move from being secret-carriers in the Christian community to being individuals who confess their sins to appropriate people at specific times. This will require detailed discussion on the nature of the community, the trusted members within it, the form of the sin that requires confession, the best way to bring about biblical restoration, and the motivation for the confession.

Encouraging confession in a community is not a recipe for the complete resolution of difficulties. In many evangelical churches sin is kept private and personal, and when confession is made, gossip and criticism take over. This is where the Christian counselor needs to set appropriate goals. To talk about communal confession is to invite a counselee into a risky interaction. There is no guarantee that it will work. He or she may be misunderstood or may experience rejection. However, confession in the context of a caring Christian community will often reap benefits. As John White and Ken Blue indicate, "Confession is most dramatically therapeutic when the person making the confession no longer cares about who knows about his or her sin, so great is the burden of concealment."[54] As Gordon MacDonald claims, "What liberation when the secrets are jettisoned and they walk out of the darkness into the light."[55]

COUNSELING FEES AND COMMUNITY

A third aspect that relates the community to the counselee is the subject of fees. While at first glance this may seem unrelated to communal concerns, a more careful examination will reveal that the link with moral-ethical issues is significant.

One of the by-products of our individualistic culture is that our connection with and interest in each other is limited. With a strong commitment to the present and to ourselves, it is difficult to genuinely care for others. In North America this trend is paired with the increasing proliferation of so-called caring professions. Among others, doctors, ministers, and counselors are perceived as people in occupations that are premised on care. They provide technical expertise but in a way that purportedly reflects a sincere commitment to humanity, and they get paid for doing so. The conclusion? Money has become a medium of exchange for care.

I have heard many counselors describe their early days in the field. Their initial motivation to pursue the profession of counseling was based on an interest in people, a desire to help others, and a service mentality. In essence, a care for others was central to their occupational motivation. However, as they started seeing people in formal sessions, they did not know how to put the fee for service together with their altruistic aspirations. Often this tension was heightened when counselees raised concerns about the amount of the fee and their ability to pay. On the other side, counselors are no different than the general population; they need to eat and pay their bills, so a fee for service can be justified.

Given this tension, it is surprising that there is a lack of writing on the topic of fees. As Alan Tulipan indicates:

> Since the literature about fees has been scant, the conclusion must be drawn that there is a general unwillingness to deal openly and actively with a transaction that may be justified within the context

of the modern commercial world, but which carries, for some, an undesirable mercenary connotation. Psychotherapists tend to want to nurture their image as beneficent purveyors of good rather than as individuals who are at least partially involved in commerce. The result has been a gap in the literature that can only be the result of some degree of "selective inattention," more than likely arising from difficulties in facing up to the attendant conflict.[56]

Much of this "selective inattention" is linked with the conflict around whether counseling is a straight business transaction or whether it a purchase of friendship.[57] Both counselors and counselees struggle with this. For instance, I have had counselees ask me: "Would you still be showing me care and giving me understanding if I were not paying you and we were just friends?" It is this concern that has led Al Dueck to argue that we are living in a "marketplace of impersonal transactions" so that counseling "in such a setting may well take on the character of an exchange of fees for friendship."[58] Philip Rieff has suggested that the fee distinguishes therapeutic interactions from mentoring. In the former, patients discharge their "debt of gratitude,"[59] while in the latter, the disciple is always in debt to his or her mentor.

In an attempt to debunk the notion of the "hired friend," William Herron and Shiela Rouslin Welt suggest that four variables distinguish friendship from therapeutic connection:

1. *Selection*—Under most circumstances, we select our friends but not our counselees.

2. *Boundaries*—Therapeutic interactions tend to have more clearly defined boundaries that influence time, duration, location, formality, and fees.

3. *Focus*—Counselees come to counseling with particular problems that become the primary focus of the interaction, so there is an absence of mutuality.

4. *Content*—Counselors focus on particular themes and patterns to help move the counselee toward resolution of difficulties. Ideally, counselors do this without any

concern for the effect on the relationship or their own personal feelings.[60]

How should Christian counselors and pastors respond to this issue? Of all people, we should have something to say about the power of money and the spiritual values that are inherent in it. We should have some understanding of the role of care that is resident in the character of the giver rather than in a business transaction between strangers. As those committed to the centrality of the community, we should be able to critique a system where fee for service runs the risks of marginalizing the socially and economically disadvantaged. If, in the words of Lewis Yablonsky, "people in the helping field are afflicted with an inner tug of war between altruism, guilt, and materialism,"[61] then Christians need to enter into the moral and ethical tensions that are resident in this war.

PASTORS AND COUNSELING FEES

1. *Educate the community on the power of money.* Money is not a neutral commodity; it has moral and spiritual dimensions that need to be understood. When Jesus spoke about the need to have treasures in heaven, he concluded his remarks with this statement:

> No one can serve two masters; for a slave will either hate the one and love the other, or be devoted to the one and despise the other. You cannot serve God and wealth (Matt. 6:24 NRSV).

In these two short sentences Jesus personifies money. He acknowledges its potential for control. It has the capacity to dominate. Surprisingly, it is even something that can be worshiped. Money is a rival of God in its demand of our allegiance. Because it is a rival, many of the parables focus on financial concerns. Jesus made more references to money than many other topics including the new birth, faith, prayer, and life after death.

Since pastors have the responsibility to educate, train, and equip those whom they lead, the biblical teaching on money cannot be overlooked. Both those in the helping professions as well as those who are receiving care in exchange for money need to grapple with the substantive issues around this topic so they can make appropriate ethical decisions. As Richard Foster says:

> The truth is that it is not really difficult to discover what the Bible teaches about money. If we will simply read it through with honest hearts, we can come to a rather clear sense of the direction of Scripture on this subject. The Bible is much more clear and straightforward about money than it is about many other issues. Our difficulty is not in understanding the teaching; our problem lies in another direction. The most difficult thing we have to deal with when we begin to look at the dark side of money is fear. If we have any sense at all, these words of Jesus really do frighten us.[62]

Only with a biblical and theological foundation can issues like the poor, accessibility of service, third-party payments, professionalism, and the like be properly understood.

2. *Provide the socially and economically disadvantaged with access to counseling.* When the church is functioning as a Christian community, there are no barriers based on socio-economic status. There is access to various ministries because they are rooted in the grace and mercy of God expressed through the community. James makes this clear in his epistle:

> My brothers and sisters, do you with your acts of favoritism really believe in our glorious Lord Jesus Christ? For if a person with gold rings and in fine clothes comes into your assembly, and if a poor person in dirty clothes also comes in, and if you take notice of the one wearing the fine clothes and say, "Have a seat here, please," while to the one who is poor you say, "Stand there," or, "Sit at my feet," have you not made distinctions among your-selves, and become judges with evil thoughts? (James 2:1–4 NRSV).

It would be easy for pastors to claim that the fee for service issue does not make sense in their context. Their church or parachurch organization pays their salary, and there is no direct fee for their service. However, the implicit message in a fee for service structure is that some can afford it and some cannot. In cases where people are economically disadvantaged, their access to the professional world is severely limited. A similar dynamic operates in pastoral counseling. If a church is middle-class in orientation, it is often set up to keep the lower classes out. The style of decoration in the building and the pastor's office, the appearance and decorum of the staff, and the physical location of many evangelical churches serve to create a barrier to ministry. It is highly unlikely that the poor and socially disadvantaged will be drawn to such a context. In translation, their socioeconomic status will get in the way of genuine ministry.

In commenting on this reality in pastoral counseling centers, Roy Smith decries the situation:

> It is a testament to the dominance of individualistic middle-class ideologies in the North American church that this situation has not drawn more criticism. . . . The dependence of pastoral counselors upon fees and their identity as professional psychotherapists virtually guarantees that they will not see many of the poor and those who are suffering the most from psychological problems.[63]

If this is true in pastoral counseling situations, then the church and a number of parachurch organizations have the opportunity to bridge this gap by making counseling opportunities available to the poor. This might be done by moving the counseling office into the physical environment where the poor are located. I know of one church where a part-time staff counselor was hired, but her office was situated in a low-income apartment complex. The counseling in this context takes on a different aura. It is not necessarily formal and regimented but may involve a level of caring that moves into the provision of groceries, financial assistance, and practical direction such as accompanying an individual to the welfare office. This approach to counseling is in stark contrast to the solely verbal orientation so typical of middle- and upper-class counseling. This may be one place where the pastor has opportunities to make a meaningful impact. Roy Smith suggests:

> Pastoral counselors might revive and develop the discipline of pastoral visiting. The disciplined use of formal rituals with troubled individuals might be considered. Far more emphasis might be placed on developing therapeutic communities within the neighborhoods where, for instance, those who are released from mental institutions are dumped into half-way houses.[64]

3. *Provide financial assistance to those involved in private counseling.* If pastors in a Christian community are aware that someone is receiving private counseling, there are ways to work with the client and the counselor to affirm the priority of the community in the healing process. One of the ways this can be done is through payment or partial payment of the counseling fee. Because money has power, it speaks loudly as a way of connecting us with others. As Edward Bauman expresses so clearly, "Money as a form of power is so intimately related to the possessor that one cannot consistently give money without giving self."[65] In translation, the community can become a partner in the counseling by participating in the cost.

This can occur in any number of ways. If there is a private counseling agency that works with a number of your people, you may want to consider giving a specified amount on a yearly basis. On the other hand, you may want to set up a fund that could be accessed by people within your community. In some churches this is overseen by one or two people, and formal request is made to them for distribution of funds. A more personalized way of dealing with financial aid is to treat each case on a personal basis. In some situations the entire fee could be paid, while in others there may need to be a specific ratio (e.g., 60 percent).

For both the church and the parachurch, this financial partnership needs to be seen as a contribution to the ministry, not just in the life of the individual, but in that of the community. For instance, some mission organizations send their personnel for help with the express purpose of strengthening the mission's ministry. By facilitating the growth of the staff, the organization can benefit. In a basic sense, it is worth the outlay of funds.

If you are willing to engage in this kind of ministry to people in your community, there are a number of questions that need to be answered in concert with the private counselor:

How will the money be given and by whom?

How will confidentiality be handled?

How much information will be revealed?

Will diagnostic labels be shared?

Will there be a limit on the fund?

Will there be a limit on the number of sessions?

How will you determine whether the counseling has been successful?

It would be wise to work these out before the counseling starts and the money is exchanged.

Private Counselors and Fees

1. *Be clear about the motivational issues in fees.* Jeffrey Kottler captures the inner tension experienced by counselors who charge fees:

> Monetary issues muddle things a lot. Once upon a time, the practice of therapy, like that of medicine or law, was a commitment to helping. There was a passion and single-minded devotion to a simpler world with simpler ideals. . . . Now competition for customers is the name of the game for many therapists and mental health organizations. . . . New clinicians are caught between images of themselves as missionaries

and behavior that is more characteristic of manufac-
turers' representatives. We feel angry about being
unappreciated and underpaid. . . . Other times we feel
guilty about being overpaid for doing nothing.[66]

Why do private counselors charge fees? Rosalea Schonbar
suggests a number of reasons. First of all, those who have
trained in the profession have invested time and energy and
have made financial sacrifices, so their fee is a form of invest-
ment on those losses. Second, like all other citizens, caregivers
have bills to pay, families to support, and homes to buy or rent.
Third, many believe that fees facilitate motivation for help and
free therapy tends to encourage resistance. However, her conclusion is striking: "I believe the statements of rigorous fee
setters that the fee is necessary for the patient's well-being to
be at best a myth."[67]

Some of the literature confirms Schonbar's conclusion.[68] As
Herron and Rouslin Welt summarize:

Clinical and research evidence makes the point
that not all patients have to be charged a fee directly
in order to gain from psychotherapy. This takes
away any universal application of the traditional jus-
tification for fees, namely, that the patient needed to
pay so that he would be properly motivated and in
turn derive therapeutic effects. At least some patients
seem to get along well without the fee.[69]

Another twist on this issue is demonstrated by the differences between male and female therapists. Mary Burnside
found that male therapists charged more than their female
counterparts. She explains this difference on the basis that
women tend to be more empathic, are better prepared cultur-
ally to be a helper and a healer, and are also more sensitive to
the financial burden involved in counseling.[70] But again, the
distinction relates to counselor variables rather than concerns
of the counselee.

Private counselors and those involved in agencies need to
struggle through these issues. If the long held belief that fees

are motivational is untrue, then we are forced to examine a fundamental question: Is the fee for the counselor or the counselee? If the former, then the counseling system and structure runs the risk of being an expression of greed:

> Greed, then, is a problem for therapists. It is a problem for those who experience unbridled, but unidentified greed, for those in other words who feel entitled and have no reservation about the fee or its limits but who are unconscious about their greed. For such therapists, the patient is there in the service of the therapist.[71]

Clearly, the broader communal good is not in focus but rather the personal economic development of the individual. The results are obvious: Not only does the counselor become wealthier at the expense of the rest of the community, but a large segment of the Christian community that does not have the resources is denied access to help.

Because so many Christian counselors are struggling to make ends meet financially, it would be easy to dismiss concerns that relate money to motivation and to attitude. However, this would be a mistake for two reasons. First of all, as we have already noted, money is intimately tied to spiritual values. Christians who are seeking to live with spiritual integrity cannot avoid this subject. Second, as William Herron and Sheila Rouslin Welt have argued, "Although therapists may feel guilty, uncomfortable, and/or unworthy, reality needs to prevail. Therapists tell their patients there are no taboo topics."[72]

2. *Develop a system of accessibility that encourages the involvement of the poor.* In a study that looked at the reasons people go to clergy or professional agencies, Dennis Morgan found that the number one reason people gave for not going to a Christian counselor was that it was too expensive. The next four reasons in order were: (2) embarrassed, (3) don't need it, (4) don't know enough, and (5) don't believe it would help.[73] This should cause counselors who are claiming to be Christian some concern. It means that accessibility is a problem for

a number of people, particularly those who would be classed as poor. As Roy Smith has expressed:

> The tendency to exclude the least of these from the care of the church is theologically unacceptable. At a minimum, the church has, throughout its history, understood its services to be available to the poor and the suffering—even if this availability has often been expressed in condescending ways. When the profession which embodies the counseling function of the church is established in such a way that the least of these tend to be excluded from receiving help, or the help they receive is less than that given those who are richer or who are suffering less, the church has betrayed its mission.[74]

Smith also emphasizes that marginalization based on economic status can sometimes be more subtle. In some agencies higher paying clients are assigned to more experienced therapists, while the poor are connected with interns or inexperienced helpers. In others, lower paying clients are encouraged to engage in short-term counseling, while long-term therapy is provided for wealthy counselees. Since, in Roy Smith's words, "the severity of psychological suffering is often positively correlated with the degree of poverty,"[75] the poor pay in more ways than one.

So how can counselors make their services more accessible to the poor? In a helpful analysis on the various fee schedules that can be utilized, Herron and Rouslin Welt suggest that fixed fees have a number of advantages. They provide a fixed income for the counselor, do not allow for negotiation, preclude playing favorites, and do not create resentment on the part of the therapist. The downside is that this form of payment is not utilized frequently, it does not appear altruistic, and it may be seen as cold and greedy. The bottom line is clear. Fixed fee schedules bring advantages to the therapist but are not sensitive to the economic diversity in the Christian community.

Sliding scales require careful investigation of the counselee's financial situation at the beginning of counseling, a reality that can be a deterrent to both parties. On the surface it may look like a sensitive way to handle the poor, but most counselors and agencies can only handle a certain number of low-paying clients.

> Too many patients at the low end may cause frustration and resentment, with the possible "curing" of too many too fast with the aim, albeit unconscious, of making room for the more affluent. In contrast, if the upper end of the scale is predominant, there may be less incentive to make room for lower-paying patients unless therapists' superegos have a persistent guilt-tilt. Lower payers may have more appeal to therapists when patients are in short supply or when one is beginning.[76]

As a private counselor, reflect on the moral-ethical dimensions of your fee structure. Who is it serving? Who is benefiting? Is it facilitating accessibility or negating it? Is your counseling ministry open to the whole body of Christ or a specified component of it? These issues are not easily resolved, but a strong commitment to community will necessarily translate into justice for the poor. This needs to be a high priority for Christian counselors since "oppressing the poor in order to enrich oneself, and giving to the rich, will lead only to loss" (Prov. 22:16 NRSV).

3. *Work with the church or parachurch as a third-party participant.* One of the ways to resolve the fee schedule conflict noted earlier is to work in a third-party format. With the proliferation of private and government health insurance plans, many individuals can receive counseling through the payment of another body. This requires the counselor to keep in mind the questions noted earlier around confidentiality and boundaries. In fact, in their discussion of third-party payment, Herron and Rouslin Welt argue that it is "a problematic development. . . . [because] it adds an outside influence to the therapy process, disturbing the frame."[77] If we can rephrase that concern in language that fits with the tone of this book, we might say that third-party payment is intrusive because it

disrupts the sanctioned retreat. No longer can counselor and counselee function autonomously; they must be part of a larger context.

Is it possible that the Christian community could become the third party? Could churches and parachurch organizations align themselves with an individual counselor or with an agency? Is it possible that this kind of arrangement could facilitate the counselor as an exemplar of the community? If a church were willing to contribute a particular amount toward the fee, then the counselor would have some accountability to that community. There may be a heightened likelihood of connection and exchange at many different levels. Given the power of money, this medium could become a bridge between the world of the private counselor and that of the Christian community. In contexts where I have seen this happen, the bridge is extremely effective.

Roy Smith has proposed a similar concept when he argues that "if pastoral counselors are going to be available to the least of these, then fees cannot be the basis for their support."[78] He suggests that local, regional, national, or even global facets of the church should be supporting counselors so they are not dependent on fees. This would have a number of dramatic effects. Counselees could talk freely about their financial struggles without a fear that it is going to impact the counselor's financial well-being. People who require frequent sessions due to the severity of their difficulties would not be prohibited from this option. Smith also suggests that traditional fee-for-service models tend to make poor clients feel shame because they know they cannot afford what is being given to them. The support of the private counselor by the church would allow the poor to feel like they are going to the minister for help, where the link of shame with economics is irrelevant.

SUMMARY

When individuals go through the process of help and healing, they are not simply receiving the warmth of a caring relationship. Christian communities have a moral-ethical foundation upon which all of life exists. To operate within a communal framework is to affirm the centrality of this foundation. From the perspective of the counselee, three particular areas are considered important: discipline, confession, and fees.

Given the gap between the sinfulness of humanity and the righteousness of God, we need to understand the place of discipline. People require education and discipline so their lives can be brought into harmony with biblical truth. This is not done in a harsh, legalistic spirit but with a view to restoration and remediation. In the current climate, pastors and private counselors need to understand this area in the context of concerns around confidentiality and the law.

One aspect of moral concern that does not receive much attention in Protestant circles is confession. We find it easier to hide our frailty and sin rather than admit to it in the context of community. At times this hiding is facilitated by pious fellowships where people function out of the way they think things ought to be, rather than the way things really are. Both pastors and private counselors need to understand the burden of secret-carrying as well as the power of confession to bring healing.

A neglected area in the counseling field is that of fees. Given the power of money and its centrality in Western culture, we cannot downplay its importance in the caring professions. Pastors need to take their biblical mandate seriously so people understand the theology of finances and its implications in the professional world. By the same token, private counselors need to confront this taboo subject head on. Otherwise, they run the risk of alienating the economically marginalized with the result that only part of the Christian community is served.

NOTES

1. I. Epstein, ed., "Sanhedrin," in *Babylonian Talmud* (London: Soncino Press, 1935), 7a.

2. B. Grant, "The Moral Nature of Psychotherapy," *Counseling and Values* 29 (1985): 141–50.

3. Mary W. Nicholas, *The Mystery of Goodness: And the Positive Moral Consequences of Psychotherapy* (New York: Norton, 1994), 10.

4. W. Clebsch and C. Jaekle, *Pastoral Care in Historical Perspective* (Englewood Cliffs, N.J.: Prentice-Hall, 1964).

5. O. Hobart Mowrer, "Some Constructive Features of the Concept of Sin," *Journal of Counseling Psychology* 7 (1960): 188.

6. Jay E. Adams, *Competent to Counsel* (Nutley, N.J.: Presbyterian and Reformed Publishing, 1970), xvi. See also an interesting article that looks at the historical connections between Calvinistic theology and Adams's nouthetic counseling: Michael W. Bobick, "Guilt and Growth: Jay Adams and John Owen on Motivating Christians with Guilt," *Journal of Pastoral Practice* 6 (1983): 38–44.

7. Nicholas, *Mystery of Goodness*, 12–14.

8. Don S. Browning, *The Moral Context of Pastoral Care* (Philadelphia: Westminster Press, 1976), 11.

9. Lynn Sharp Paine, "Managing for Organizational Integrity," *Harvard Business Review* (March-April 1994): 106.

10. Stanely Hauweras and William H. Willimon, *Resident Aliens: Life in the Christian Colony* (Nashville: Abingdon, 1989), 79.

11. Samuel Southard, *Theology and Therapy: The Wisdom of God in a Context of Friendship* (Dallas: Word, 1989), 160.

12. Marlin Jeschke, *Discipling the Brother* (Scottdale, Pa.: Herald, 1972), 181–82.

13. John White, *Eros Defiled* (Downers Grove, Ill.: InterVarsity, 1977), 158–59.

14. J. Carl Laney, *A Guide to Church Discipline* (Minneapolis: Bethany House, 1985), 21.

15. It is not the intent of this section to present all the intricacies of discipline. The reader is encouraged to examine the following: Jay E. Adams, *Handbook of Church Discipline* (Grand Rapids: Zondervan, 1986); Don Baker, *Beyond Forgiveness: The Healing Touch of Church Discipline* (Portland: Multnomah, 1984); Lynn R. Buzzard and Laurence Eck, *Tell It to the Church: Reconciling Out of Court* (Elgin, Ill.: David C. Cook, 1982); Joy P. Gage and Kenneth G. Gage, *Restoring Fellowship* (Chicago: Moody, 1984); Gordon MacDonald, *Rebuilding Your Broken World* (Nashville: Oliver-Nelson, 1988); E. Schweizer, *Church Order in the New Testament* (London: SCM Press, 1961); John White and Ken Blue, *Healing the Wounded: The Costly Love of Church Discipline* (Downers Grove, Ill.: InterVarsity, 1985); and John Howard Yoder, "Binding and Loosing," *Concern* (1967).

16. Karl Menninger, *Whatever Became of Sin?* (New York: Bantam, 1973), 228.

17. White and Blue, *Healing the Wounded*, 30.

18. Paul R. Gilchrist, "Not a Sledgehammer," *Presbyterian Journal* 44 (1986): 9–11.

19. White and Blue, *Healing the Wounded*, 31.

20. James M. Houston, "The Independence Myth," *Christianity Today*, 15 January 1990, 32.

21. White and Blue, *Healing the Wounded*, 70.

22. Gerald T. Blanchard, "Sexually Abusive Clergymen: A Conceptual Framework for Intervention and Recovery," *Pastoral Psychology* 39 (1991): 244–45.

23. Steve Levicoff, *Christian Counseling and the Law* (Chicago: Moody, 1991), 112–13.

24. Terrance Steven Carter, "A Legal Analysis of Church Discipline in Canada," *CCCC Bulletin* (25 May 1992): 6–7.

25. Ibid., 7.

26. Al Dueck, "Ethical Contexts of Healing: Peoplehood and Righteousness," *Pastoral Psychology* 35 (1987): 242.

27. Ibid.

28. Laney, *Church Discipline*, 37.

29. Philip E. Slater, *The Pursuit of Loneliness: American Culture at the Breaking Point* (Boston: Beacon Press, 1970), 21.

30. Mark R. Laaser, "Sexual Addiction and Clergy," *Pastoral Psychology* 39 (1991): 215.

31. W. W. Becker, "The Paraprofessional Counselor in the Church: Legal and Ethical Considerations," *Journal of Psychology and Christianity* 6 (1987): 79.

32. Adams, *Church Discipline*, 30–31.

33. Levicoff, *Christian Counseling*, 81.

34. Siang-Yang Tan, *Lay Counseling: Equipping Christians for a Helping Ministry* (Grand Rapids: Zondervan, 1991), 250.

35. For a summary of key issues on the topic of confessing sin, see John R. W. Stott, *Confess Your Sins: The Way of Reconciliation* (Dallas: Word, 1974).

36. Richard E. Butman, "Confession," in *Baker Encyclopedia of Psychology*, ed. David G. Benner (Grand Rapids: Baker Book House, 1985), 213.

37. Ibid.

38. For more detail in this area, see Dietrich Bonhoeffer, *Spiritual Care* (Philadelphia: Fortress Press, 1985); Laney, *Church Dicipline*; Menninger, *Whatever Became of Sin?*; White and Blue, *Healing the Wounded*.

39. Bonhoeffer, *Spiritual Care*.

40. MacDonald, *Rebuilding*, 67.

41. V. Worthen has argued that this is one of the features of confession that distinguishes it from traditional psychotherapy. V. Worthen, "Psychotherapy and Catholic Confession," in *Wholeness and Holiness*, ed. H. N. Maloney (Grand Rapids: Baker Book House, 1983), 319–30.

42. Dietrich Bonhoeffer, *Life Together* (New York: Harper and Row, 1954), 110.

43. Cathryn I. Hill, "A Developmental Perspective on Adolescent 'Rebellion' in the Church," *Journal of Psychology and Theology* 14 (1986): 315.

44. MacDonald, *Rebuilding*, 73.

45. Clifford Williams, "When Mercy Hurts," *Christianity Today*, 3 February 1989, 16.

46. Bonhoeffer, *Life Together*, 112.

47. White, *Eros Defiled*, 62.

48. Henri J. M. Nouwen, *In the Name of Jesus: Reflections on Christian Leadership* (New York: Crossroad, 1993), 45–46.

49. Menninger, *Whatever Became of Sin?*, 228–29.

50. Houston, "Independence Myth," 32.

51. MacDonald, *Rebuilding*, 69.

52. Ibid., 79.

53. Everett L. Worthington, Jr., et al., "Christian Therapists' and Clients' Perceptions of Religious Psychotherapy in Private and Agency Settings," *Journal of Psychology and Theology* 16 (1988): 282–93.

54. White and Blue, *Healing the Wounded*, 19.

55. MacDonald, *Rebuilding*, 82.

56. Alan B. Tulipan, "Fee Policy as an Extension of the Therapist's Style and Orientation," in *The Last Taboo: Money as Symbol and Reality in Psychotherapy and Psychoanalysis*, ed. David W. Krueger (New York: Brunner/Mazel, 1986), 79.

57. W. Schoefield, *The Purchase of Friendship* (Englewood Cliffs, N.J.: Prentice Hall, 1964).

58. Al Dueck, "North American Psychology: Gospel of Modernity?" *Conrad Grebel Review* 3 (1985): 171.

59. Philip Rieff, *The Triumph of the Therapeutic: Uses of Faith after Freud* (New York: Harper and Row, 1966), 75.

60. William G. Herron and Sheila Rouslin Welt, *Money Matters: The Fee in Psychotherapy and Psychoanalysis* (New York: Guilford Press, 1992).

61. Lewis Yablonsky, *The Emotional Meaning of Money* (New York: Gardner, 1991), 150.

62. Richard Foster, *Money, Sex and Power: The Challenge of the Disciplined Life* (New York: Harper and Row, 1985), 21–22

63. Roy Herndon Steinhoff Smith, "Fees, Confidentiality, and Pastoral Counseling," *Pastoral Psychology* 39 (1990): 104.

64. Ibid., 108.

65. E. W. Bauman, *Where Your Treasure Is* (Arlington, Va.: Bauman Bible Telecasts, 1980), 133.

66. Jeffrey A. Kottler, *On Being a Therapist* (San Francisco: Jossey-Bass, 1987), 65.

67. Rosalea A. Schonbar, "The Fee as Focus of Transference and Countertransference in Treatment," in *The Last Taboo: Money as Symbol and Reality in Psychotherapy and Psychoanalysis*, ed. David W. Krueger (New York: Brunner/Mazel, 1986), 33–47.

68. See R. C. Friedman, "Psychotherapy Without Fee," in *Money and Mind*, ed. S. Klebanow and E. L. Lowenkopf (New York: Plenum, 1991), 207–21; William G. Herron and S. Sitkowski, "Effect of Fees on Psychotherapy: What Is the Evidence," *Professional Psychology: Research and Practice* 17 (1986): 347–51; and N. Manos, "Free Psychotherapy: The Therapist's and the Patient's View," *Psychotherapy and Psychosomatics* 37 (1982): 137–43.

69. Herron and Rouslin Welt, *Money Matters*, 55.

70. Mary A. Burnside, "Fee Practices of Male and Female Therapists," in *The Last Taboo: Money as Symbol and Reality in Psychotherapy and Psychoanalysis*, ed. David W. Krueger (New York: Brunner/Mazel, 1986), 48–54.

71. Herron and Rouslin Welt, *Money Matters*, 40.

72. Ibid., 7.

73. Dennis D. Morgan, "Needs Assessment in Churches: A Christian Community's Need for Professional Counseling Services," *Journal of Psychology and Theology* 10 (1982): 242–50.

74. Smith, "Fees, Confidentiality, and Pastoral Counseling," 105.

75. Ibid., 104.

76. Herron and Rouslin Welt, *Money Matters,* 134.

77. Ibid., 148.

78. Smith, "Fees, Confidentiality, and Pastoral Counseling," 106.

Chapter Eight

A Vision for Community

It is my hope that an ethic of God's reign, a normative people and our personal character as disciples of Christ might more significantly shape the therapeutic process.

—Al Dueck

CHRISTIAN COMMUNITY IS THE VISIBLE MANIFESTATION of the work of God, through Jesus Christ, in the church. While God prizes a relationship with individuals, his heart is with a body—a fellowship, a community, a people. Because of this, those of us in the field of counseling need to take the role of the community seriously. Whether we are pastors or private counselors, we need a view of help and healing that roots people in their Christian community. To do this is to move away from the traditional emphasis on the intrapsychic person and to fly in the face of the individualistic emphasis of Western culture. However countercultural a communal orientation may be, it is consistent with a fundamental theological thread that runs through Scripture and throughout history: We were created to be interdependent and relational.

REACTIONS

"This is idealistic and utopian." An emphasis on community runs the risk of seeming like wish fulfillment. We all aspire for a

sense of belonging and connection in the Christian community, but most of us are aware of the cruel realities that characterize many of these communities. It seems that so many of them are hard and harsh, debilitating and demotivating. So to talk of community seems to present an ideal that can never be realized. However, Christian communities are no different than individuals. They are not perfect. They have not arrived. They are not sinless. They need an infusion of the grace and mercy of God. They need an experience of forgiveness so they can start again. This book is an attempt to cultivate an interest in Christian communities learning to function as they were intended.

"We don't need private Christian counselors." The thesis of this book should not be construed as a negation of the private counseling enterprise. I fear that those who have a penchant for criticizing counseling will use the arguments contained in these pages and assert that private counselors should seek alternative employment. I am also concerned that some private counselors will see this book as a repudiation of their sense of call before God. Having spent many years in the profession, this is neither my intent nor interest. However, I have attempted to employ an irenic spirit in suggesting that private counselors need to examine their assumptions in light of the biblical mandate that stresses community. To read this book and miss that point is to miss the heart of the argument.

"The church is the answer." One of the corollaries of the "we don't need private Christian counselors" thesis is the affirmation that the church is the answer. Fundamentally, I agree with that conclusion, but with one proviso: When the church is functioning as the church, it will be communally oriented. It will not be characterized by rampant individualism and self-serving autonomy. It will not simply nurture individuals into personal decisions and privatized religion without due consideration for the importance of the body of Christ. A church that takes its call as the people of God seriously will affirm all its members as individuals-in-community. The cure of souls does not happen when the church simply exists to maintain itself and perpetuate its rituals. However, when the community of faith takes its mandate seriously, its role in the healing process cannot be underestimated.

"There is so much more to consider." The metaphor for this project is the introductory textbook in a first-year course. This book raises key issues and concerns and attempts to lay the foundation for further exploration. The role of community in the field of counseling needs further exploration. Lectures need to be developed. Debates need to occur. Books need to be written. Cross-disciplinary interchange needs to take place. There is no question that many areas have been left out in this study, and many of those that were noted are embryonic and preliminary. Further reflection on the part of the Christian community will only add to this body of knowledge.

WHERE DO WE GO FROM HERE?

1. *More communication.* One of the major reasons that the private counseling world and the world of the church are having problems with each other is because they do not communicate enough. Pastors read their particular literature and go to their own conferences. Counselors pull from their body of knowledge and attend professional meetings. Knowledge for each of these groups is contextualized, and the interchange is minimal. The result is a lack of communication and a lack of mutuality in the process of caregiving. This can only be rectified by more communication where pastors and counselors sit down together and talk about concerns, issues, and key questions. Whether this is in the form of cross-disciplinary writing, conferences, or informal connection, more communication is needed. In a fundamental sense, reconciliation between these two groups will only enhance the work of both.

2. *Training for Christian counselors.* The current thesis raises many questions about the nature of training for Christian counselors. There is no question that the educational system has prized specialization, individual accomplishment, and discipline-specific training. In a sense, modern Western education has enshrined privatization and negated a communal consciousness. So we need to ask whether the training for Christian counselors is facilitating communal approaches to counseling or not. When we refer to Christian educational institutions, what does the adjective *Christian* describe? Is it Christian in the sense

of personal piety and devotion, or is it Christian in that it encourages a communal sensibility and an awareness of social justice concerns? Do graduating counseling students have an intrapsychic preoccupation or a commitment to the communal good? These questions need to be answered by those who are mandated to educate and train.

3. *Interdisciplinary study.* The study of community is not discipline-specific. It does not fall exclusively within the domain of counseling, theology, ethics, biblical studies, sociology, philosophy, or pastoral studies. These fields cannot take the topic as their own and negate the input of others. However, one of the negative by-products of Western specialization is that most of us are confined by our discipline. It is not easy to find the time to read books, attend conferences, and connect collegially outside our own areas. Most of our disciplines have such a large body of knowledge that we cannot keep up with it, much less anything else. But the study of community demands this. We must break down the artificial walls between our fields and work together to understand community.

For those of us in the social sciences this is particularly important. Our field has become popular, fashionable, and revered in the Western mind. This has served to facilitate our own arrogance and kept us distant from other bodies of knowledge, notably those in the biblical and theological realm. Being well read is a must when you tackle the topic of community.[1]

4. *View of self.* This book has not dealt with an issue that needs to be addressed for a full understanding of the nature of community: What is the self? In asserting the priority of community, do we lose the self? Is the individual still important? How do we understand the self in the postmodern world? How do we link the relational with individuality? If we do not deal with these questions, we may find a pendulum effect where the lack of community in Western culture is replaced by a repudiation of the individual. Somehow we need to find a healthy tension where self and individuality can be understood and respected while communal concerns are given priority. Again, this is where the input of scholars from different disciplines can be invaluable.

5. *Community as a biblical criterion.* In the field of Christian counseling there are extensive debates about a multitude of counseling approaches based on the soundness of their theology and the validity of their biblical understanding. An understanding of community could bring a new criterion to the field that might help separate the wheat from the chaff. It is not just that community is an interesting notion that can be utilized by Christians. Community is central if we understand God and his work in the world. So we need to do more structural analyses of the counseling field. We need to ask about the influence of Western culture in the world of Christian counseling. We need to reflect on the biblical viability of the sanctioned retreat. At the core, we need to possess sufficient humility to look at our field with integrity and repentance.

NOTES

1. Some of the recent literature illustrates the cross-disciplinary nature of community. Stanley J. Grenz, *Theology and the Community of God* (Nashville, Tennessee: Broadman and Holman, 1994), presents the doctrines of the Christian faith using the concept of community as an integrative theme. Rex A. Koivisto, *One Lord, One Faith* (Wheaton, Ill.: BridgePoint, 1993), suggests we need to move beyond our own denominational boundaries and recapture the catholicity of the church. Ian Nicholson, "From the Kingdom of God to the Beloved Community, 1920–1930: Psychology and the Social Gospel in the Work of Goodwin Watson and Carl Rogers," *Journal of Psychology and Theology* 22 (1994): 196–206, argues that psychology has appealed to religiously minded people because of its promise to construct a community. David F. Wells, *No Place for Truth: Or Whatever Happened to Evangelical Theology* (Grand Rapids: Eerdmans, 1993), posits that evangelical theology has become watered down partially due to our contemporary obsession with individuality and Everyperson. Robert Wuthnow, *Sharing the Journey: Support Groups and America's New Quest for Community* (New York: Free Press, 1994), notes that support groups are part of the fabric of Western culture and reflect our yearning for community.

Epilogue

One night I dreamed a dream:
I was walking through dense woods.
At times I appeared to be walking alone;
it seemed that no one was around.
No one cared
or expressed interest.
But when I looked more closely, they were there.
Some hid behind the trees,
thinking that they too were alone.
Others were further ahead, leading the way.
Still others were behind, following my trail.
A small group was right beside me
with outstretched arms and welcoming smiles,
at times visible,
at others, hidden from view.
And behind them all, and in them all,
and through them all—
those that hid, those that led,
those that followed, and those close at hand—
God.
And then I saw a city.
It was majestic and exquisite,
like a new bride,
radiant and perfect.
A city teeming with people beyond number.
Those that used to hide, those that led,
those that followed, and those that expressed care—
they were all there.
And I was among them.
And then I heard a loud voice,
"The home of God is among mortals.
He will dwell with them as their God;
they will be his peoples,
and God himself will be with them."
I wept.
But then He wiped every tear from my eye.

Amen.

Appendix A

A friend of mine, who is involved in a counseling ministry within his local church, took a twenty-hour course with me on this material and then read through a major portion of the manuscript when the course was over. One of his comments was telling: "There are lots of questions that are frustratingly accurate, but we are not going to work them out with a one, two, three approach. We need to work it out in our faith community." To facilitate this task, let me suggest the following.

If you are in a church or parachurch organization, have everyone in your leadership group read the first four chapters and then agree to come together for interaction. Since part 1 is foundational in nature, it would be helpful to see whether you are all coming from a similar perspective. Consider the following questions in one or more sessions:

1. Do you agree with the basic thesis that is outlined in the first chapter?

2. Of all the issues noted in chapter 1, which one do you, as an individual leader, need to grapple with the most?

3. From your experience in Western culture, which issues in chapter 2 are most relevant?

4. From your observation, does counseling tend to be a sanctioned retreat?

5. As you reflect on your own reading of Scripture, does it tend to be individualistic or communal in orientation?

In subsequent meetings, work through the twenty-seven points that apply to pastors. Assess your own individual ministry as well as that of the leadership.

It is rather odd trying to give private counselors suggestions on how to discuss a book on community in a group setting! First of all, I would suggest that a couple of private counselors get together for interaction. This often happens in larger centers where there are a number who are involved in the field. Start with the foundational questions, noted above, and then move through the twenty-seven implications for private counselors. Counselors employed by an agency can utilize this time to reflect not only on their individual practice but also to ask questions about the culture of the agency or organization. This latter emphasis is extremely important: What do we as an agency/organization communicate about our view of the Christian community in general and the church in particular?

IMPLICATIONS FOR PASTORS

1. Grasp the culture of the community you represent.

2. Understand the moral-ethical framework that is embedded in the community you represent.

3. Practice accountability to your community so there is interdependence.

4. Seek warm and caring relationships within your community.

5. Recognize the power inherent in the pastoral role and the potential danger that this brings to communal relationships.

6. Admit to your legitimate needs for affirmation and care without imposing on the community to fulfill them.

7. Make sure your private performance squares with your public performance.

8. Recognize the relationship between intimacy and self-disclosure.

9. Elevate the ministry of the community above the expressions of your own giftedness.

10. Define the limits of confidentiality for the church or parachurch context.

11. Recognize the dangers of the pastoral role.

12. Facilitate community awareness with permission.

13. Call the community to communal repentance.

14. Take the suffering of individuals seriously.

15. Guard against institutional cruelty.

16. Be aware of the power of language.

17. Preach with communal sensitivity.

18. Emphasize the importance of communion.

19. Learn to distinguish caring instruction from legalistic rules.

20. Make remediation a key component of discipline.

21. Identify the place of confidentiality and legal concerns.

22. Acknowledge the dangers of a pious community.

23. Take the sin of others seriously.

24. Facilitate confession in the community.

25. Educate the community on the power of money.

26. Provide the socially and economically disadvantaged with access to counseling.

27. Provide financial assistance to those involved in private counseling.

IMPLICATIONS FOR PRIVATE COUNSELORS

1. Determine the centrality of the Christian community in your practice.

2. Reflect on your moral-ethical presuppositions and their relationship to the Christian community.

3. Move from a utilitarian to a reciprocal mode in terms of your relationship with the Christian community.

4. Revisit the dual-relationship issue and its application in your own context.

5. Acknowledge that all relationships are ambiguous.

6. Separate dual-relationship concerns from the potential for exploitation.

7. Recognize the integrity problem built into the counseling process.

8. Accept your own dependency needs and allow yourself to be vulnerable.

9. Acknowledge your own weakness as a key component of the healing process.

10. Identify boundaries as they relate to Christian communities.

11. Encourage the client to broaden boundaries.

12. Work directly with the leadership of Christian communities.

13. Develop an understanding of sin in social structures.

14. Facilitate community intervention.

15. Grapple with social injustice.

16. Bridge the gap between community liturgy and the counseling context.

17. Emphasize the importance of community in the realization of forgiveness.

18. Explore the humanizing qualities of counseling and of liturgy.

19. Do not jettison moral concerns due to a fear of being moralistic.

20. Affirm the true nature of the church in its mandate to discipline.

21. Develop a position on confidentiality and work with the church.

22. Recognize the self-deception in sin.

23. Acknowledge the pain of keeping secrets in community.

24. Encourage counselees to confess sin.

25. Be clear about the motivational issues in fees.

26. Develop a system of accessibility that encourages the involvement of the poor.

27. Work with the church or parachurch as a third-party participant.

Bibliography

Adams, Jay E. *Competent to Counsel*. Nutley, N.J.: Presbyterian and Reformed Publishing, 1970.

——. *Handbook of Church Discipline*. Grand Rapids: Zondervan, 1986.

Albee, G. "The Protestant Ethic, Sex, and Psychotherapy." *American Psychologist* 32 (1977): 150–61.

Almond, R. *The Healing Community: Dynamics of the Therapeutic Milieu*. New York: Jason Aronson, 1974.

American Association of Marriage and Family Therapy. *Code of Ethical Principles for Marriage and Family Therapists*. American Association of Marriage and Family Therapy, Washington, D.C., 1988.

Anderson, Neil T., and Charles Mylander. *Setting Your Church Free: A Biblical Plan to Help Your Church*. Ventura, Calif.: Regal Books, 1994.

Anderson, Ray S. *On Being Human: Essays in Theological Anthropology*. Grand Rapids: Eerdmans, 1982.

Aune, Michael B. "'But Only Say the Word': Another Look at Christian Worship as Therapeutic." *Pastoral Psychology* 41 (1993): 145–57.

Bach, G., and L. Torbet. *A Time for Caring: How to Enrich Your Life through an Interest and Pleasure in Others*. New York: Delacorte, 1982.

Backus, William. *Telling the Truth to Troubled People*. Minneapolis: Bethany House, 1985.

Baker, Don. *Beyond Forgiveness: The Healing Touch of Church Discipline*. Portland: Multnomah, 1984.

Bakke, Ray. *The Urban Christian: Effective Ministry in Today's Urban World*. Downers Grove, Ill.: InterVarsity, 1987.

Ballinger, Bruce. "We Have Come Into His House." Beverly Hills, Calif.: All Nations Music/Sound III, Inc., 1976.

Barber, Cyril J. *Nehemiah and the Dynamics of Effective Leadership*. Neptune, N.J.: Loizeaux, 1984.

Barrett, D. *World Class Cities and World Evangelization*. Birmingham, Ala.: New Hope, 1986.

Barry, M. *Bellevue Is a State of Mind*. New York: Berkley, 1971.

Barth, Karl. *Evangelical Theology: An Introduction*. Grand Rapids: Eerdmans, 1979.

Bauman, E. W. *Where Your Treasure Is*. Arlington, Va.: Bauman Bible Telecasts, 1980.

Becker, W. W. "The Paraprofessional Counselor in the Church: Legal and Ethical Considerations." *Journal of Psychology and Christianity* 6 (1987): 78–82.

Bellah, Robert N. "Conclusion: Competing Visions of the Role of Religion in American Society." In *Uncivil Religion: Interreligious Hostility in America*. Ed. Robert N. Bellah and F. E. Greenspan. New York: Crossroad, 1987, 219–32.

Bellah, Robert N., Richard Madsen, William M. Sullivan, Ann Swidler, and Steven M. Tipton. *Habits of the Heart: Individualism and Commitment in American Life*. New York: Harper and Row, 1985.

Bender, Harold S. *The AnaBaptist Vision*. Kitchener, Ontario: Herald, 1944.

―――. *These Are My People*. Scottdale, Pa.: Herald, 1962.

Bender, R. T. *The People of God*. Scottdale, Pa.: Herald, 1971.

Benner, David G. *Psychotherapy and the Spiritual Quest*. Grand
Rapids: Baker Book House, 1988.
————. *Strategic Pastoral Counseling: A Short-Term Structured
Model*. Grand Rapids: Baker Book House, 1992.
Berman, J. S., and N. C. Norton, "Does Professional Training
Make a Therapist More Effective?" *Psychological Bulletin* 98
(1985): 401–7.
Bernard, J. *The Sociology of Community*. Glenview, Ill.: Scott,
Foresman, 1973.
Bettelheim, Bruno. *Home for the Heart*. London: Thames and
Hudson, 1974.
Bibby, Reginald W. *Mosaic Madness: The Poverty and Potential of
Life in Canada*. Toronto, Ontario: Stoddart, 1990.
Bishop, Leigh C. "Healing in the Koinonia: Therapeutic Dy-
namics of Church Community." *Journal of Psychology and
Theology* 13 (1985): 12–20.
Blackbird, Tegan, and Paul H. Wright. "Pastors' Friendships,
Part 1: Project Overview and an Exploration of the Pedestal
Effect." *Journal of Psychology and Theology* 13 (1985): 274–83.
Blanchard, Gerald T. "Sexually Abusive Clergymen: A Concep-
tual Framework for Intervention and Recovery." *Pastoral
Psychology* 39 (1991): 237–46.
Bloom, Allan. *The Closing of the American Mind*. New York:
Simon and Schuster, 1987.
Bloor, Michael, Neil McKeganey, and Dick Fonkert. *One Foot
in Eden: A Sociological Study of the Range of Therapeutic
Community Practice*. London: Routledge, 1988.
Blue, Ken. *Healing Spiritual Abuse: How to Break Free from Bad
Church Experiences*. Downers Grove, Ill.: InterVarsity, 1993.
Bobick, Michael W. "Guilt and Growth: Jay Adams and John
Owen on Motivating Christians with Guilt." *Journal of
Pastoral Practice* 6 (1983): 38–44.
Bonhoeffer, Dietrich. *Life Together*. New York: Harper and Row,
1954.
————. *The Communion of Saints: A Dogmatic Inquiry into the
Sociology of the Church*. New York: Harper and Row, 1960.
————. *Spiritual Care*. Philadelphia: Fortress Press, 1985.
Bouma, M. *Divorce in the Parsonage*. Minneapolis: Bethany
House, 1979.

Bowen, Murray. *Family Therapy in Clinical Practice*. New York: Jason Aronson, 1978.

Browning, Don S. *The Moral Context of Pastoral Care*. Philadelphia: Westminster Press, 1976.

Brueggemann, Walter. *The Creative Word: Canon as a Model for Biblical Education*. Philadelphia: Fortress Press, 1982.

Buechner, Frederick. *Telling Secrets*. New York: HarperCollins, 1991.

Bufford, Rodger K., and R. E. Buckler. "Counseling in the Church: A Proposed Strategy for Ministering to Mental Health Needs in the Church." *Journal of Psychology and Christianity* 6 (1987): 21–29.

Bullis, Ronald K. "When Confessional Walls Have Ears: The Changing Clergy Privileged Communications Law." *Pastoral Psychology* 39 (1990): 75–84.

Burkholder, J. R. and C. Redekop. *Kingdom, Cross and Community*. Kitchener, Ontario: Herald, 1976.

Burnside, Mary A. "Fee Practices of Male and Female Therapists." In *The Last Taboo: Money as Symbol and Reality in Psychotherapy and Psychoanalysis*, ed. David W. Krueger. New York: Brunner/Mazel, 1986, 48–54.

Butman, Richard E. "Confession." In *Baker Encyclopedia of Psychology*, ed. David G. Benner. Grand Rapids: Baker Book House, 1985, 212–14.

Buzzard, Lynn R., and Laurence Eck. *Tell It to the Church: Reconciling Out of Court*. Elgin, Ill.: David C. Cook, 1982.

Carkuff, R. R. "Differential Functioning of Lay and Professional Helpers." *Journal of Counseling Psychology* 15 (1968): 117–28.

Carter, Terrance Steven. "A Legal Analysis of Church Discipline in Canada." *CCCC Bulletin* (25 May 1992): 1–12.

Clapp, Rodney. *Families at the Crossroads: Beyond Traditional and Modern Options*. Downers Grove, Ill.: InterVarsity, 1993.

Clebsch, W., and C. Jaekle. *Pastoral Care in Historical Perspective*. Englewood Cliffs, N.J.: Prentice-Hall, 1964.

Code, Michael. "Guarantees of Freedom of Religion Affecting the Law of Confidentiality." In *Constitutional Issues in Religion and the Law*. (Toronto: Social Planning Council of Metropolitan Toronto (1988): 3–21.

Collins, Gary R. "Lay Counseling: Some Lingering Questions for Professionals." *Journal of Psychology and Christianity* 6 (1987): 7–9.

Covey, Stephen R. *The Seven Habits of Highly Effective People: Restoring the Character Ethic.* New York: Simon and Schuster, 1989.

Crabb, Lawrence J., Jr. and Dan B. Allender. *Encouragement: The Key to Caring.* Grand Rapids: Zondervan, 1984.

———. "Basic Biblical Counseling." In *Christian Counseling and Psychotherapy,* ed. David G. Benner. Grand Rapids: Baker Book House, 1987.

Cramer, J. L. "The Special Characteristics of Suicide in Hospital In-Patients." *British Journal of Psychiatry* 145 (1984): 460–76.

De Dietrich, S. *The Witnessing Community: The Biblical Record of God's Purpose.* Philadelphia: Westminster Press, 1958.

Driver, John. *Community and Commitment.* Kitchener, Ontario: Herald, 1976.

Dueck, Al. "American Psychology in Cross-Cultural Context." *Journal of Psychology and Theology* 11 (1983): 172–80.

———. "North American Psychology: Gospel of Modernity?" *Conrad Grebel Review* 3 (1985): 165–78.

———. "Ethical Contexts of Healing: Peoplehood and Righteousness." *Pastoral Psychology* 35 (1987): 239–53.

———. "Ethical Contexts of Healing: Character and Ritual." *Pastoral Psychology* 36 (1987): 69–83.

———. "Ethical Contexts of Healing: Ecclesia and Praxis." *Pastoral Psychology* 36 (1987): 49–62.

Dulles, Avery. *Models of the Church.* New York: Image, 1987.

Durlak, J. A. "Comparative Effectiveness of Paraprofessional and Professional Helpers." *Psychological Bulletin* 86 (1979): 80–92.

Ellison, H. L. *The Old Testament Prophets: Studies in the Hebrew Prophets.* Grand Rapids: Zondervan, 1978.

Emerson, James G., Jr. *The Dynamics of Forgiveness.* Philadelphia: Westminster Press, 1964.

Empereur, James L. "Liturgy as Humanizing or as Therapeutic." *Exploring the Sacred.* (Washington, D.C.: The Pastoral Press, 1986), 85–96.

Engleberg, S. and J. Symansky. "Ethics and the Law." *Family Therapy Networker* 13 (1989): 30–31.

Enroth, Ronald M. *Churches that Abuse.* Grand Rapids: Zondervan, 1992.

Epstein, I., ed. "Sanhedrin." In *Babylonian Talmud.* London: Soncino Press, 1935.

Evans, C. Stephen. *Wisdom and Humanness in Psychology.* Grand Rapids: Baker, 1989.

Fine, Reuben. *Troubled Men: The Psychology, Emotional Conflicts and Therapy of Men.* San Francisco: Jossey-Bass, 1988.

Foster, Richard J. *Money, Sex and Power: The Challenge of the Disciplined Life.* New York: Harper and Row, 1985.

Friedman, R. C. "Psychotherapy Without Fee." In *Money and Mind,* ed. S. Klebanow and E. L. Lowenkopf. New York: Plenum, 1991: 207–21.

Gage, Joy P. and Kenneth G. Gage. *Restoring Fellowship.* Chicago: Moody, 1984.

Gallup Poll. *The Unchurched American.* Princeton, N.J.: Princeton Religious Research Center, 1978.

George, Rickey L., and Therese S. Cristiani, *Counseling Theory and Practice.* 3d ed. Englewood Cliffs, N.J.: Prentice-Hall, 1990.

Geyer, Melanie C. "Dual Relationships and Christian Counseling." *Journal of Psychology and Theology* 22 (1994): 187–95.

Gilchrist, Paul R. "Not a Sledgehammer." *Presbyterian Journal* 44 (1986): 9–11.

Githumbi, Stephen. "I Am Because You Are; If You Are Not, I Cannot Be!" *Theology, News and Notes* (1991): 6–9.

Gorman, Julie A. *Community That Is Christian: A Handbook for Small Groups.* Wheaton, Ill.: Victor Books, 1993.

Grant, B. "The Moral Nature of Psychotherapy." *Counseling and Values* 29 (1985): 141–50.

Grayson, Paul A., and Kate Cauley, eds. *College Psychotherapy.* New York: Guilford Press, 1989.

Grenz, Stanley J. *Revisioning Evangelical Theology: A Fresh Agenda for the 21st Century.* Downers Grove, Ill.: InterVarsity, 1993.

———. *Theology and the Community of God.* Nashville: Broadman and Holman, 1994.

Gunton, C. E. "The Church on Earth: The Roots of Community." In *On Being the Church: Essays on the Christian Community*, ed. C. E. Gunton and D. W. Hardy. (Edinburgh, Scotland: Clark, 1989) 48–80.

Gunton, C. E., and D. W. Hardy, eds. *On Being the Church: Essays on the Christian Community*. Edinburgh, Scotland: Clark, 1989.

Guy, James D., and Gary P. Liaboe. "Isolation in Christian Psychotherapeutic Practice." *Journal of Psychology and Theology* 13 (1985): 167–71.

Haley, Jay. *Problem-Solving Therapy*. San Francisco: Jossey-Bass, 1987.

Halleck, S. L. *The Politics of Therapy*. New York: Harper, 1971.

Hallie, Philip. *The Paradox of Cruelty*. Middletown, Conn.: Wesleyan University, 1969.

Hanna, Sharon L. *Person to Person: Positive Relationships Don't Just Happen*. Englewood Cliffs, N.J.: Prentice-Hall, 1991.

Hardy, D. "Created and Redeemed Sociality." In *On Being the Church: Essays on the Christian Community*, ed. C. E. Gunton and D. W. Hardy (Edinburgh, Scotland: Clark, 1989).

Hauagaard, Jeffrey J., and N. Dickon Reppucci, *The Sexual Abuse of Children: A Comprehensive Guide to Current Knowledge and Intervention Strategies*. San Francisco: Jossey-Bass, 1988.

Hauerwas, Stanley. *Unleashing the Scripture: Freeing the Bible from Captivity to America*. Nashville: Abingdon, 1993.

Hauerwas, Stanley, and William H. Willimon. *Resident Aliens: Life in the Christian Colony*. Nashville: Abingdon, 1989.

Healey, Bede J. "Self-Disclosure in Religious Spiritual Direction: Antecedents and Parallels to Self-Disclosure in Psychotherapy." In *Self-Disclosure in the Therapeutic Relationship*, ed. George Stricker and Martin Fisher. New York: Plenum, 1990, 17–27.

Hedgespeth, Joanne. "Integrative Inquiry: Response 2." *Journal of Psychology and Theology* 19 (1991): 287–88.

Herron, William G., and S. Sitkowski. "Effect of Fees on Psychotherapy: What Is the Evidence." *Professional Psychology: Research and Practice* 17 (1986): 347–51.

Herron, William G., and Sheila Rouslin Welt. *Money Matters: The Fee in Psychotherapy and Psychoanalysis*. New York: Guilford Press, 1992.

Hesselgrave, David J. *Counseling Cross-Culturally: An Introduction to Theory and Practice for Christians*. Grand Rapids: Baker Book House, 1984.

Hill, Cathryn I. "A Developmental Perspective on Adolescent 'Rebellion' in the Church." *Journal of Psychology and Theology* 14 (1986): 306–18.

Hoekema, Anthony. *The Christian Looks at Himself*. Grand Rapids: Eerdmans, 1975.

Houston, James M. "The Independence Myth." *Christianity Today*, 15 January 1990, 31–33.

Hug, William F. "Beyond Therapy and Technique: Reflections on the Process of Becoming." In *Pastoral Counseling*, ed. Barry K. Estadt, Melvin Blanchette, and John R. Compton. Englewood Cliffs, N.J.: Prentice-Hall, 1983.

Hunter, James D. *American Evangelicalism: Conservative Religion and the Quandry of Modernity*. New Brunswick, N.J.: Rutgers University, 1983.

Ignatieff, Michael. *The Needs of Strangers*. New York: Viking Penguin, 1985.

Illich, Ivan D. *Toward a History of Needs*. New York: Pantheon, 1978.

"Integrative Inquiry." *Journal of Psychology and Theology* 19 (1991): 285–90.

Isely, Paul J., and Peter Isely. "The Sexual Abuse of Male Children by Church Personnel: Intervention and Prevention." *Pastoral Psychology* 39 (1990): 85–99.

Jeschke, Marlin. *Discipling the Brother*. Scottdale, Pa.: Herald, 1972.

Johnson, David, and Jeff VanVonderen. *The Subtle Power of Spiritual Abuse*. Minneapolis: Bethany House, 1991.

Johnson, Timothy J. "Empowerment as a Christian Helping Strategy: Bridging the Chasm Between Client and Institutional Oppression." *Social Work and Christianity* 17 (1990): 66–78.

Jones, Maxwell. *The Therapeutic Community*. New York: Basic Books, 1953.

————. *Beyond the Therapeutic Community*. New Haven: Yale University Press, 1968.

Karpel, Mark A., and Eric S. Strauss, *Family Evaluation*. New York: Gardner Press, 1983.

Kirwan, William T. *Biblical Concepts for Christian Counseling: A Case for Integrating Psychology and Theology*. Grand Rapids: Baker Book House, 1984.

Koivisto, Rex A. *One Lord, One Faith*. Wheaton, Ill.: BridgePoint, 1993.

Kolbenschlag, M. *Lost in the Land of Oz: The Search for Identity and Community in American Life*. New York: Harper and Row, 1988.

Kottler, Jeffrey A. *On Being a Therapist*. San Francisco: Jossey-Bass, 1987.

Kottow, Michael H. "Medical Confidentiality: An Intransigent and Absolute Obligation," *Journal of Medical Ethics* 12 (1986): 117–22.

Kraus, C. Norman. *The Community of the Spirit*. Grand Rapids: Eerdmans, 1974.

————. *Evangelicalism and Anabaptism*. Kitchener, Ontario: Herald, 1979.

Krebs, Richard L. "Why Pastors Should Not Be Counselors." *The Journal of Pastoral Care* 34 (1980): 229–33.

Krueger, David W., ed. *The Last Taboo: Money as Symbol and Reality in Psychotherapy and Psychoanalysis*. New York: Brunner/Mazel, 1986.

Kung, Hans. *The Church*. Garden City, N.Y.: Image, 1976.

Laaser, Mark R. "Sexual Addiction and Clergy." *Pastoral Psychology* 39 (1991): 213–35.

Laney, J. Carl. *A Guide to Church Discipline*. Minneapolis: Bethany House, 1985.

Lasch, Christopher. *Haven in a Heartless World: The Family Besieged*. New York: Basic Books, 1977.

————. *The Culture of Narcissism: American Life in an Age of Diminishing Expectations*. New York: Norton, 1978.

————. *The Minimal Self: Psychic Survival in Troubled Times*. New York: Norton, 1984.

————. *The True and Only Heaven: Progress and Its Critics*. New York: Norton, 1991.

Lebacqz, Karen. *Professional Ethics*. Nashville: Abingdon, 1985.

Lebacqz, Karen, and Ronald G. Barton. *Sex in the Parish*. Louisville: Westminster/John Knox, 1991.

Leech, Kenneth. *Soul Friend: The Practice of Christian Spirituality*. New York: Harper and Row, 1977.

Leggett, Donald A. *Loving God and Disturbing Men: Preaching from the Prophets*. Burlington, Ontario: Welch, 1990.

Levicoff, Steve. *Christian Counseling and the Law*. Chicago: Moody, 1991.

Lipsett, S. *Continental Divide: The Values and Institutions of the United States and Canada*. Toronto, Ontario: C. D. Howe Institute, 1989.

Loeschen, John R. *The Divine Community: Trinity, Church, and Ethics in Reformation Theologies*. Kirksville, Mo.: Sixteenth Century Journal Publishers, 1981.

Lohfink, G. *Jesus and Community: The Social Dimensions of the Christian Faith*. Philadelphia: Fortress Press, 1984.

Lowen, A. *Narcissism*. New York: Macmillan, 1983.

MacDonald, Gordon. *Rebuilding Your Broken World*. Nashville: Oliver-Nelson, 1988.

Malherbe, Abraham J. *Paul and the Thessalonians: The Philosophic Tradition of Pastoral Care*. Philadelphia: Fortress Press, 1987.

Manos, N. "Free Psychotherapy: The Therapist's and the Patient's View." *Psychotherapy and Psychosomatics* 37 (1982): 137–43.

Marney, C. *Priests to Each Other*. Valley Forge, Pa.: Judson, 1974.

Maslow, Abraham. *Toward a Psychology of Being*. 2d ed. New York: Van Nostrand, 1968.

———. *Motivation and Personality*. 2d ed. New York: Harper and Row, 1970.

Meloy, J. Reid. "Narcissistic Psychopathology and the Clergy." *Pastoral Psychology* 35 (1986): 50–55.

Menninger, Karl. *Whatever Became of Sin?* New York: Bantam, 1973.

Meth, Richard L., Robert S. Pasick, Barry Gordon, Jo Ann Allen, Larry B. Feldman, and Sylvia Gordon. *Men in Therapy: The Challenge of Change*. New York: Guilford Press, 1990.

Miller, William R., and Kathleen A. Jackson. *Practical Psychology for Pastors*. Englewood Cliffs, N.J.: Prentice-Hall, 1985.

Minirth, Frank B. *Christian Psychiatry*. Old Tappan, N.J.: Revell, 1977.

Moody, Christopher. "Pastors or Counselors?" *Theology* 91 (1988): 387–92.

Morgan, Dennis D. "Needs Assessment in Churches: A Christian Community's Need for Professional Counseling Services." *Journal of Psychology and Theology* 10 (1982): 242–50.

Mowrer, O. Hobart. "Some Constructive Features of the Concept of Sin." *Journal of Counseling Psychology* 7 (1960): 185–88.

Newbigin, Lesslie. *The Gospel in a Pluralistic Society*. Grand Rapids: Eerdmans, 1989.

Nicholas, Mary W. *The Mystery of Goodness: And the Positive Moral Consequences of Psychotherapy*. New York: Norton, 1994.

Nichols, Michael P. *The Self in the System: Expanding the Limits of Family Therapy*. New York: Brunner/Mazel, 1987.

Nichols, Michael P., and Richard C. Schwartz. *Family Therapy: Concepts and Methods*. 2d ed. Toronto, Ontario: Allyn and Bacon, 1991.

Nicholson, Ian. "From the Kingdom of God to the Beloved Community, 1920–1930: Psychology and the Social Gospel in the Work of Goodwin Watson and Carl Rogers." *Journal of Psychology and Christianity* 22 (1994): 196–206.

Niebuhr, H. Richard. *Man's Nature and His Communities: Essays on the Dynamics and Enigmas of Man's Personal Existence*. London: Geoffrey Bles, 1965.

Nouwen, Henri J. M. *The Wounded Healer: Ministry in Contemporary Society*. Garden City, N.Y.: Image, 1972.

————. *Clowning in Rome: Reflections on Solitude, Celibacy, Prayer, and Contemplation*. Garden City, N.Y.: Image, 1979.

————. *Making All Things New: An Invitation to the Spiritual Life*. San Francisco: Harper and Row, 1981.

————. *In the Name of Jesus: Reflections on Christian Leadership*. New York: Crossroad, 1993.

Noyce, Gaylord. *Pastoral Ethics: Professional Responsibilities of the Clergy*. Nashville: Abingdon, 1988.

————. *The Minister as Moral Counselor*. Nashville: Abingdon, 1989.

Olthius, James H. "Being-With: Toward a Relational Psychotherapy." *Journal of Psychology and Christianity* 13 (1994):
217–31.

———. "God-With-Us: Toward a Relational Psychotherapeutic
Model." *Journal of Psychology and Christianity* 13 (1994):
37–49.

Osherson, Samuel. *Wrestling with Love: How Men Struggle with
Intimacy with Women, Children, Parents, and Each Other.*
New York: Fawcett Columbine, 1992.

Paine, Lynn Sharp. "Managing for Organizational Integrity."
Harvard Business Review (March–April 1994): 106–17.

Parson, Talcott. *Social Structure and Personality.* New York: Free
Press, 1964.

Patrick, Dale. *Old Testament Law.* Atlanta: Knox, 1985.

Peck, M. Scott. *The Different Drum: Community-Making and Peace.*
New York: Touchstone, 1987.

———. *A World Waiting to Be Born: Civility Rediscovered.* New
York: Bantam, 1993.

Peterson, Marilyn R. *At Personal Risk: Boundary Violations
in Professional-Client Relationships.* New York: Norton,
1992.

Poloma, M. M. "Christian Covenant Communities: An Adap-
tion of the Intentional Community for Urban Life." In
A Reader in Sociology: Christian Perspectives, ed. C. P. De
Santo, C. Redekop, and W. L. Smith Hinds. Kitchener,
Ontario: Herald, 1980: 609–30.

Prior, David. *Creating Community: An Every-Member Approach to
Ministry in the Local Church.* Colorado Springs: NavPress,
1992.

Pytches, Mary. *A Healing Fellowship: A Guide to Practical Counseling in the Local Church.* London: Hodder and Stoughton,
1988.

Rauch, Gerry. "Confidentiality: Just Between You and Me
and . . . ?" *Pastoral Renewal* 46 (1984): 38–39, 46.

Rendall, Ted S. *Nehemiah: Laws of Leadership.* Three Hills, Alberta:
Prairie, 1980.

Ridley, Charles R. "Cross-Cultural Counseling in Theological
Context," *Journal of Psychology and Theology* 14 (1986):
288–97.

Rieff, Philip. *The Triumph of the Therapeutic: Uses of Faith after Freud.* New York: Harper and Row, 1966.

Rolfe, David J. "The Destructive Potential of Psychological Counseling for Pastor and Parish." *Pastoral Psychology* 34 (1985): 61–68.

Rosenthal, Peggy. *Words and Values: Some Leading Words and Where They Lead Us.* New York: Oxford, 1984.

Rutter, Peter. *Sex in the Forbidden Zone.* New York: Ballantine Books, 1989.

Ryan, Dale, and Juanita Ryan. *Recovering from Spiritual Abuse.* Downers Grove, Ill.: InterVarsity, 1992.

Ryder, Robert, and Jeri Hepworth. "AAMFT Ethical Code: 'Dual Relationships.'" *Journal of Marital and Family Therapy* 16 (1990): 127–32.

Sappington, A. A. "Psychology for the Practice of the Presence of God: Putting Psychology at the Service of the Church." *Journal of Psychology and Christianity* 13 (1994): 5–16.

Sarason, S. *Psychology Misdirected.* New York: Free Press, 1981.

Schoefield, W. *The Purchase of Friendship.* Englewood Cliffs: Prentice Hall, 1964.

Schonbar, Rosalea A. "The Fee as Focus of Transference and Countertransference in Treatment." In *The Last Taboo: Money as Symbol and Reality in Psychotherapy and Psychoanalysis,* ed. David W. Krueger. New York: Brunner/Mazel, 1986, 33–47.

Schweizer, E. *Church Order in the New Testament.* London: SCM Press, 1961.

Scudder, H. Steven. "Social Work and Pastoral Counseling Perspectives: An Exploratory Comparative Analysis," *Social Work and Christianity* 17 (1990): 37–51.

Sebert, S. R., and W. G. Ross, eds. *The Meditations of Elton Trueblood.* New York: Harper and Row, 1975.

Shedd, Russell Philip. *Man in Community: A Study of St. Paul's Application of Old Testament and Early Jewish Conceptions of Human Solidarity.* London: Epworth, 1958.

Slater, Philip E. *The Pursuit of Loneliness: American Culture at the Breaking Point.* Boston: Beacon Press, 1970.

Smith, David. *The Friendless American Male.* Ventura, Calif.: Regal Books, 1984.

Smith, James Bryan. *A Spiritual Formation Workbook: Small Group Resources for Nurturing Christian Growth.* San Francisco: Harper, 1993.

Smith, Roy Herndon Steinhoff. "Fees, Confidentiality, and Pastoral Counseling." *Pastoral Psychology* 39 (1990): 101–9.

Snyder, H. A. *The Community of the King.* Downers Grove, Ill.: InterVarsity, 1977.

Southard, Samuel. *Theology and Therapy: The Wisdom of God in a Context of Friendship.* Dallas: Word, 1989.

Stanelle, Herb. "The Emotionally Isolated Christian Male." *Social Work and Christianity* 18 (1991): 104–15.

Stevens, R. Paul. "Analogy or Homology? An Investigation of the Congruency of Systems Theory and Biblical Theology in Pastoral Leadership." *Journal of Psychology and Theology* 22 (1994): 173–81.

Stott, John R. W. *Confess Your Sins: The Way of Reconciliation.* Dallas: Word, 1974.

———. *I Believe in Preaching.* London: Hodder and Stoughton, 1982.

Stricker, George, and Martin Fisher, eds. *Self-Disclosure in the Therapeutic Relationship.* New York: Plenum, 1990.

Tan, Siang-Yang. *Lay Counseling: Equipping Christians for a Helping Ministry.* Grand Rapids: Zondervan, 1991.

———. "Lay Counseling: A Christian Approach," *Journal of Psychology and Christianity* 13 (1994): 264–69.

Taylor, Glenn C. "The Christian Campus as a Therapeutic Community." *The Bulletin: Christian Association for Psychological Studies* 4 (1978): 17–23.

———. "Therapeutic Community." In *Baker Encyclopedia of Psychology,* ed. D. G. Benner. Grand Rapids: Baker Book House, 1985: 1149–54.

Toennies, F. *Community and Society.* New York: Harper and Row, 1957.

Toh, Y. M., S. Y. Tan, C. D. Osburne, and D. E. Faber. "The Evaluation of a Church-Based Lay Counseling Program: Some Preliminary Data," *Journal of Psychology and Christianity* 13 (1994): 270–75.

Tournier, Paul. *Secrets.* Atlanta: John Knox, 1965.

Trobisch, Walter. *Love Yourself: Self-Acceptance and Depression.* Downers Grove, Ill.: InterVarsity, 1977.

Tulipan, Alan P. "Fee Policy as an Extension of the Therapist's Style and Orientation." In *The Last Taboo: Money as Symbol and Reality in Psychotherapy and Psychoanalysis,* ed. David W. Krueger. New York: Brunner/Mazel, 1986, 79–87.

VanderMey, Randall J. *God Talk: The Triteness and Truth in Christian Cliches.* Downers Grove, Ill.: InterVarsity, 1993.

Vander Vennen, Mary. "The Encounter with the Family of Origin." In *Christian Counseling and Psychotherapy,* ed. David G. Benner. Grand Rapids: Baker Book House, 1987: 111–17.

Vanier, Jean. *Community and Growth.* London: Darton, Longman and Todd, 1989.

Van Leeuwen, Mary Stewart. *Gender and Grace: Love, Work and Parenting in a Changing World.* Downers Grove, Ill.: InterVarsity, 1990.

Vitz, Paul C. *Psychology as Religion: The Cult of Self-Worship.* Grand Rapids: Eerdmans, 1977.

Von Rad, G. *Wisdom in Israel.* New York: Abingdon, 1972.

Waanders, David D. "Ethical Reflections on the Differentiation of Self in Marriage." *The Journal of Pastoral Care* 41 (1987): 100–110.

Wallis, Jim. "Community." *Sojourners.* (October 1981): 25–28.

Walter, Tony. *Need: The New Religion.* Downer's Grove, Ill.: InterVarsity, 1985.

Watkins, C. Edward. "The Effects of Counselor Self-Disclosure: A Research Review." *The Counseling Psychologist* 18 (1990): 477–500.

Webber, Robert E. *Liturgical Evangelism: Worship as Outreach and Nurture.* Harrisburg, Pa.: Morehouse, 1986.

Webster, Douglas D. *Selling Jesus: What's Wrong with Marketing the Church.* Downers Grove, Ill.: InterVarsity, 1992.

Wells, David F. *No Place for Truth: Or Whatever Happened to Evangelical Theology.* Grand Rapids: Eerdmans, 1993.

White, John. *Eros Defiled.* Downers Grove, Ill.: InterVarsity, 1977.

————. *Excellence in Leadership: Reaching Goals with Prayer, Courage and Determination.* Downers Grove, Ill.: InterVarsity, 1986.

White, John, and Ken Blue. *Healing the Wounded: The Costly Love of Church Discipline.* Downers Grove, Ill.: InterVarsity, 1985.

Whitehead, Evelyn Eaton, and James D. Whitehead. *Christian Life Patterns: The Psychological Challenges and Religious Invitations of Adult Life.* Garden City, N.Y.: Image Books, 1979.

Wicker, Tom. *One of Us: Richard Nixon and the American Dream.* New York: Random House, 1991.

Wiest, Walter E., and Elwyn A. Smith. *Ethics in Ministry: A Guide for the Professional.* Minneapolis: Augsburg Fortress, 1990.

Wiley, Mary O'Leary, and Philip B. Ray. "Counseling Supervision by Developmental Level." *Journal of Counseling Psychology* 33 (1986): 439–45.

Williams, Clifford. "When Mercy Hurts." *Christianity Today* 3 February 1989, 16–19.

Williams, Melvin. *Community in a Black Pentecostal Church.* Pittsburg: University of Pittsburg, 1974.

Wind, James P. "Leading Congregations, Discovering Congregational Cultures." *The Christian Century* 3–10 February 1993, 105–10.

Wink, Walter. *Naming the Powers: The Language of Power in the New Testament.* Philadelphia: Fortress Press, 1984.

———. *Unmasking the Powers: The Invisible Forces that Determine Human Existence.* Philadelphia: Fortress Press, 1986.

———. *Engaging the Powers: Discernment and Resistance in a World of Domination.* Minneapolis: Augsburg Fortress, 1992.

Worthen, V. "Psychotherapy and Catholic Confession," in *Wholeness and Holiness,* ed. H. N. Maloney. Grand Rapids: Baker Book House, 1983, 319–30.

Worthington, Everett L. Jr. *When Someone Asks for Help: A Practical Guide to Counseling.* Downers Grove, Ill.: InterVarsity, 1983.

Worthington, Everett L., Jr., Philip D. Dupont, James T. Berry, and Loretta A. Duncan. "Christian Therapists' and Clients' Perceptions of Religious Psychotherapy in Private and Agency Settings." *Journal of Psychology and Theology* 16 (1988): 282–93.

Wright, G. E. *The Biblical Doctrine of Man in Society.* London: SCM Press, 1954.

Wright, Paul H., and Tegan Blackbird. "Pastors' Friendships, Part 2: The Impact of Congregational Norms." *Journal of Psychology and Theology* 14 (1986): 29–41.

Wuthnow, Robert. *Sharing the Journey: Support Groups and America's New Quest for Community.* New York: Free Press, 1994.

Xavier, N. S. *The Two Faces of Religion: A Psychiatrist's View.* Tuscaloosa, Ala.: Portals, 1987.

Yablonsky, Lewis. *The Emotional Meaning of Money.* New York: Gardner, 1991.

Yoder, John Howard. "Binding and Loosing." *Concern* (1967).

Index

About the Author

Dr. Rod Wilson is the former director of the counseling program at Ontario Theological Seminary in Toronto, Ontario. Currently, he is the vice president of Ontario Bible College in Toronto, Ontario, as well as the teaching elder at Forest Brook Bible Chapel in Pickering, Ontario. He is involved in a speaking ministry both in church and parachurch contexts.

Dr. Wilson holds an M.A. and Ph.D. in clinical-counseling psychology from York University, Toronto, and is completing an M.T.S. from Conrad Grebel College in Waterloo, Ontario.

Dr. Wilson resides in Pickering, Ontario, with his wife, Bev, and their daughter, Jessica.